Managing and Maintaining a Microsoft® Windows® Server 2003 Environment

Project Lab Manual

Exam 70-290

Managing and Maintaining a Microsoft® Windows® Server 2003 Environment

Project Lab Manual
Exam 70-290

First Edition

Kenneth C. Laudon, Series Designer
Russell Jones, MCSE

The Azimuth Interactive MCSE/MCSA Team
Carol G. Traver, Series Editor
Kenneth Rosenblatt
Robin L. Pickering
Russell Polo
David Langley
Richard Watson, MCSE
Stacey McBrine, MCSE, MCSA
Brien Posey, MCSE
Simon Sykes-Wright, MCSE
Nigel Kay, MCSE
David Lundell, MCSE, MCT
Wale Soyinka, MCP
David W. Tschanz, MCSE
Mark Maxwell

PEARSON
Prentice Hall

Upper Saddle River, New Jersey, 07458

Senior vice President/Publisher: Natalie Anderson
Executive Editor: Steven Elliot
Senior Marketing Manager: Steven Rutberg
Assistant Editor: Laura Burgess
Manager, Print Production: Christy Mahon
Production Editor & Buyer: Carol O'Rourke
Composition: Azimuth Interactive, Inc.
Quality Assurance; Digital Content Factory, Ltd.
Printer/Binder: Courier, Bookmart Press

PEARSON
Prentice Hall

10 9 8 7 6 5 4
ISBN 0-13-144974-5

To our families,
for their love, patience,
and inspiration.

Brief Contents

Contents

Preface

The purpose of this Project Lab Manual is to provide you, the student, with another opportunity to review Windows Server 2003 concepts and skills, and to apply them to situations that you are likely to encounter on the job. The Prentice Hall Certification Series textbooks contain a great deal of conceptual and hands-on material. The Prentice Hall Certification Series Project Lab Manuals are designed to give you an opportunity to put those concepts and skills to work in a variety of different real-world on-the-job situations, and to understand the textbook contents in greater depth.

The Project Lab Manuals are organized in the same two-page highly illustrated format with conceptual material and instructions on the left-hand page, and screenshots and conceptual diagrams on the right-hand page. The Lessons in the Project Lab Manuals follow the Lessons in the textbook. Each Project Lab Manual Lesson is composed of a number of projects that reinforce the concepts and skills taught in the accompanying textbooks.

Project Lab Manual Lesson Contents

The Project Lab Manual Lessons have a number of elements designed to speed your learning and help you understand key concepts and skills.

Introductory Page: Each Lesson begins with an introductory page that reviews the key concepts and skills that you will be asked to apply in the lesson.

Scenario: Each Lesson has a brief scenario that describes the setting in which the projects take place. These scenarios provide you with a sense of how the concepts and skills that you have learned in the book are used in realistic business settings.

Project/Objective Table: Each Lesson includes a table that lists the Lesson projects and the corresponding exam objective supported. Where the project relates to a basic understanding of the subject matter, this is referred to as "Basic knowledge." You will always know how a project relates to MCSE/MCSA exam requirements.

General Requirements: At the beginning of each Lesson, there is a description of the hardware and software that you will need to complete the projects in the Lesson.

Project's Exam Objective: For each project there is a description of the specific MCSA/MCSE exam objective supported by the project.

Overview: Each project presents a specific assignment that builds on the Lesson's main scenario.

Learning Objective: Each project includes a specific learning objective that describes what you will be able to do after completing the project.

Specific Requirements: A list of specific requirements for each project is provided.

Estimated Completion Time: For each project, there is an estimated time for completion based on the experience of MCSE/MCSA professionals and instructors in colleges and training institutes. You should use these estimates only as a guide because your actual completion times will depend on your prior experience with Windows Server 2003.

Project Steps: Each project includes a set of step-by-step instructions for completing the project. These instructions are similar to those in the main textbook, but often differ because new options and pathways may be explored in the Project Lab Manuals.

Tips: Throughout the Project Lab Manuals you will find Tips and Cautions that offer you suggestions or comments about completing the project and working with Windows Server 2003.

Graphics and Illustrations: As you can expect from the Prentice Hall Certification Series, there are many screenshots and conceptual graphics provided that show you how the software should look at various points in the project. These are intended to familiarize you with the Windows Server 2003 environment and assure you that you are on the right track.

Quality Assurance

We have made every effort to ensure that the Project Lab Manuals are written to the same quality standards as the main textbook and the Interactive Solution CD-ROM. The Project Lab Manuals are written by MCSE and MCSA professionals with many years of real-world experience. The initial instructions and scenarios are then reviewed by independent technical editors who test each project, and each step. These results are then verified by the MCSE/MCSA team at Azimuth and the Series Designer and Editor. The end result is a product that students and instructors can understand and trust.

Notice

The projects in the Project Lab Manuals have been built using the most recent release of Windows Server 2003, Windows 2000 Server, and Windows XP Professional software. Your school or other institution may be using an earlier release of the software, or its environment may differ in some respects from the environment in which the projects were built. At times, these variations in environment and service packs can cause variations in the progression of steps and screenshots so that a screenshot in the book does not precisely match the screen you may be looking at. If this should occur, please report this to the authors at the Web site for this book.

LESSON

1 Introducing Windows Server 2003

The Windows Server 2003 operating system offers many of the same features introduced in the Windows 2000 environment, with the addition of many new security and management-related features and improvements to Active Directory services. The Windows Server 2003 family of operating systems includes:

- **Windows Server 2003, Standard Edition**: the operating system designed to meet the needs of small- to medium-sized businesses.
- **Windows Server 2003, Enterprise Edition**: the platform of choice for medium-sized company applications.
- **Windows Server 2003, Datacenter Edition**: built for the highest levels of scalability and reliability required by medium- to large-sized organizations.
- **Windows Server 2003, Web Edition**: offers dedicated Web serving and hosting, as well as a platform for building and hosting Web applications.

Windows Server 2003 comes with various services that were included with the Windows 2000 Server operating system. These include file and print services, application services, and Web services that enable a computer on which Windows Server 2003 is installed to function as a file server, print server and/or Web server. The operating system also includes networking services such as DHCP (Dynamic Host Configuration Protocol), DNS (Domain Name System), and RAS (Remote Access Services).

Additionally, the Windows Server 2003 operating system comes with new automated management tools, including Microsoft Software Update Services (SUS) and Group Policy Management Console (GPMC). Advances in data backup/restoration and improved utilization of storage area networks (SANs) are also available in the Windows Server 2003 family. Another important component of the Windows Server 2003 product line is IIS 6.0. This version has significant enhancements that improve reliability, scalability, and performance.

This lesson contains a variety of projects that will help you become more familiar with various versions of Windows Server 2003, its features and benefits, its underlying architecture and the network services, network protocols and security services that it offers.

Scenario

You have been hired as a network consultant for AcmePrint, Inc., a large commercial printing company, to investigate the viability of implementing a Windows Server 2003 environment. To do so, you must convince senior management to invest funds in upgrading systems across the organization.

Lesson 1 Introducing Windows Server 2003

Project	Exam 70-290 Objective
1.1 Describing the Windows 2003 Family of Operating Systems	Basic knowledge
1.2 Exploring the Features of Windows Server 2003	Basic knowledge
1.3 Examining Windows Server 2003 Architecture	Basic knowledge
1.4 Examining Network Services in Windows Server 2003	Basic knowledge
1.5 Examining Network Protocols and Security Services	Basic knowledge

General Requirements

There are no special requirements for this lesson. However, you may find it helpful to refer to Lesson 1 in your Prentice-Hall Certification Series Exam 70-290 textbook for further information about the topics covered by the projects in this lesson.

project 1.1

Describing the Windows Server 2003 Family of Operating Systems

exam objective

Basic knowledge

overview

Implementing a Windows Server 2003 environment is a large-scale operation involving considerable investments in time, money, and effort. You must convince John Seidel, the CEO of AcmePrint, Inc., of the viability of an organization-wide implementation of this operating system. The first step is to understand the similarities and differences of the various versions of the Windows Server 2003 family of operating systems **(Table 1-1)** to enable you to better suggest the appropriate software.

learning objective

After completing this project, you will be more familiar with the similarities and differences of the various versions of Windows Server 2003 and be able to recommend the version that is most appropriate for a particular situation.

specific requirements

None

estimated completion time

15 minutes

project steps

1. Create a table that compares and contrasts the features of Windows Server 2003, Standard Edition; Windows Server 2003, Enterprise Edition; Windows Server 2003, Web Edition; and Windows Server 2003, Datacenter Edition in the areas of processor support, hardware support, and file/print services.
2. Describe the differences among the four versions of Windows Server 2003 in the areas of networking services and security. Include the topics of VPNs, RADIUS support, and PKI support.

Table 1-1 Comprehensive list of features included in Windows Server 2003 family of operating systems

	Standard	Enterprise	Datacenter	Web
Hardware Support				
32-bit Intel x86 systems	✓	✓	✓	✓
64-bit Itanium-based systems		✓	✓	
Maximum number of processors	4	8	32 128 in 64-bit version	2
Maximum amount of RAM	4 GB	32 GB 64 GB in 64-bit version	64 GB 512 GB in 64-bit version	2 GB
Hot-add memory support		✓	✓	
Non-Uniform Memory Access (NUMA) support		✓	✓	
File Systems and Storage				
Distributed File System (DFS)	✓	✓	✓	✓
Volume Shadow Copy Restore (requires 2000 or XP client)	✓	✓	✓	✓
Removable and remote storage	Removable storage only	✓	✓	
Management Features				
IntelliMirror technologies	✓	✓	✓	Partial
Group Policy Results	✓	✓	✓	Partial
Windows Management Instrumentation (WMI) command line features	✓	✓	✓	✓
Image-based remote installation	✓	✓	✓	✓
Remote Installation Services (RIS)	✓	✓	✓	
Windows System Resource Manager (WSRM) and administrative GUI		✓	✓	
Active Directory				
Active Directory member server	✓	✓	✓	✓
Active Directory domain controller	✓	✓	✓	
Metadirectory Services (MMS)		✓	✓	
Security				
Encrypting File System (EFS)	✓	✓	✓	✓
Internet Connection Firewall (ICF)	✓	✓		
Public Key Infrastructure (PKI), Certificate Services, and Smart Card	Partial	✓	✓	Partial
Terminal Server				
Terminal Server	✓	✓	✓	
Terminal Server Session Directory		✓	✓	
Administered through Remote Desktop available	✓	✓	✓	✓
Networking				
Virtual Private Networking (VPN)	✓	✓	✓	Partial
Maximum number of VPN clients	1000	Unlimited	Unlimited	1
Internet Authentication Service (IAS)	✓	✓	✓	
Maximum number of RADIUS network access servers for IAS	50	Unlimited	Unlimited	
Maximum number of remote RADIUS groups for IAS	2	Unlimited	Unlimited	
Network bridging	✓	✓	✓	
Internet Connection Sharing (ICS)	✓	✓		
IPv6 supported	✓	✓	✓	✓
Clustering				
Network Load Balancing (NLB)	✓	✓	✓	✓
Cluster Service		✓	✓	
Maximum number of cluster nodes		8	8	
Application Services				
.NET Framework	✓	✓	✓	✓
Internet Information Services (IIS) 6.0	✓	✓	✓	✓
IIS 6.0 installed by default				✓
ASP .NET	✓	✓	✓	✓
Enterprise UDDI Services	✓	✓	✓	
Miscellaneous				
Windows Media Services 9 Series	✓	✓	✓	
Fax service	✓	✓	✓	
Services for Macintosh	✓	✓	✓	

project 1.2

Exploring the Features of Windows Server 2003

exam objective

Basic knowledge

overview

You now have a basic understanding of the different versions of Windows Server 2003 and are ready to convince CEO John Seidel of the viability of an organization-wide implementation of this operating system. The next step is to prepare a presentation that highlights the important features and benefits of Windows Server 2003. This presentation should include features such as Active Directory, network protocols, multi-lingual capabilities, Volume Shadow Copy Restore, and the Group Policy Management Console **(Figure 1-1)**.

learning objective

After completing this project, you will be more familiar with the features and benefits offered by Windows Server 2003.

specific requirements

None

estimated completion time

15 minutes

project steps

1. Discuss some of the features of Windows Server 2003 that increase reliability and scalability, lower the cost of computing, and provide a solid foundation for running business applications.
2. Summarize the key features of Active Directory, DHCP, DNS, and security services offered by Windows Server 2003.
3. List specific ways in which implementing Windows Server 2003 will benefit AcmePrint, Inc.

Figure 1-1 Windows Server 2003 Features

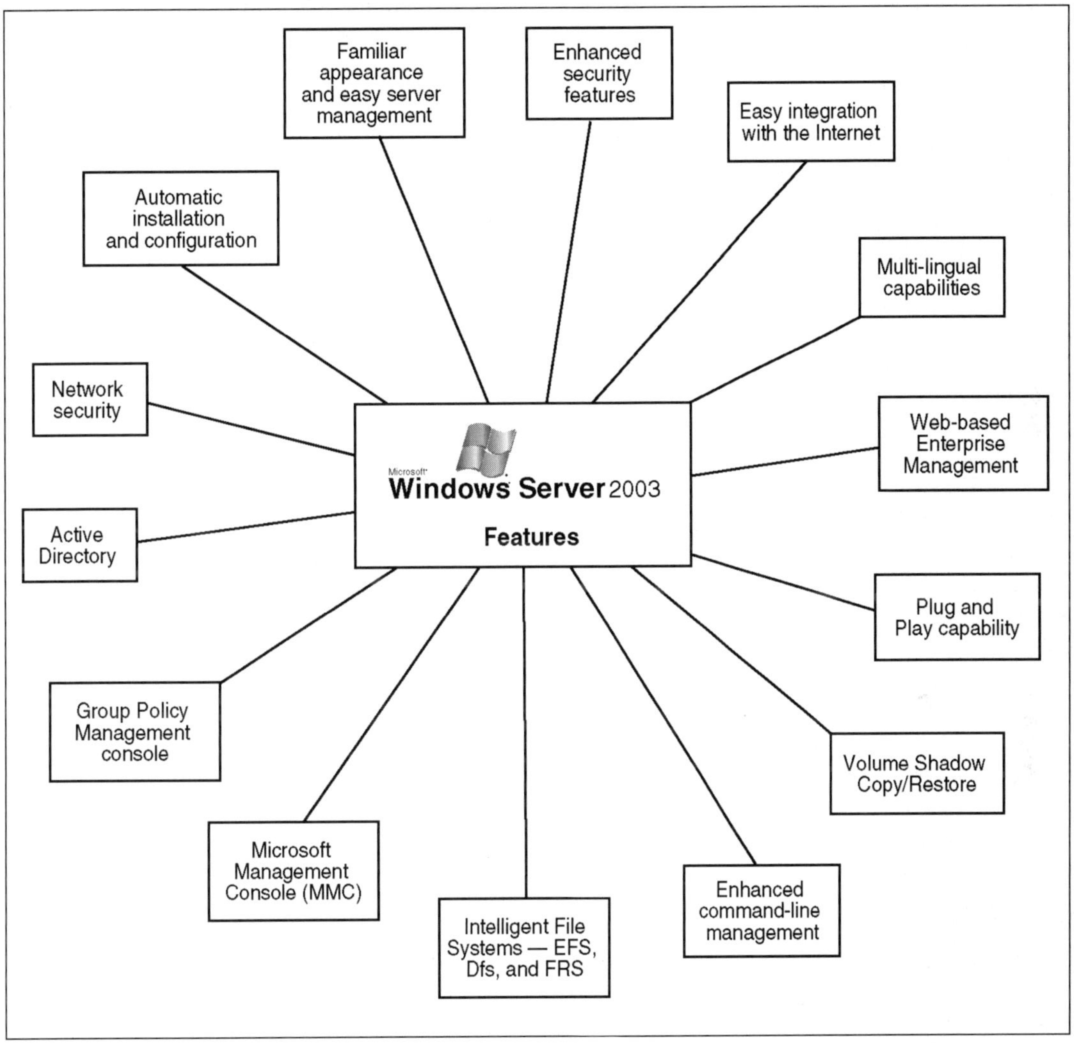

project 1.3

Examining Windows Server 2003 Architecture

exam objective

Basic knowledge

overview

As part of your role as a network consultant at AcmePrint, Inc., you are responsible for training the other networking personnel on the intricacies of the new Windows Server 2003 environment being rolled out. The topic for today's training session is Windows Server 2003 architecture.

learning objective

After completing this project, you will be more familiar with the underlying architecture of Windows Server 2003.

specific requirements

None

estimated completion time

15 minutes

project steps

1. Provide an overview of Windows Server 2003 architecture using a diagram to show all of the parts.
2. Explain user mode and kernel mode **(Figure 1-2)**.
3. Explain the user mode subsystems, including the environmental subsystems and integral subsystems.
4. Explain the Executive Services subsystem.
5. List the components of the Executive Services subsystem **(Figure 1-3)**.

Figure 1-2 User mode and kernel mode

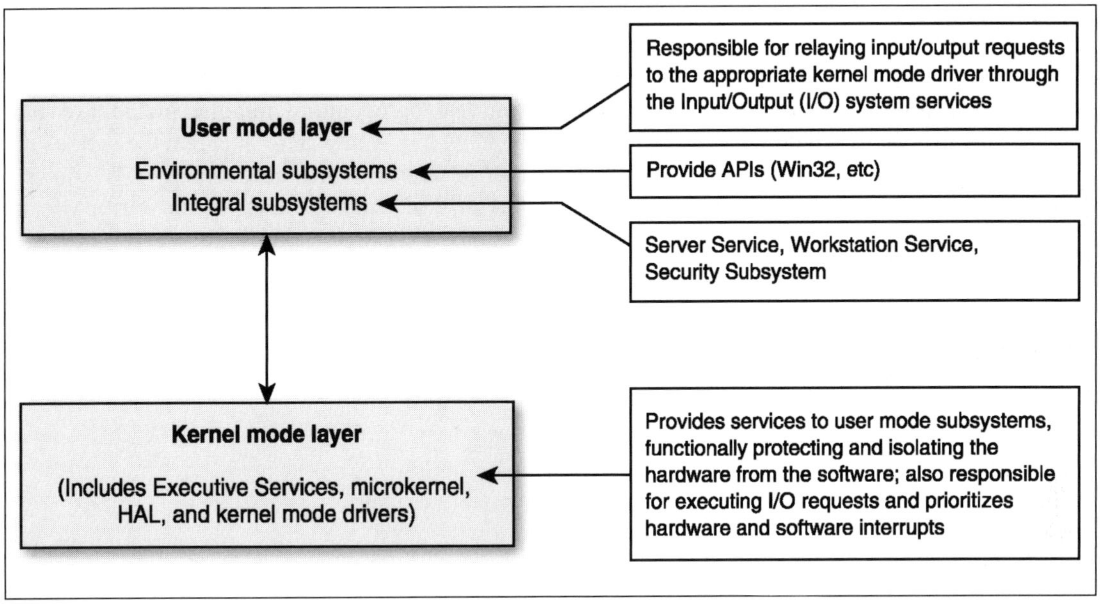

Figure 1-3 Components of the Executive Services Subsystem

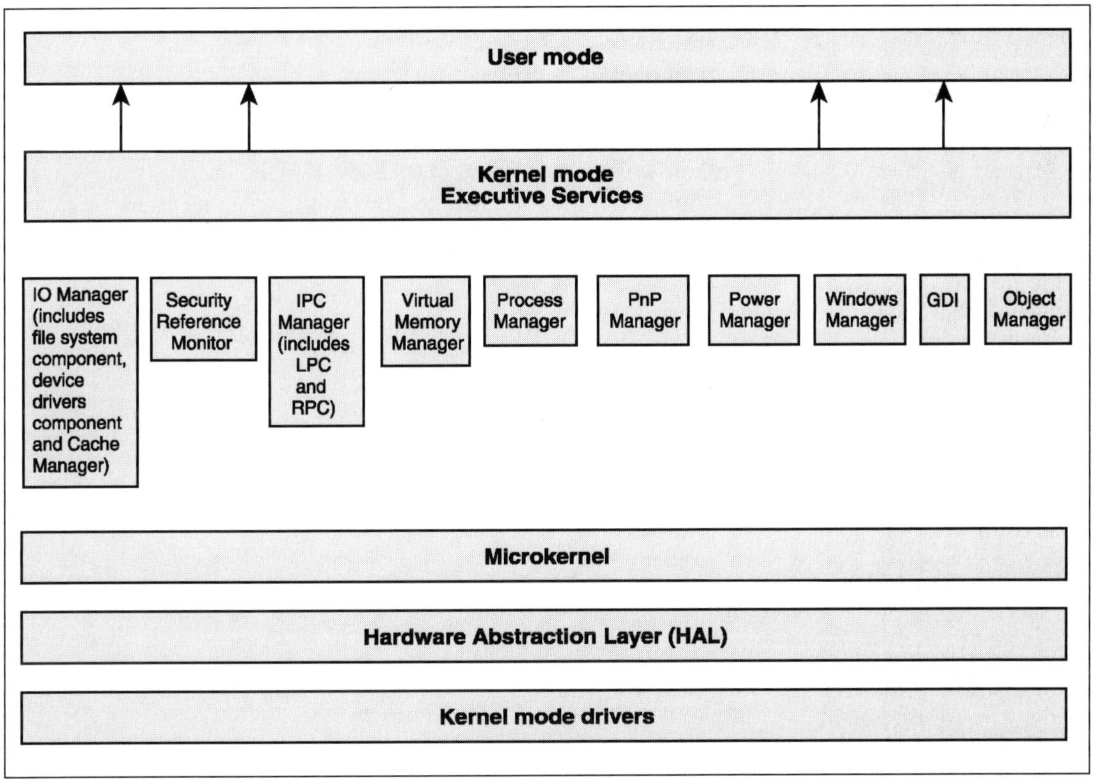

project 1.4 Examining Network Services in Windows Server 2003

exam objective

Basic knowledge

overview

AcmePrint, Inc. has many employees who work from their home and from offsite locations. AcmePrint also hires many contract employees who work exclusively from their home offices. These users run different desktop operating systems, including Windows XP and Windows 98. You must show the CEO how you plan to integrate the various desktops at the corporate headquarters and the offsite users into the company's Windows Server 2003 network. This demonstration requires an understanding of the various network services provided by the Windows Server 2003 operating system **(Figure 1-4)**.

learning objective

After completing this project, you will more familiar with the network services offered in Windows Server 2003.

specific requirements

None

estimated completion time

15 minutes

project steps

1. Describe the differences between the workgroup network model and the domain network model.
2. Decide which of the models in Step 1 would be appropriate for this organization, and explain your reasoning.
3. Decide whether you would use VPN connections for some of your remote users, and explain why or why not.
4. Discuss how you would implement RAS and RADIUS services for your remote users.
5. Explain how you will use DNS to integrate the remote users' computers into your network.

Figure 1-4 Network Services provided by Windows Server 2003

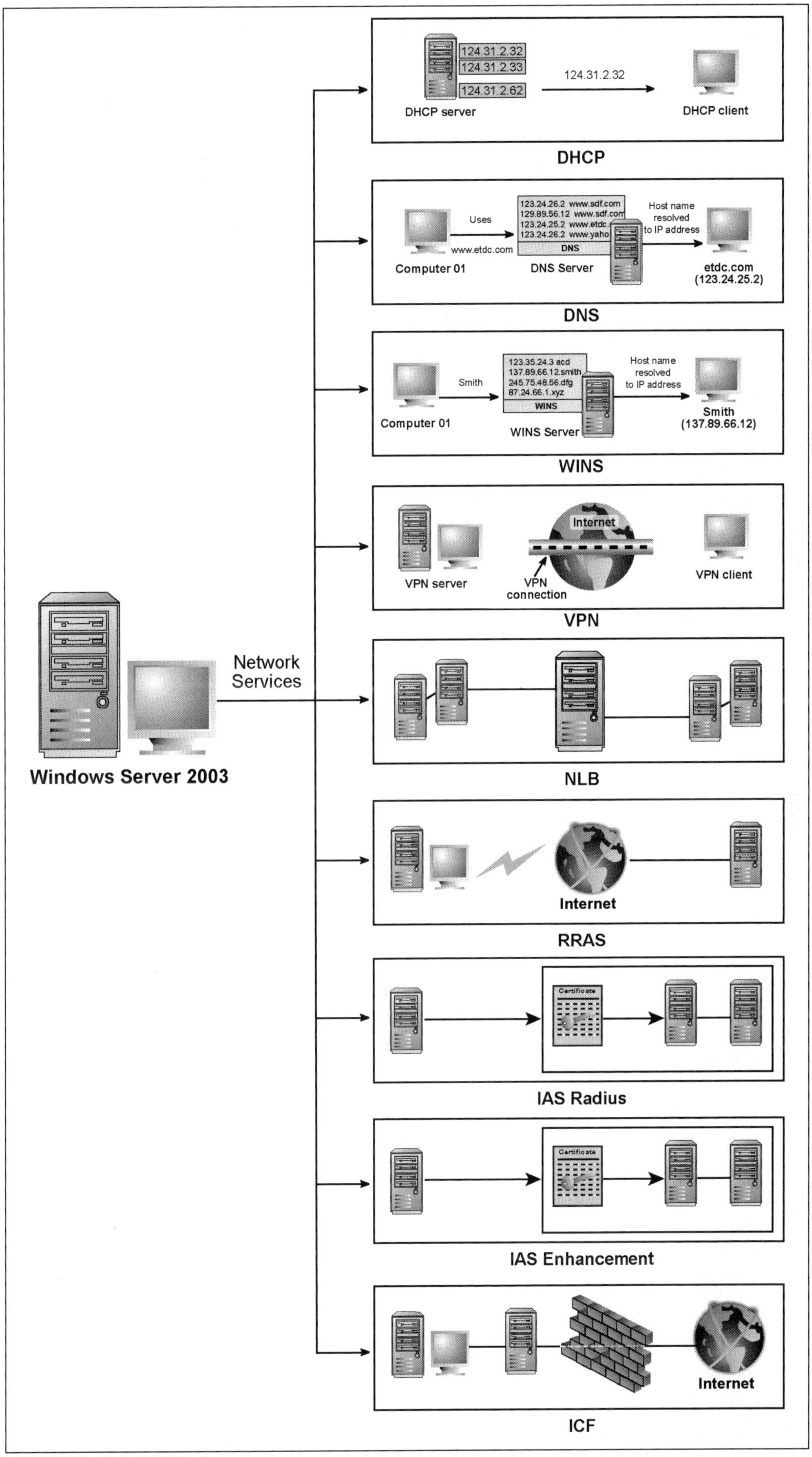

project 1.5

Examining Network Protocols and Security Services

exam objective

Basic knowledge

overview

Windows Server 2003 provides various networking protocols, such as TCP/IP, PPTP, L2TP, and HTTP. It also provides security services: Kerberos v.5, PKI, EFS, and IPSec. As a network consultant to AcmePrint, Inc., you want to offer the company a strong and secure networking environment for all of its clients. You need to show CEO Seidel the need for greater network security and the viability of implementing Windows Server 2003. Prepare documentation that highlights the increasing need for security to protect all the user data from the various security threats posed by hackers and viruses.

learning objective

After completing this project, you will more familiar with the various network protocols and security services offered by Windows Server 2003.

specific requirements

None

estimated completion time

15 minutes

project steps

1. Summarize the advantages provided by the fact that Windows Server 2003 supports a large number of different network protocols.
2. Describe the TCP/IP, L2TP, and PPTP network protocols (**Figure 1-5**).
3. Define Kerberos, PKI, EFS, and IPSec (**Figure 1-6**).
4. Identify the advantages of implementing these security services in a networking environment.

Figure 1-5 Network protocols supported by Windows Server 2003

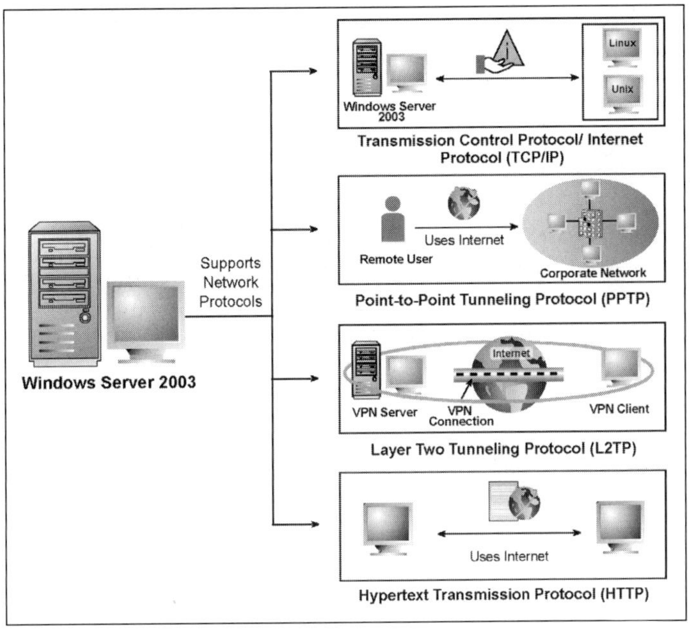

Figure 1-6 Security Services provided by Windows Server 2003

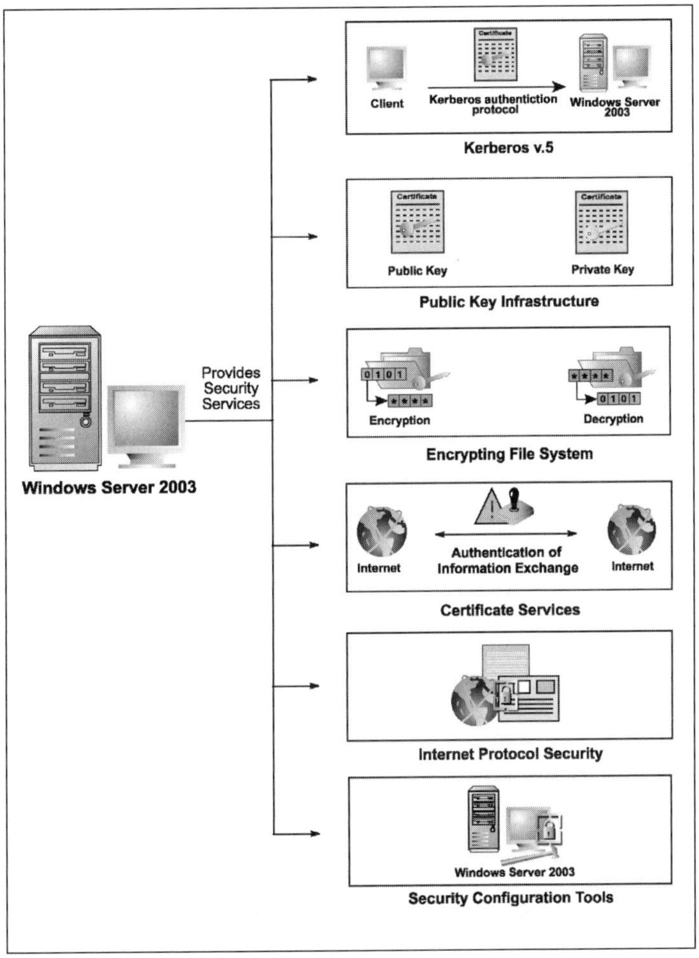

LESSON

2 Installing Windows Server 2003 and Server Hardware Devices

Windows Server 2003 is a user-friendly operating system that you can easily install and configure. You can perform a new installation or upgrade your old version of Windows 2000 Server or Windows NT Server 4.0 to Windows Server 2003. You can install Windows Server 2003 using either an attended or unattended installation. An attended installation allows you to install and configure Windows Server 2003 in several easy-to-follow steps. An attended installation can be performed by either:

- Using the Windows Server 2003 installation CD-ROM
- Running Winnt.exe or Winnt32.exe over the network from a share

The Windows Server 2003 installation process consists of three phases:

1. The Pre-copy phase
2. The Text mode phase
3. The GUI mode phase

During an upgrade, Windows Server 2003 automatically retains all existing settings for users, groups, permissions, and rights. You do not need to reconfigure them after upgrading your system. You can upgrade Windows NT Server 4.0 and Windows 2000 Server to Windows Server 2003, but not versions earlier than Windows NT 4.0. For earlier versions, you must first upgrade to at least Windows NT 4.0. You cannot upgrade Windows 2000 Professional, Windows 98 or Windows 95 to Windows Server 2003.

A critical activity in the upgrade process is to back up the server you will be upgrading. After running the backup, you must verify that the files on the backup media are restorable. If the upgrade is not successful, use the backup you created to restore the server to its pre-upgrade configuration. To avoid installation problems, perform some pre-installation tasks such as checking for hardware and software compatibility, using the Windows Server Catalog on either the installation CD-ROM or the Microsoft Web site.

This lesson contains projects that will enable you to practice performing pre-installation tasks and then installing Windows Server 2003 on a clean hard drive using the installation CD. You will also be able to practice troubleshooting failed installations.

Once Windows Server 2003 is installed, you may need to install various server hardware devices. This lesson also includes projects that will enable you to practice working with the Add Hardware Wizard and Device Manager, and configuring driver signing options.

Scenario

You are the network administrator for Craighead College. You are responsible for the installation and maintenance of all of the hardware and networking software for your school. Craighead College is expanding its campuses into several new cities. To facilitate this geographical expansion, you have selected Windows Server 2003, Enterprise Edition to handle your networking needs. The school will then be able to utilize the multi-protocol support in Windows Server 2003, which will enhance its software development efforts. You must install Windows 2003 Server on the new computers purchased for the expansion.

Lesson 2 Installing Windows Server 2003 and Server Hardware Devices

Project	Exam 70-290 Objective
2.1 Performing Pre-installation Tasks	Basic knowledge
2.2 Performing an Attended Installation of Windows Server 2003 on a Clean Hard Drive	Basic knowledge
2.3 Troubleshooting Failed Installations	Basic knowledge
2.4 Working with the Add Hardware Wizard	Install and configure server hardware devices. Monitor server hardware. Tools might include Device Manager, the Hardware Troubleshooting Wizard, and appropriate Control Panel items.
2.5 Configuring Driver Signing	Install and configure server hardware devices. Monitor server hardware. Tools might include Device Manager, the Hardware Troubleshooting Wizard, and appropriate Control Panel items. Configure driver signing options.
2.6 Configuring Hardware Profiles and Working with Device Manager	Install and configure server hardware devices. Monitor server hardware. Tools might include Device Manager, the Hardware Troubleshooting Wizard, and appropriate Control Panel items. Configure device properties and settings.

General Requirements

To complete the projects in this lesson, you will need a computer that meets the minimum hardware requirements for Windows Server 2003, Enterprise Edition, or Standard Edition, as indicated in Table 2-1. These *minimum* requirements include a Pentium 133 MHz processor, a VGA monitor, 128 MB of RAM, at least 3 GB of hard disk space (since you will need additional space beyond the 2.5 GB recommended for installation to complete all of the projects), a 12X CD-ROM drive, a network interface card (NIC), a mouse pointing device, and a keyboard. You also will need a Windows Server 2003, Enterprise Edition, or Standard Edition installation CD-ROM. In addition, you may find it helpful to refer to Lesson 2 in your Prentice-Hall Certification Series Exam 70-290 textbook for more information about the topics covered by the projects in this lesson.

project 2.1 Performing Pre-Installation Tasks

exam objective

Basic knowledge

overview

Before installing Windows Server 2003 on the new computers purchased by Craighead College for the expansion, you must perform several pre-installation tasks that will help you avoid problems during and after the installation.

learning objective

After completing this project, you will know how to perform pre-installation tasks for Windows Server 2003.

specific requirements

See general requirements.

estimated completion time

15 minutes

project steps

Create and complete a checklist for the following pre-installation tasks:

1. Check that the computer meets minimum hardware requirements **(Table 2-1)**, including:
   - Pentium 133 MHz of faster processor.
   - VGA monitor.
   - 128 MB RAM (256 MB for more than five clients).
   - 1.5 GB hard drive space (2.5 GB recommended).
   - A 12X or higher CD-ROM drive.
   - A network interface card (NIC).
   - Mouse and keyboard.
2. Check the hardware components of your systems against the Windows Server Catalog.
3. Determine the file system that you are going to use to format the partition on your hard drive. Windows Server 2003 supports FAT16, FAT32, and NTFS.
4. Decide whether the computer will be part of a workgroup or a domain.
5. Decide what optional Windows components you wish to install.
6. Disconnect any UPS devices.
7. Decide which licensing mode you will use on the computer: Per Server licensing mode or Per Device or Per User licensing mode **(Figure 2-1)**.

Table 2-1 Minimum and Recommended Hardware Requirements

Windows Server 2003 System Requirements				
Requirement	**Standard Edition**	**Enterprise Edition**	**Datacenter Edition**	**Web Edition**
Minimum CPU Speed	133 MHz	133 MHz for x86-based computers 733 MHz for 64-bit Itanium-based computers*	400 MHz for x86-based computers 733 MHz for 64-bit Itanium-based computers*	133 MHz
Recommended CPU Speed	550 MHz	733 MHz	733 MHz	550 MHz
Minimum RAM	128 MB	128 MB	512 MB	128 MB
Recommended Minimum RAM	256 MB	256 MB	1 1 GB	256 MB
Maximum RAM	4 GB	32 GB for x86-based computers 64 GB for 64-bit Itanium-based computers*	64 GB for x86-based computers 512 GB for 64-bit Itanium-based computers*	2 GB
Multiprocessor Support	Up to 4	Up to 8	Minimum of 8 required Maximum of 64	Up to 2
Minimum Disk Space for Setup	1.5 GB	1.5 GB for x86-based computers 2.0 GB for 64-bit Itanium-based computers*	1.5 GB for x86-based computers 2.0 GB for 64-bit Itanium-based computers*	1.5 GB
Recommended Disk Space	2.5 GB	2.5 GB	2.5 GB	2.5 GB

* The 64-bit versions of Windows Server 2003, Enterprise Edition and Windows Server 2003, Datacenter Edition cannot be successfully installed on 32-bit systems. They are only compatible with 64-bit Itanium-based systems.

Figure 2-1 Windows Server 2003 Licensing Options

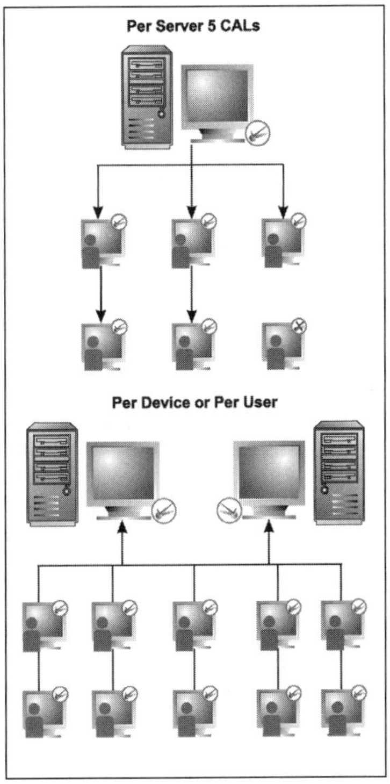

project 2.2

Performing an Attended Installation of Windows Server 2003 on a Clean Hard Drive

exam objective

Basic knowledge

overview

Now that you have completed your pre-installation checklist, you are ready to install Windows Server 2003 on the new computers purchased by Craighead College for the expansion. These computers have no prior operating system installed, and you will use the Windows Server 2003 installation CD-ROM. The installation will consist of three phases **(Figure 2-2)**: pre-copy, text-based, and GUI.

learning objective

After completing this project, you will know how to perform an attended installation of Windows Server 2003 using the installation CD-ROM.

specific requirements

See general requirements. The project assumes that the computer does not have an operating system installed (i.e., it has a "clean" hard drive), but you can still do the project even if it does. Note that some steps may differ as a result.

estimated completion time

Approximately 75 minutes, depending on your computer.

project steps

Install Windows Server 2003 on a clean hard drive using the installation CD-ROM.

1. Reboot your computer with the **Windows Server 2003 installation CD-ROM** in the CD-ROM or DVD drive of your computer. If you receive the prompt to **Press any key to boot from CD**, press the **[Spacebar]** to boot the computer with the Windows Server 2003 installation CD.
2. The **Windows Server 2003 Setup** screen will appear. Depending on the licensing arrangements with respect to the software you are installing, you may also see a message telling you that you have only a certain period of time in which to activate the installation before it is deactivated. Press **[Enter]**. The Setup program will then begin loading files to be used during the text-based portion of the installation.
3. The text phase of the installation begins when the **Welcome to Setup** screen appears and gives you a choice to either set up Windows, repair Windows or quit **(Figure 2-3)**. Press **[Enter]** to select set up.
4. Read the **Windows Licensing Agreement** when it appears **(Figure 2-4);** press **[F8]** to accept its terms and conditions. Setup will search for previous installations of Windows.
5. Windows Setup next displays a list of the existing partitions (if any exist) and available unpartitioned space. Since this is supposed to be a clean hard drive, all available space should be listed as unpartitioned space. You will create a new partition. Use the **[Up]** and **[Down]** arrow keys to select the Unpartitioned space and press **[Enter]**. Then, press the **[C]** key to create a partition in the unpartitioned space of the first available drive.
6. The **Create a New Partition** screen appears. Type **2000** as the partition size and press **[Enter]** to create the partition.
7. The **Existing Partitions** screen appears. Verify the newly created partition is highlighted and press **[Enter]** to continue with the installation.
8. The next screen informs you that the partition that you have just created is not formatted. Select **Format the partition using the NTFS file system (Figure 2-5)**, and press **[Enter]** to continue the installation.
9. After the format of the partition is completed, Setup will examine your disks, copy files to the Windows Server 2003 installation folders, and initialize your Windows Server 2003 configuration. This may take several moments.

tip

If you are not prompted to boot from the CD at all, possibly your computer's boot options are not set correctly. Usually, the boot order should be set to Floppy, CD, Hard Disk. If this is not so, you may need to edit your BIOS configuration settings.

tip

If existing partitions are listed, delete them by first highlighting each partition and then pressing D, and then confirming the deletion by pressing L. If there is any data on these partitions, make sure that you have a working backup before deleting them.

Figure 2-2 Three Phases of a Windows Server 2003 Installation

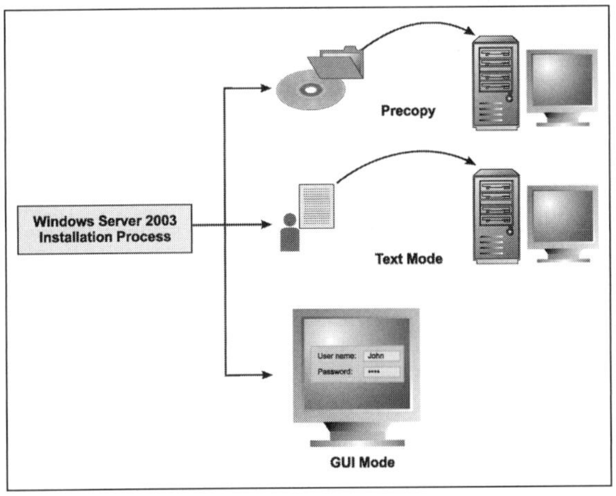

Figure 2-3 Welcome to Setup

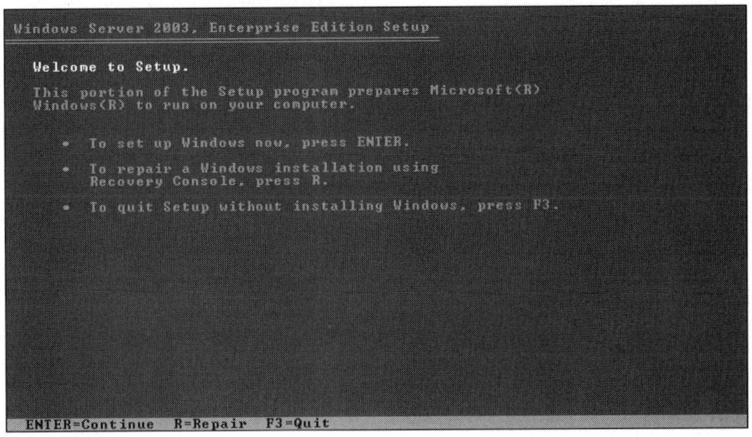

Figure 2-4 Windows Licensing Agreement

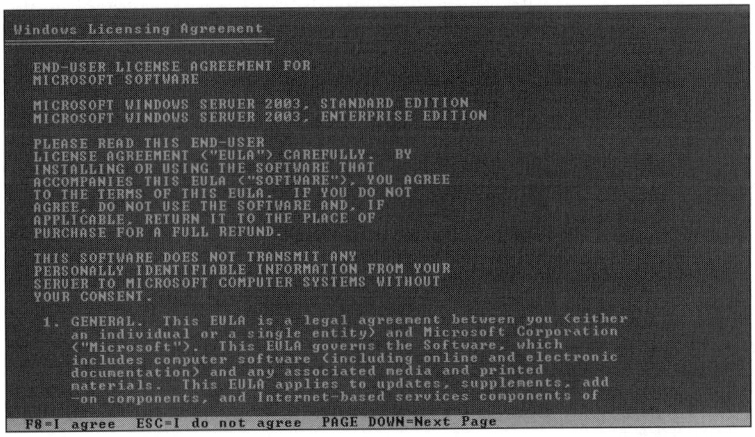

Figure 2-5 Formatting the partition

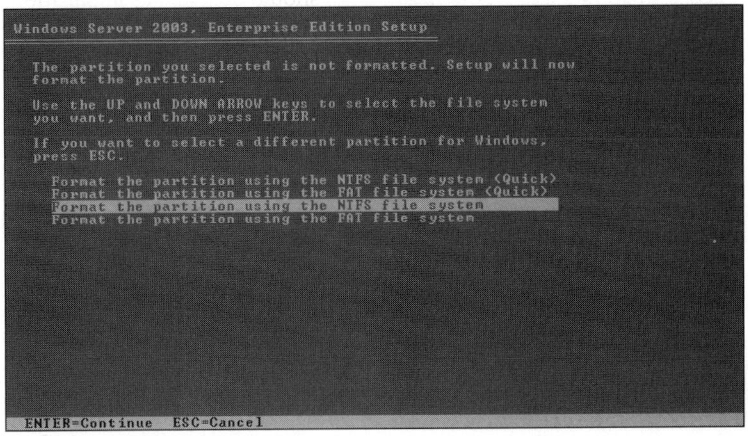

project 2.2

Performing an Attended Installation of Windows Server 2003 on a Clean Hard Drive (cont'd)

exam objective

Basic knowledge

project steps

10. When completed, the computer will reboot, and the GUI phase of installation begins. The **Windows Server 2003** splash screen appears, followed by the **Windows Server 2003 Setup** screen. Then, Setup detects and installs the devices on your computer. An **Installing Devices** progress bar shows you how far the process has progressed **(Figure 2-6)**. The computer screen may flicker during this process.
11. Next, the **Regional and Language Options** screen opens. Here, you can customize settings for different regions and languages. Accept the default settings and click **Next**.
12. The **Personalize Your Software** screen opens. Type:
    - Your name in the **Name** text box.
    - **Craighead College** in the **Organization** text box.

    Click **Next**.
13. The **Your Product Key** screen opens. Type the product key (located on the back cover of the Windows Server 2003 CD jewel box) in the spaces provided and click **Next**.
14. Click **Next**. The **Licensing Modes** screen opens. Choose the **Per Server** option and type **5** in the **Number of Concurrent Connections** spin box if it is not already present by default (remember, in the business world, you will enter the number of licenses you have purchased) **(Figure 2-7)**.
15. Click **Next**. The **Computer Name and Administrator Password** screen opens. Type:
    - A computer name, such as **Server1**, in the **Computer Name** text box.
    - An Administrator password in the **Administrator Password** text box. Note that if you do not select a password that meets Microsoft's criteria for strong passwords, a message box will appear, recommending that you select a different password that meets those criteria.
    - The Administrator password again in the **Confirm password** text box.
16. If a modem is detected, the **Modem Dialing Information** screen will appear. Specify the required information about the modem, such as the area code or city code, and click **Next**. If the computer does not have a modem, you will proceed directly to Step 17.
17. The **Date and Time Settings** screen opens. Set the correct date, time and time zone and click **Next**.
18. The Windows Server 2003 Setup screen reappears, and Setup now installs network software that enables you to communicate with other computers, networks, and the Internet. When the **Installing Network** progress bar reaches 100%, the **Networking Settings** screen opens. Select **Custom Settings** and click **Next**.
19. Click **TCP/IP**, and then click **Properties**. Click the **Use the following IP Address** option button, and type **10.0.0.1** in the **IP address** text box. Type **255.0.0.0** in the **Subnet Mask** text box. Click the **Use the following DNS server** option button, and type **10.0.0.1** in the **Preferred DNS server** text box. Click **OK**, and then click **Next**.
20. The **Workgroup or Computer Domain** screen opens. Accept the default selection **No, this computer is not on a network, or is on a network without a domain. Make this computer a member of the following workgroup** and the default Workgroup name, **WORKGROUP**, by clicking **Next**.
21. The Windows Server 2003 Setup screen reappears once more. Setup now copies files and completes installation, including installing Start menu items, registering components, saving settings, and removing any temporary files used. Progress bars will appear, indicating the progress and completion of each of these tasks, which may take a total of 20–30 minutes.
22. When all tasks have been completed, the computer will reboot to the **Welcome to Windows Microsoft Windows Server 2003** initial logon screen. Press **[Ctrl] + [Alt] + [Delete]**.
23. The **Log on to Windows** dialog box appears. Enter the password for the Administrator account and click **OK**.

Figure 2-6 Windows Server 2003 Setup screen — Installing Devices progress bar

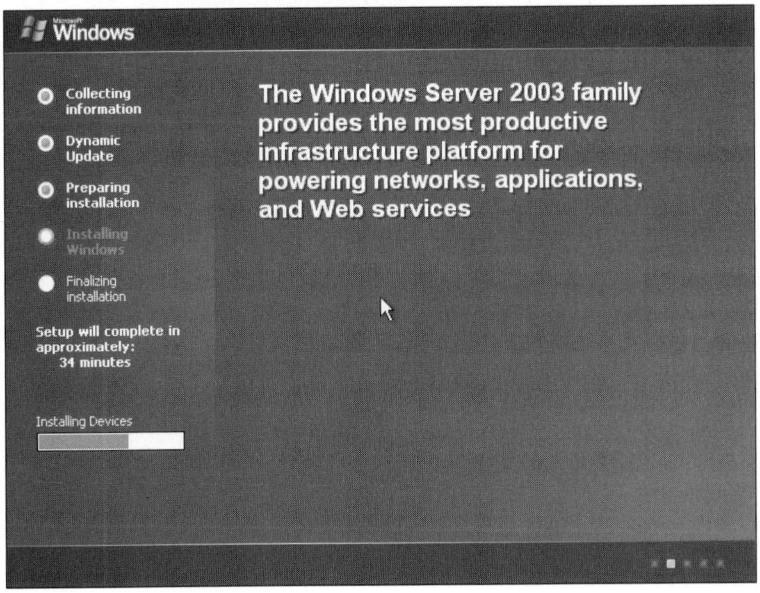

Figure 2-7 Licensing Modes screen

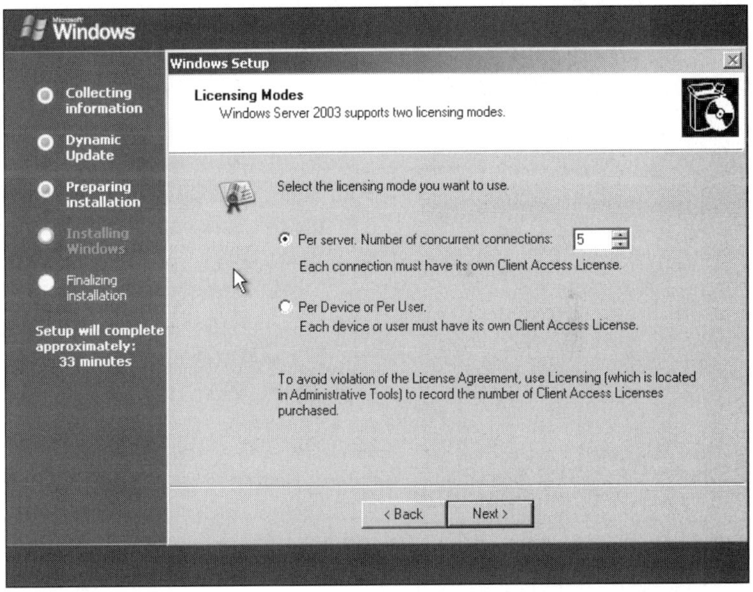

Figure 2-8 Setting TCP/IP Properties

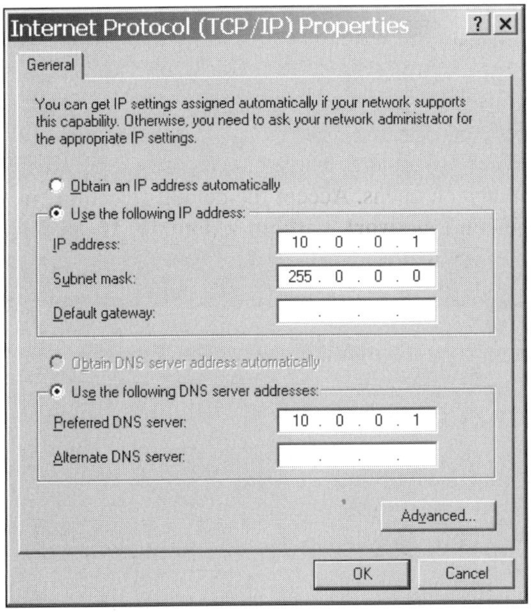

project 2.3

Troubleshooting Failed Installations

exam objective

Basic knowledge

overview

When you install Windows 2003 Server, you may encounter hardware or software-related problems (**Figure 2-9**). In order to achieve a successful installation, it is important to be able to troubleshoot these problems.

learning objective

After completing this project, you will know how to troubleshoot a failed Windows 2003 Server installation.

specific requirements

None

estimated completion time

30 minutes

project steps

1. Give possible solutions to the following problems that may occur during installation:
   - Media errors
   - Insufficient disk space
   - Hardware driver errors
   - Missing installation files
2. Some installation malfunctions will generate STOP errors. Give possible solutions for the following STOP error messages:
   - IRQL_NOT_LESS_OR_EQUAL
   - KMODE_EXCEPTION_NOT_HANDLED
   - UNKNOWN_HARD_ERROR
   - DRIVER_POWER_STATE_FAILURE
   - INACCESSIBLE_BOOT_DEVICE

Figure 2-9 Problems that cause failed installations

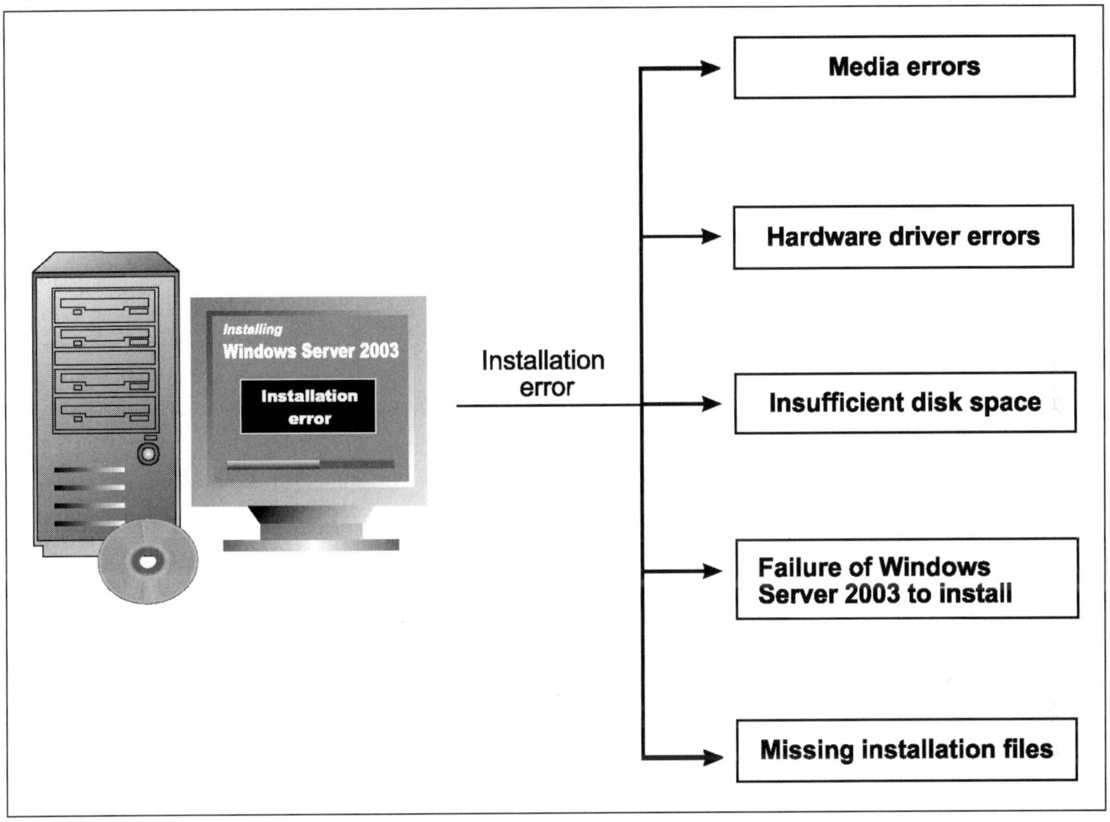

project 2.4

Working with the Add Hardware Wizard

exam objective

Install and configure server hardware devices. Monitor server hardware. Tools might include Device Manager, the Hardware Troubleshooting Wizard, and appropriate Control Panel items.

overview

Installing and configuring hardware devices in the Windows Server 2003 environment is typically an easy and problem-free procedure because the operating system is Plug and Play compatible, which means that most common devices will be located and installed automatically. However, Plug and Play may not work for all devices because some of them may be too old, too new, or too minor to have a device driver included on the installation CD. When Windows Server 2003 does not automatically detect and install a new hardware device (and its associated driver) that is attached to your system, you may need to use the **Add Hardware Wizard (Figure 2-10)** or run a setup program from a manufacturer's supplied CD. Note that only an Administrator can install non-Plug and Play devices.

learning objective

After completing this project, you will know how to install a hardware device on a Windows Server 2003 computer using the Add Hardware Wizard.

specific requirements

Administrative rights on a Windows Server 2003 computer on which a CD-ROM or DVD drive is physically present but has not been installed or has been uninstalled.

estimated completion time

30 minutes

project steps

1. Click **Start**, point to **Control Panel**, and click **Add Hardware** to initiate the **Add Hardware Wizard**. The **Welcome to the Add Hardware Wizard** screen opens.
2. Click **Next**. The Add Hardware Wizard will search for, locate, install the device drivers for and configure the DVD or CD-ROM drive automatically **(Figure 2-11)**.
3. The **Completing the Add Hardware Wizard** screen opens **(Figure 2-12)**. Click **Finish** to close the **Add Hardware Wizard**.
4. If the **System Settings Change** dialog box opens, click **No**. You do not need to restart the computer.
5. Click **Start**, and click **My Computer**. The DVD or CD-ROM drive icon appears.
6. Close the **My Computer** window.

Figure 2-10 The Add Hardware Wizard

Figure 2-11 Searching for new hardware

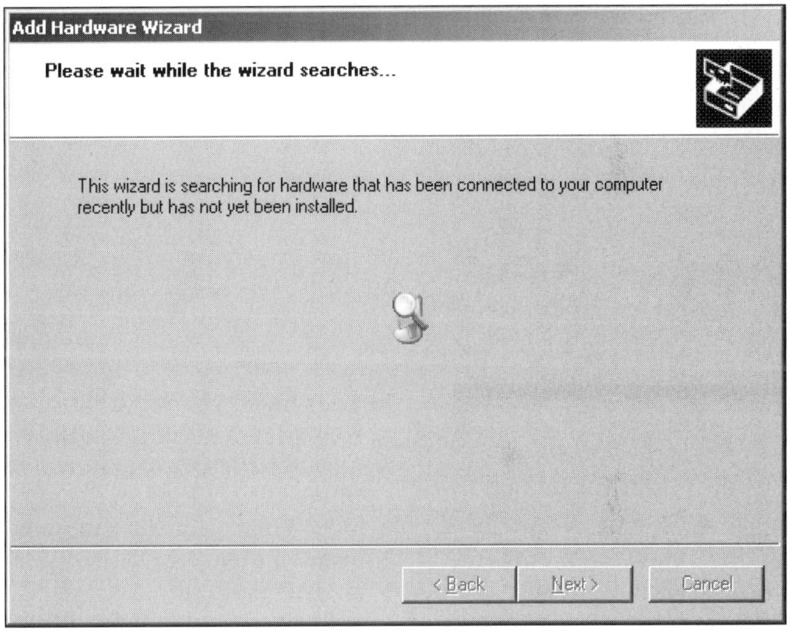

Figure 2-12 The Completing the Add Hardware Wizard screen

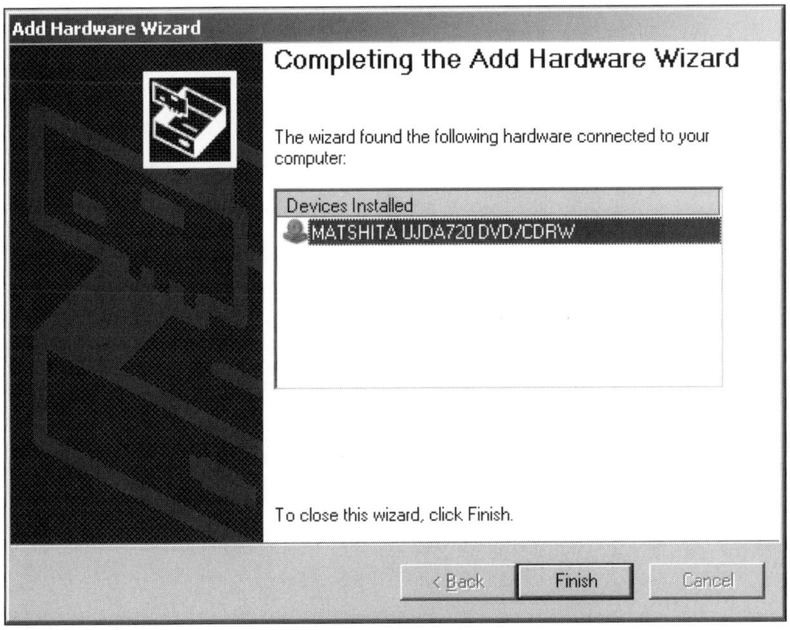

project 2.5

Configuring Driver Signing

exam objective

Install and configure server hardware devices. Monitor server hardware. Tools might include Device Manager, the Hardware Troubleshooting Wizard, and appropriate Control Panel items. Configure driver signing options.

overview

To ensure that all hardware devices installed on the new Windows 2003 computers purchased by Craighead College are reliable, it is crucial that you load compatible driver files for the devices. You have decided to install only devices that have passed the Microsoft certification process. To pass the certification process, the devices are submitted to Windows Hardware Quality Labs (WHQL) for testing. If the drivers pass the WHQL tests, they receive a Microsoft digital signature.

learning objective

After completing this project, you will know how to change the driver signing option to allow only devices with a Microsoft digital signature to be installed.

specific requirements

See general requirements.

estimated completion time

15 minutes

project steps

1. Log on to the server as an **Administrator**.
2. Click **Start**, point to **Control Panel**, and click **System (Figure 2-13)** to open the **Systems Properties** dialog box **(Figure 2-14)**. Click each of the tabs and record the information you find on a sheet of paper.
3. Click the **Hardware** tab, and then click **Driver Signing** to open the **Driver Signing Options** dialog box.
4. In the **What action do you want Windows to take?** section, click the **Block — Never install unsigned driver software** option button to prevent unsigned files from being installed on the server. Notice that **Warn — Prompt me each time to choose an action** is the default setting at installation.
5. In the **Administrator option** section, place a check mark in the **Make this action the system default** check box **(Figure 2-15)**. Click **OK** to close the **Driver Signing Options** dialog box.
6. Click **OK** to close the **System Properties** dialog box.

Figure 2-13 Opening the Systems Properties dialog box

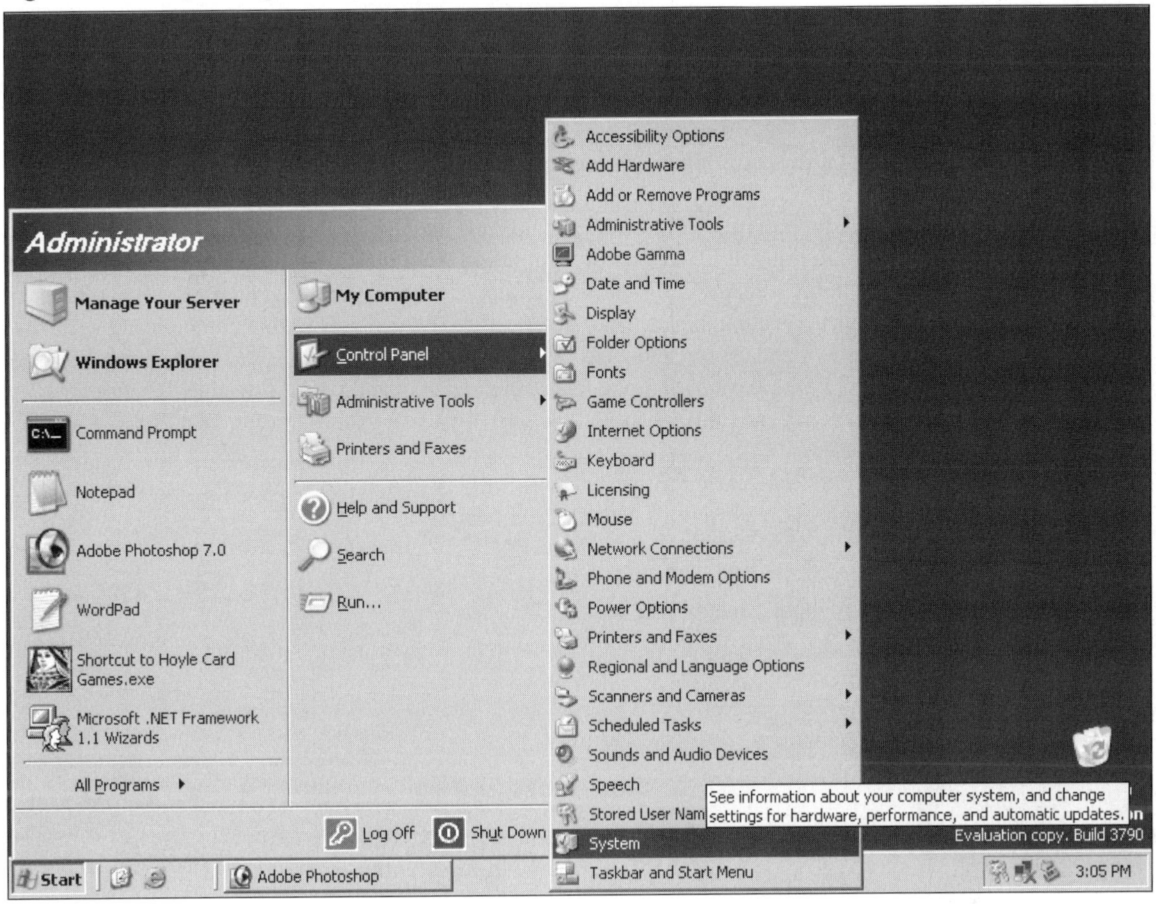

Figure 2-14 The Systems Properties dialog box

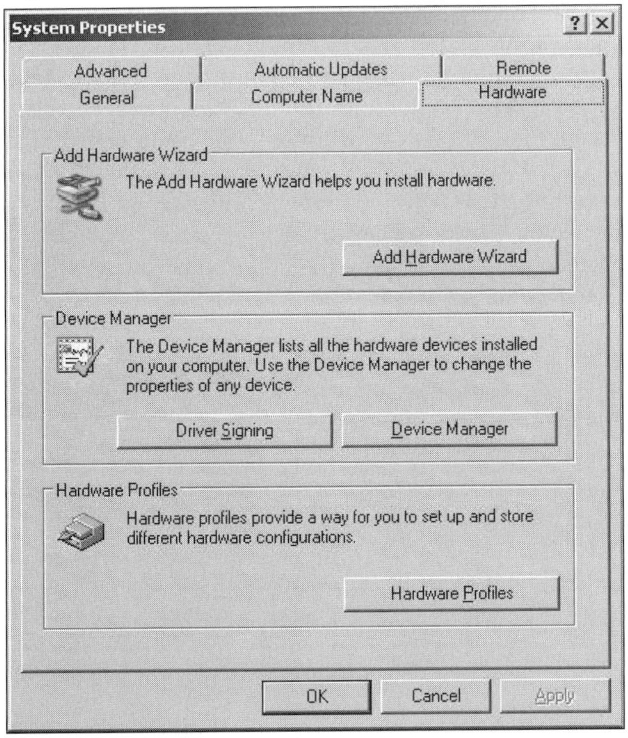

Figure 2-15 The Driver Signing Options dialog box

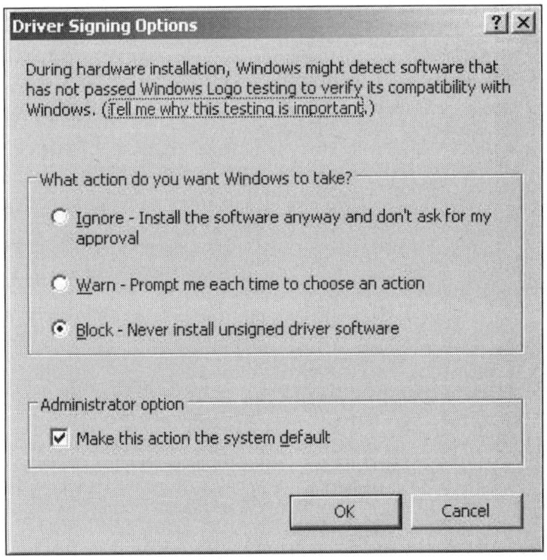

project 2.6

Configuring Hardware Profiles and Working with Device Manager

exam objective

Install and configure server hardware devices. Monitor server hardware. Tools might include Device Manager, the Hardware Troubleshooting Wizard, and appropriate Control Panel items. Configure device properties and settings.

overview

A hardware profile describes the configuration of specific computer equipment. You can use the profile so that it meets the hardware needs of several different users, or has a different hardware configuration depending on how you are using it. Hardware profiles are most commonly used on laptop computers. One of the employees at Craighead College has Windows Server 2003 running on a portable computer that he uses at home on the weekends. Since the computer will not be on a LAN when used in this manner, you want to disable the network board when the user is not at the office. To do this, you will create an additional hardware profile (one is automatically created at installation) to disable the network card when the LAN will not be available.

learning objective

After completing this project, you will know how to create and customize multiple hardware profiles on a Windows Server 2003 computer.

specific requirements

See general requirements.

estimated completion time

30 minutes

project steps

1. Log on to the computer as an **Administrator**.
2. Click **Start**, point to **Control Panel**, and click **System**.
3. The **Systems Properties** dialog box opens. Click the **Hardware** tab.
3. Click **Hardware Profiles**. Highlight the **Profile 1(Current)** profile **(Figure 2-16)** under **Available hardware profiles**, and click **Copy**. In the **Copy Profile** dialog box, type **No Network (Figure 2-17)** in the **To** text box, and click **OK**. Click **OK** again in the **Hardware Profiles** dialog box. Click **OK** in the **Systems Properties** dialog box.
4. Click **Start** and select **Shut Down**. In the **Shut Down Windows** dialog box, select **Restart** in the **What do you want the Computer to do?** list box, and then select **Hardware: Maintenance (Planned)** in the **Option** list box in the **Shutdown Event Tracker** section **(Figure 2-18)**. Click **OK**.
5. Upon reboot, select **No Network** from the **Hardware Profile/Configuration Recovery Menu**, and press **[Enter]**. Log on as an **Administrator**.
6. Click **Start**, point to **Control Panel**, and click **System**. Select the **Hardware** tab in the System Properties dialog box, and then click **Device Manager**. The **Device Manager** console window opens.

Figure 2-16 Hardware Profiles dialog box

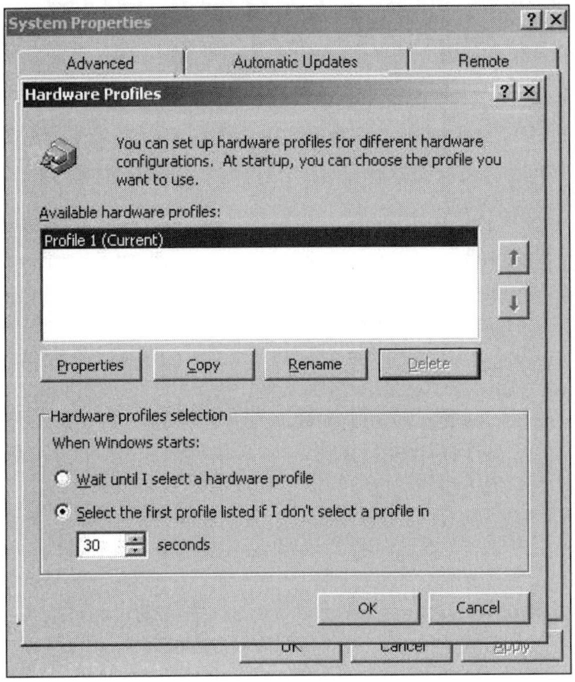

Figure 2-17 Copy Profile dialog box

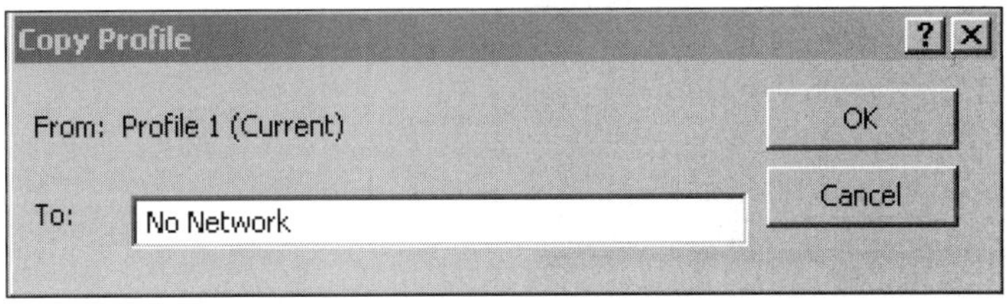

Figure 2-18 Shut Down Windows dialog box

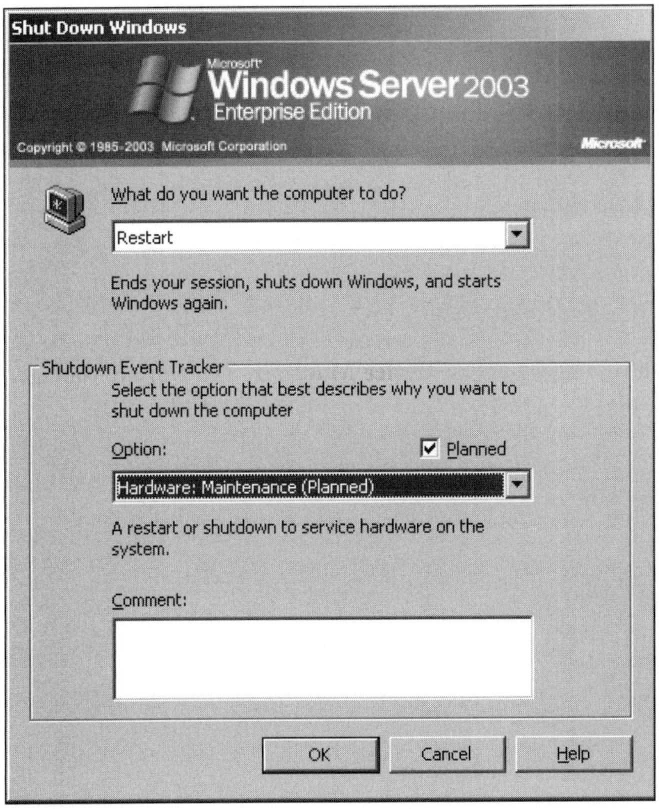

project 2.6

Configuring Hardware Profiles and Working with Device Manager (cont'd)

exam objective

Install and configure server hardware devices. Monitor server hardware. Tools might include Device Manager, the Hardware Troubleshooting Wizard, and appropriate Control Panel items. Configure device properties and settings.

project steps

7. Click the **Network adapters** node to expand it **(Figure 2-19)**, and then double-click the network adapter that is listed. The **Properties** dialog box for the adapter opens. On the **General** tab, click the drop-down arrow under **Device usage** to display the list of options, and select **Do not use this device in the current hardware profile (disable) (Figure 2-20)**. Click **OK**. (Notice that the adapter now has a red **X** on the icon.)
8. Close the **Device Manager** console window, and click **OK** in the **Systems Properties** dialog box. Repeat Step 4. Upon reboot, select **Profile 1** (the default profile) as the hardware profile, and log on as an **Administrator**.
9. To remove the **No Network** hardware profile, select **Start**, point to **Control Panel**, and click **System**. Select the **Hardware** tab in the **System Properties** dialog box, and then click **Hardware Profiles**.
10. Select **No Network** under **Available hardware profiles**, and click **Delete (Figure 2-21)**. Click **Yes** in the confirmation box. Click **OK** to close the **Hardware Profiles** dialog box, and click **OK** to close the **System Properties** dialog box.

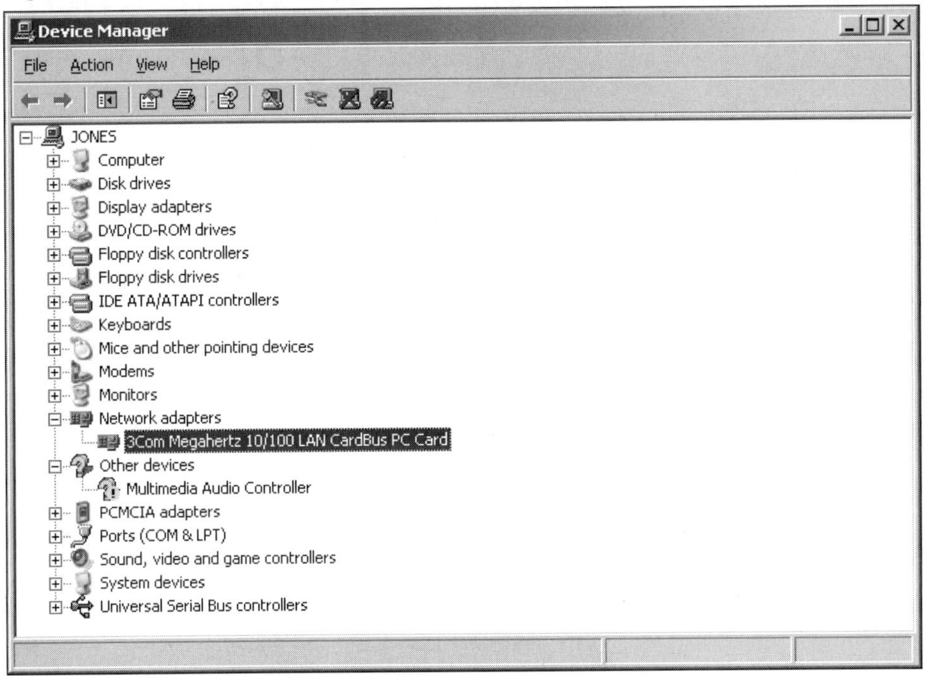

Figure 2-19 The Network adapters node in the Device Manager window

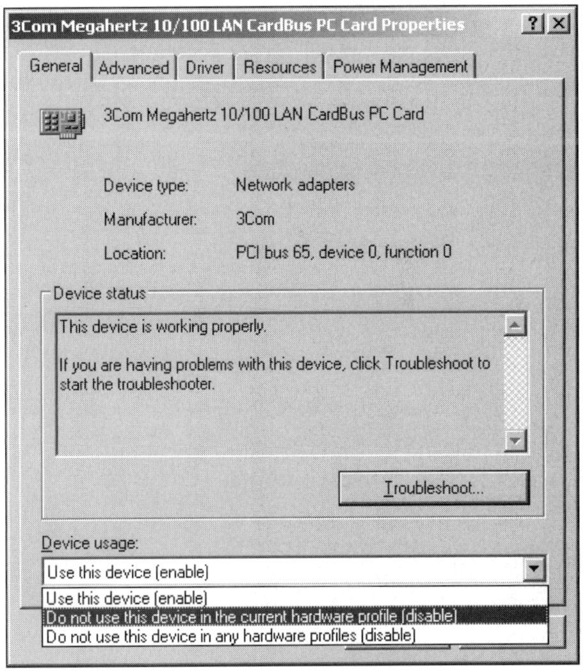

Figure 2-20 Disabling a component

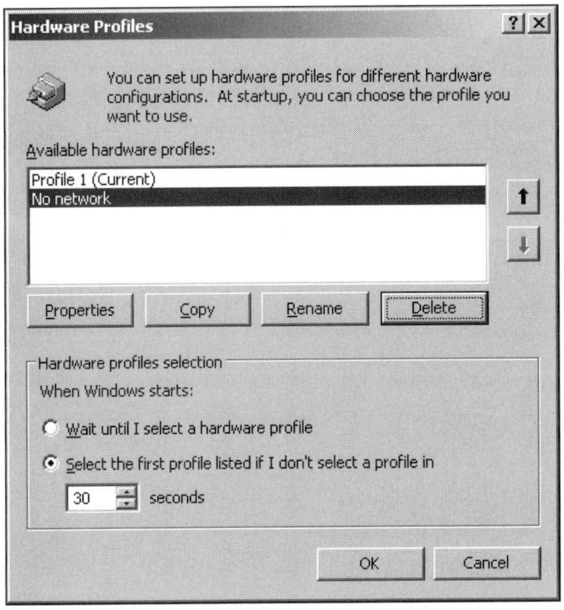

Figure 2-21 Deleting an existing hardware profile

LESSON

3 Introducing Active Directory

Active Directory facilitates the management of resources on multiple servers and multiple clients in the Windows Server 2003 environment. Active Directory enables organizations to centrally manage and share information on a network while acting as the central authority for network security. The central database stores information about users and groups, and manages logging on to the network. Active Directory stores information about how the network is structured and organized, and users access it to identify and locate resources on the network.

Active Directory's database is often simply called the directory. The directory is stored on servers, known as domain controllers, which can be accessed by network applications or services. To provide fault tolerance and load balancing, a domain should have more than one domain controller. The directory provides a logical organization of physical resources on the network—users, groups, computers, domains, organizational units, and security policies.

Like other directory services, Active Directory serves as a designated area where the names that people use to identify objects are converted into the numbers that computers use to identify information. This process is called name resolution, and Active Directory uses four different naming conventions: Distinguished Name (DN), Relative Distinguished Name (RDN), Globally Unique Identifiers (GUID), and User Principal Names (UPN). The architecture consists of three layers: Directory Service Agent (DSA), Database, and Extensible Storage Engine (ESE). The core protocol that facilitates communication between the clients and the directory is Lightweight Directory Access Protocol (LDAP).

This lesson includes projects that will help you become more familiar with the basic elements and features of Active Directory, and underlying Active Directory concepts. You will also be able to practice installing Active Directory, promoting a member server to a domain controller, creating a forest and a tree, creating organizational units and managing Active Directory objects.

Scenario

You are a network administrator for Craighead College, a private educational institution. The college has decided to use Active Directory to control access to its domain and has chosen Windows Server 2003 as its operating system. You have already completed the installation of Windows Server 2003 on a compatible computer, but no domain exists. All users currently work in a workgroup environment. You must install Active Directory, create the domain and organizational units, and place user accounts in the appropriate container.

Lesson 3 Introducing Active Directory

Project	Exam 70-290 Objective
3.1 Identifying the Basic Features and Elements of Active Directory	Basic knowledge
3.2 Examining Underlying Active Directory Concepts	Basic knowledge
3.3 Installing Active Directory	Basic knowledge
3.4 Creating Organizational Units	Basic knowledge
3.5 Managing Active Directory Objects	Basic knowledge

General Requirements

To complete the projects in this lesson, you will need administrative rights on the Windows Server 2003 computer you used in Lesson 2. You will also need your Windows 2003 Server, Enterprise Edition, or Standard Edition installation CD-ROM. In addition, you may find it helpful to refer to Lesson 3 in your Prentice-Hall Certification Series Exam 70-290 textbook for more information about the topics covered by the projects in this lesson.

project 3.1

Identifying the Basic Features and Elements of Active Directory

exam objective

Basic knowledge

overview

Before installing the directory service for Windows 2003 Server, you should understand the features and basic elements of Active Directory to facilitate a more efficient configuration. You should also understand the appropriate hierarchical structure **(Figure 3-1)** of Active Directory.

learning objective

After completing this project, you will be more familiar with the basic elements and features of Active Directory.

specific requirements

None

estimated completion time

1 hour

project steps

1. Describe how the following features of Active Directory will benefit Craighead College:
- Centralized management
- Security
- Hierarchical organization
- Integration with DNS
- Scalability

2. Define the following basic elements, and describe how they will be utilized in your implementation of Active Directory:
- Organizational units
- Tree **(Figure 3-2)**
- Domain
- Forest **(Figure 3-3)**
    - Domain controller
    - Member server
    - Client computers
- Objects
    - User
    - Printer
    - Group
    - Computer

Figure 3-1 Hierarchical Structure of Active Directory

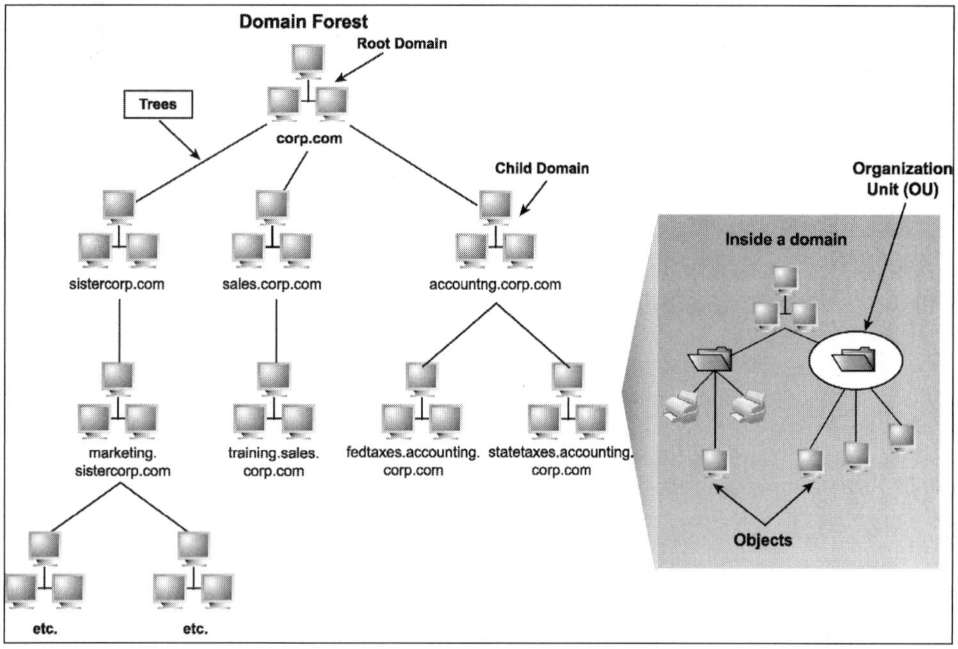

Figure 3-2 Contiguous Namespace—Tree

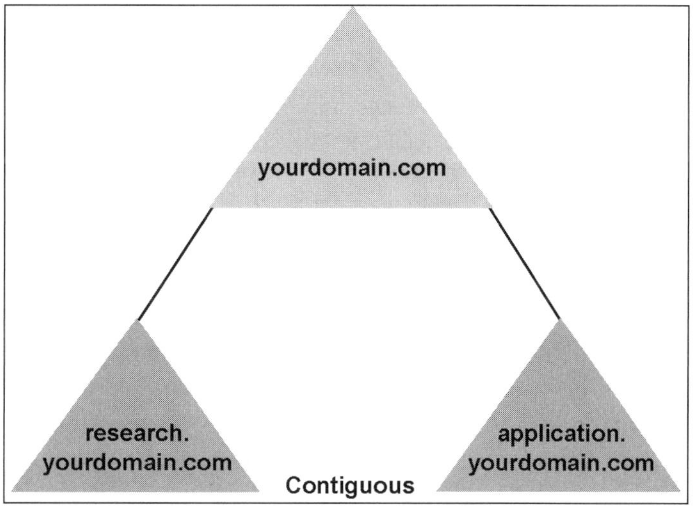

Figure 3-3 Disjointed Namespace—Forest

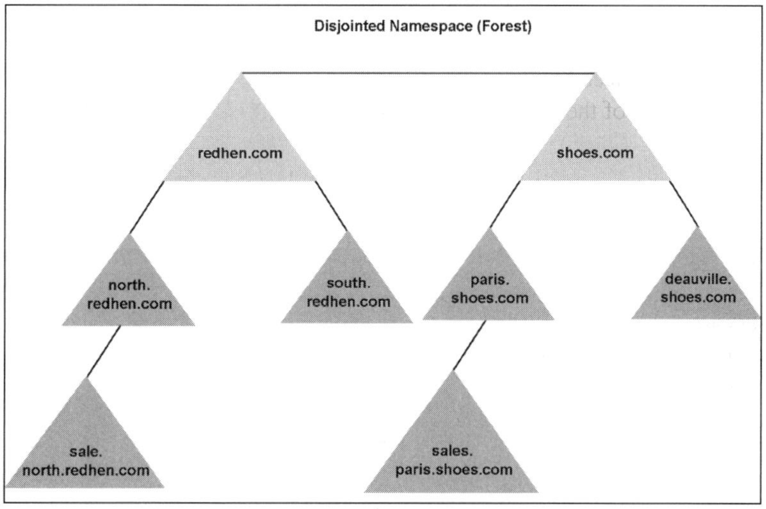

project 3.2 Examining Underlying Active Directory Concepts

exam objective

Basic knowledge

overview

For you to understand Active Directory fully, you should be aware of the ways that the directory identifies each object. Also, you should understand the concepts of schemas, global catalogs, and namespaces.

learning objective

After completing this project, you will be more familiar with the process of name resolution **(Figure 3-4)** and other underlying Active Directory concepts.

specific requirements

None

estimated completion time

30 minutes

project steps

1. Define what the schema is and its role in Active Directory.
2. Explain the purpose of the global catalog. Why does it store only a partial replica of objects? What would be the major reasons for having multiple global catalog servers?
3. Explain the difference between **contiguous namespace** and **disjointed namespace**. How are the different types of namespace related to the terms tree and forest? (Refer to **Figures 3-2** and **3-3**.)
4. Explain the differences among the Distinguished Name, Relative Distinguished Name, and User Principal Name naming conventions. Give an example of how you might use each at Craighead College.

Figure 3-4 Naming Conventions

Distinguished Name	Domain Name/Users/Business Development Group/Team Leaders/Gregory Johnson
Relative Distinguished Name	Gregory Johnson
Globally Unique Identifier	128-bit number → GUID → Retrieves regardless of DN
User Principal Name	Gregory Johnson in yourdomain.com Gregory_J@yourdomain.com

project 3.3 Installing Active Directory

exam objective

Basic knowledge

overview

Now that you are familiar with the different components of the directory, you can install Active Directory to better manage your network at Craighead College. By installing Active Directory, you are promoting this computer to a domain controller. Because you are installing Active Directory for the first time, you will also create the root domain, domain tree, and a new forest. During installation, the database, database log files, and shared system volume will be created automatically.

learning objective

After completing this project, you will know how to promote a member server to a domain controller by installing Active Directory, create a forest, and create a tree.

specific requirements

See general requirements.

estimated completion time

1 hour

project steps

1. Log on as an **Administrator** to the computer on which you previously installed Windows Server 2003 in Lesson 2. This computer currently functions in a workgroup environment.
2. Click **Start**, click **Run**, and type **dcpromo** in the **Open** text box. Click **OK** or press **[Enter]**. This command will start the **Active Directory Installation Wizard (Figure 3-5)**. Click **Next**.
3. The **Operating System Compatibility** screen **(Figure 3-6)** informs you of some compatibility issues with legacy operating systems. Click **Next**.
4. On the **Domain Controller Type** screen, select the option button for **Domain controller for a new domain (Figure 3-7)**. Click **Next**.
5. Choose the **Domain in a new forest** option button on the **Create New Domain** screen. Click **Next**.
6. The **New Domain Name** screen opens. Enter **craighead.com** as the **Full DNS name for new domain. (Figure 3-8)**. Click **Next**. Accept the default name, **CRAIGHEAD**, as the **NetBIOS Domain Name**. Click **Next**.
7. Accept the default locations provided on the **Database and Log Folders** screen. Click **Next**. Also, accept the default location for the **Shared System Volume**. Click **Next**.
8. The wizard will detect that no DNS services are installed. Because DNS is required for Active Directory, the **DNS Registration Diagnostics** screen will display. Select the **Install and configure the DNS server on this computer, and set this computer to use this DNS server as its preferred DNS server** option button **(Figure 3-9)**. Click **Next**.
9. Since you will not run any pre-Windows 2000 operating systems on the network, select **Permissions compatible only with Windows 2000 or Windows Server 2003 operating systems** on the **Permissions** screen **(Figure 3-10)**. Click **Next**.

Figure 3-5 Active Directory Installation Wizard Welcome screen

Figure 3-6 Operating System Compatibility screen

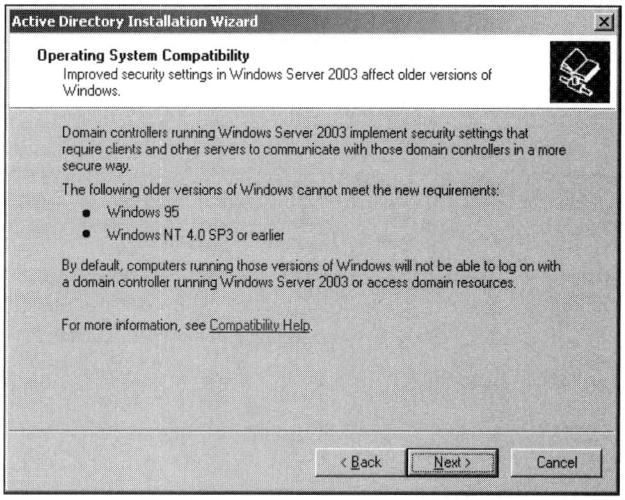

Figure 3-7 Domain Controller Type screen

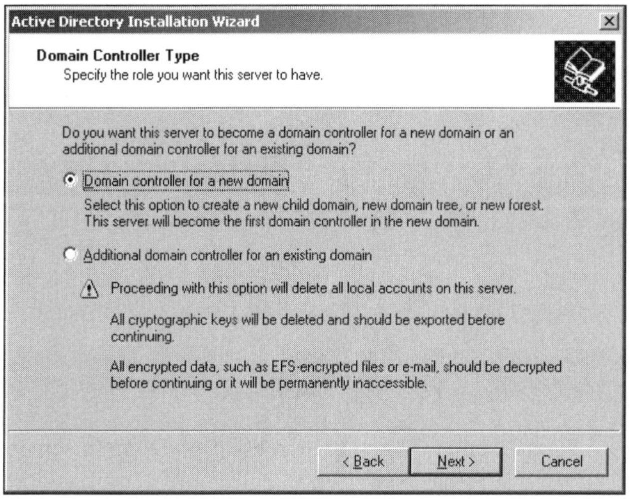

Figure 3-8 New Domain Name screen

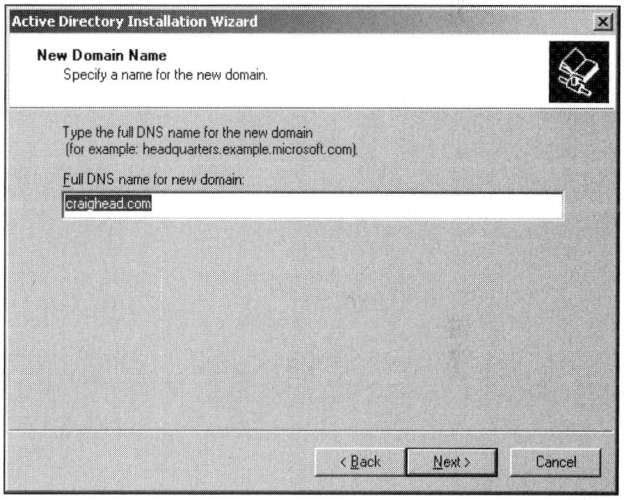

Figure 3-9 DNS Registration Diagnostics screen

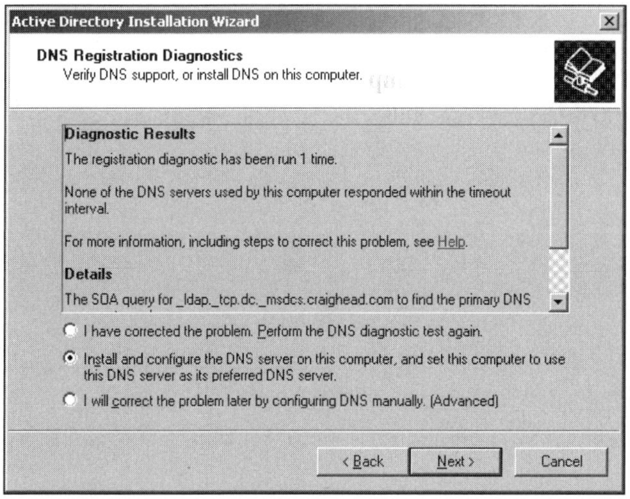

Figure 3-10 Permissions screen

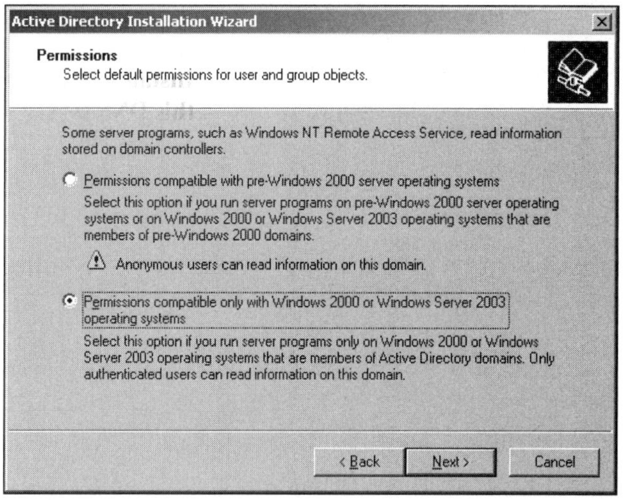

project 3.3

Installing Active Directory (cont'd)

exam objective

Basic knowledge

project steps

10. The **Directory Services Restore Mode Administrator Password** screen appears. You will be prompted to enter a password. This password is used ONLY to restore a backup of directory services and can differ from the normal administrator account password. Enter **Restore** in both the **Restore mode password** text box and in the **Confirm password** text box. Click **Next**.
11. The **Summary** screen will display. After reviewing the configuration, click **Next**. The Wizard will now configure Active Directory **(Figure 3-11)**. During this process, you may be prompted to insert your Windows 2003 Server Installation CD-ROM.
12. After the wizard has completed the installation, click **Finish**, and then click **Restart Now** to reboot.

Figure 3-11 Configuring Active Directory

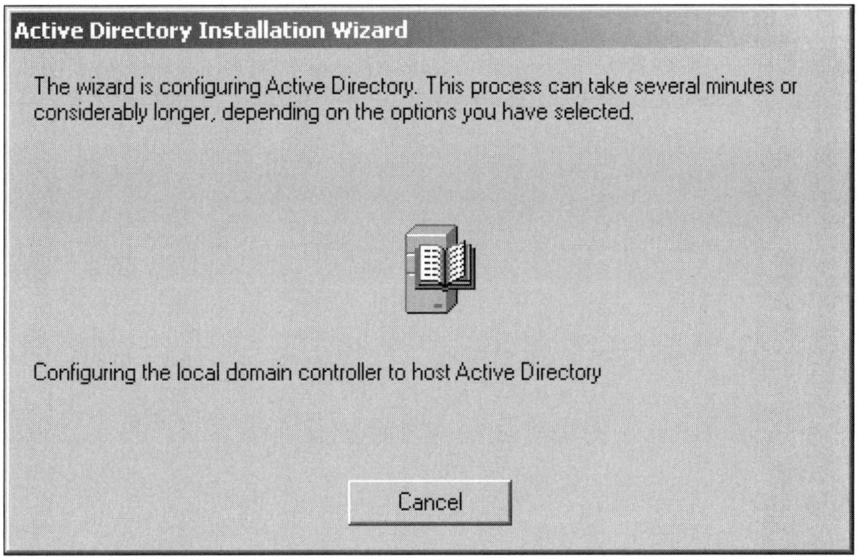

project 3.4 Creating Organizational Units

exam objective

Basic knowledge

overview

An organizational unit (OU) is a container object for organizing objects within a domain. OUs can contain users, groups, resources, and other OUs. OUs are used to simplify the management and administration of objects within Active Directory. Grouping objects into OUs allows you to create and organize child OUs, delegate permissions within specific OUs and assign group policy links.

At Craighead College, most users are either faculty members or students. You must create two OUs to hold domain user accounts by using the Active Directory Users and Computers console. By default, Windows Server 2003 grants permission to members of the Administrators group to create an OU.

learning objective

After completing this project, you will know how to organize your Active Directory tree by creating organizational unit containers for more efficient management and ease of use.

specific requirements

See general requirements. You must have also successfully completed Project 3.3.

estimated completion time

30 minutes

project steps

Create two organizational units in the Craighead College domain you created in Project 3.3, and create a user account within each of the organizational units.

1. Log on as an **Administrator**. Click **Start**, point to **Administrative Tools**, and click **Active Directory Users and Computers**.
2. The **Active Directory Users and Computers** console opens. Expand the domain, **craighead.com**, in the left pane of the console **(Figure 3-12)** to display all of the containers and the Domain Controllers OU that were automatically created at installation.
3. Right-click the **craighead.com** domain, point to **New**, and select **Organizational Unit. The New Object-Organizational Unit** dialog box opens. In the **Name t** text box **(Figure 3-13)**, type **Faculty**, and click **OK**.
4. Repeat Step 3 to create an OU named **Students**.
5. Right-click the new **Faculty** OU, point to **New**, and click **User**.
6. In the **New Object – User** dialog box **(Figure 3-14)**, enter **Amy** as the first name, leave the **Initials** text box blank, enter **Bradshaw** as the last name, and **AmyB** as the user logon name. Notice that the Full name text box and pre-Windows 2000 text box are automatically completed for you. Click **Next**.
7. Type **p@$$w0rd** in the **Password** text box, and retype **p@$$w0rd** in the **Confirm password** text box **(Figure 3-15)**. This password meets the complexity required by Windows Server 2003. Clear the check box next to **User must change password at next logon**, and place a check mark in the **Password never expires** check box. Click **Next**, and then click **Finish** to create the user account.

Figure 3-12 Active Directory Users and Computers Console

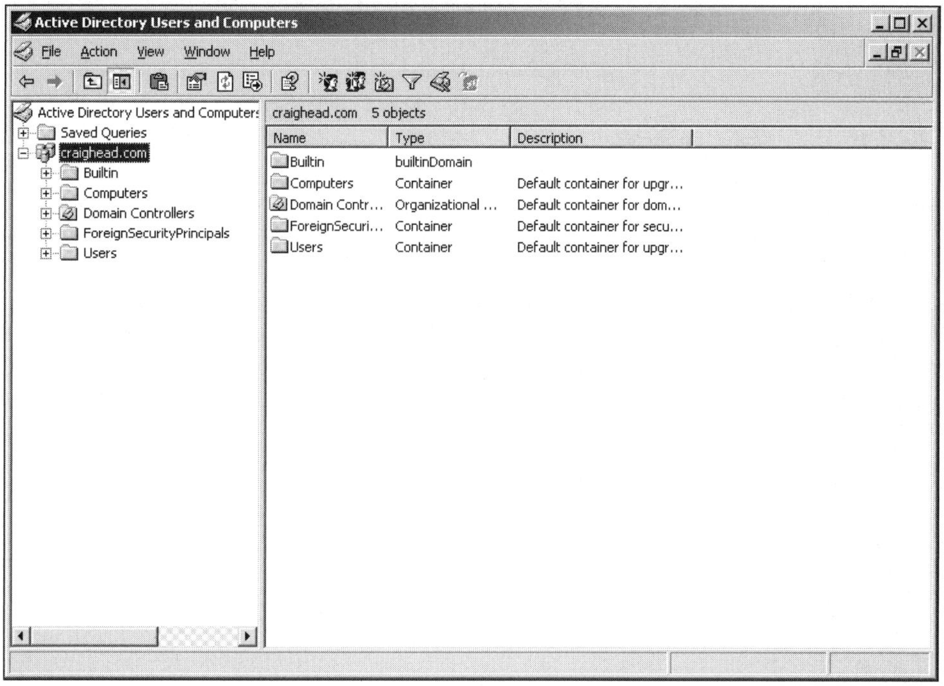

Figure 3-13 New Object - Organizational Unit dialog box

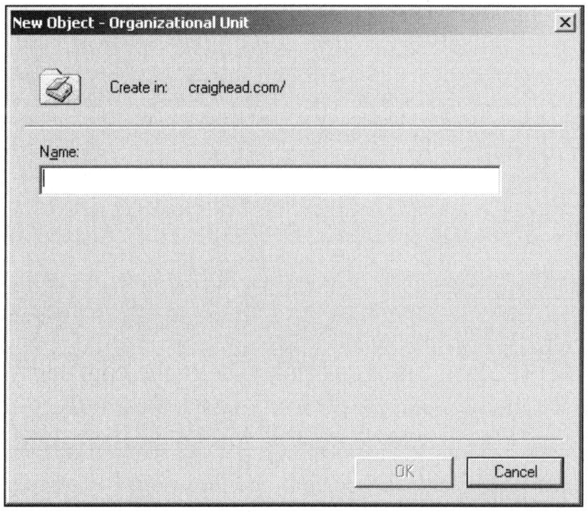

Figure 3-14 New Object - User dialog box

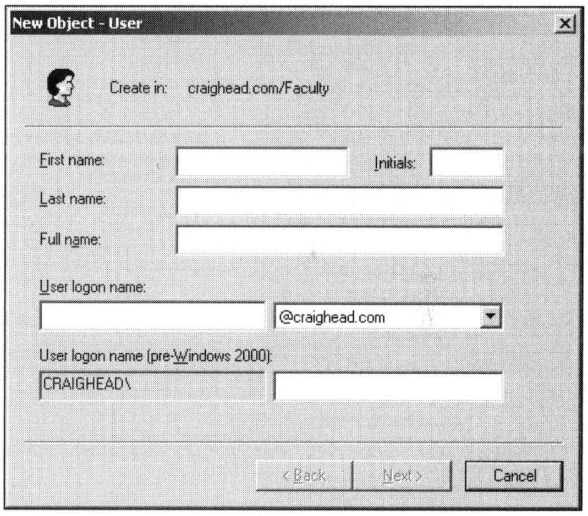

Figure 3-15 Setting the password

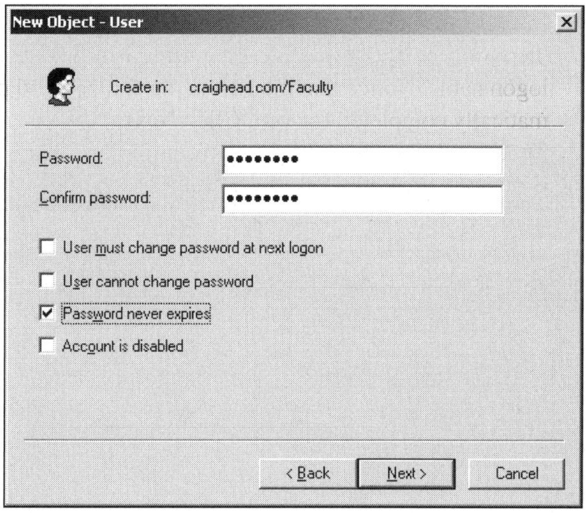

project 3.4 Creating Organizational Units (cont'd)

exam objective

Basic knowledge

project steps

8. Repeat Steps 5–7 to create a user with the first name **Nathan**, the last name **Swanson**, and the logon name **NathanS**. Use the same password as in the previous step.
9. Right-click the **Nathan Swanson** user object, and choose **Properties (Figure 3-16)**. The **Properties** dialog box for the object opens. On the **General** tab, enter **555-0999** as the **Telephone number**.
10. Select the **Telephones** tab. Enter **555-1234** as the **Home** number, and enter **555-9999** as the **Mobile** number.
11. Select the **Address** tab, and enter **13 Indian Trails** as the **Street**. Also, enter **State College** as the **City**, and enter **Arkansas** as the **State**. Use **72000** as the **Zip**. Click **OK.**

Figure 3-16 *<User Account>* Properties dialog box

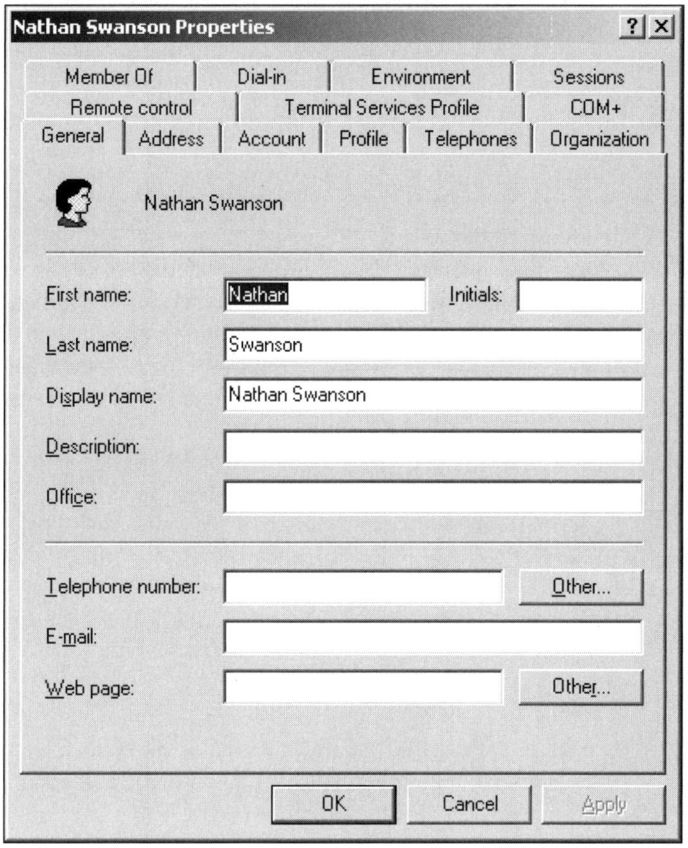

project 3.5 Managing Active Directory Objects

exam objective

Basic knowledge

overview

In addition to the creation of organization units and objects, you will periodically have to perform other managerial tasks. You may need to search for objects in the directory, modify the attributes of objects, and move objects within Active Directory.

learning objective

After completing this project, you know how to modify and move objects with Active Directory.

specific requirements

See general requirements. You must also have successfully completed Projects 3.3 and 3.4.

estimated completion time

30 minutes

project steps

1. You realize that you should have created the Nathan Swanson user object in the **Students** OU instead of the **Faculty** OU. Log on to the computer as an **Administrator**.
2. Click **Start**, point to **Administrative Tools**, and click **Active Directory Users and Computers**.
3. Click the **Faculty** OU in the left pane of the console window.
4. Right-click the **Nathan Swanson** user object and select **Move**. Click the **Students** OU, and click **OK**. Notice that the **Nathan Swanson** object no longer appears in the right pane of the console window. Verify that the move has occurred by clicking the **Students** OU in the left pane.
5. You must find a user in your domain named **Amy**, but you are not sure in which OU the object is located. Right-click the **craighead.com** domain, and select **Find**.
6. In the **Find Users**, **Contacts**, **and Groups** dialog box **(Figure 3-17)**, enter **Amy** in the **Name** text box, and then click **Find Now**. The user object will appear in the **Search results** window.
7. The phone company in your area has changed the local telephone prefix **555** to **815**. You must find all of your users that have been affected. Click the **Clear All** button to remove the previous search results, and then click **OK** to confirm.
8. Click the **Advanced** tab to allow for more complex searches **(Figure 3-18)**. Click **Field**, point to **User**, and then click **Home Phone**. In the **Value** text box, type **555**, and then click **Find Now**. Click **Yes** in the **Find in the Directory** text box. All users that meet the criteria will display in the **Search results** window.
9. Double-click the user object displayed. In the **Telephone number** text box, replace the **555** prefix with **815**. Click **OK** to close the User Properties dialog box. Close the Find Users, Contacts, and Groups dialog box. Close the Active Directory Users and Computers console.

Figure 3-17 Find Users, Contacts, and Groups dialog box

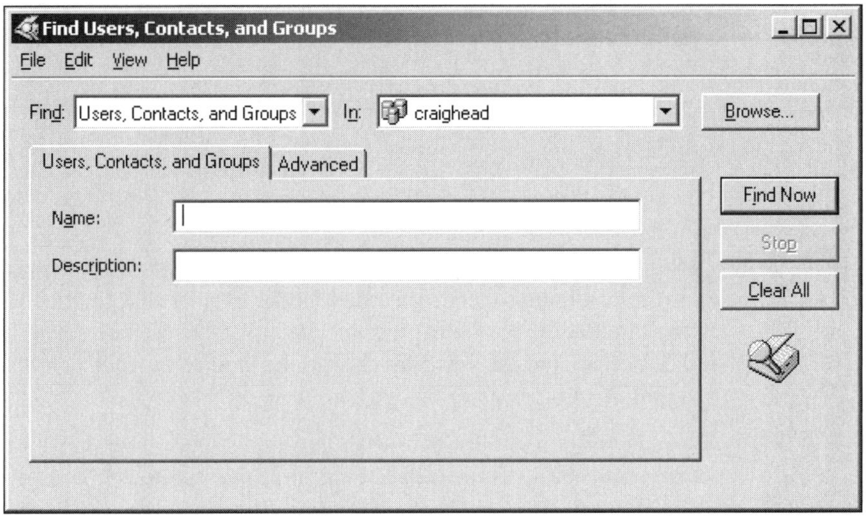

Figure 3-18 Advanced search options

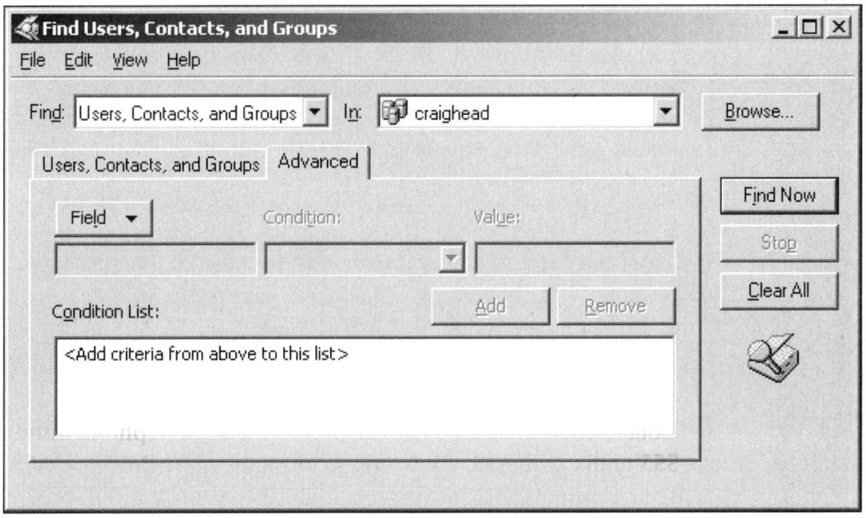

LESSON

4 Organizing a Disk for Data Storage

In any server environment, storage management is always very important. Windows Server 2003 supports a variety of storage types and file systems to allow the administrator to configure secondary storage in the manner that best fits the organization's needs. During installation, the Setup program can be used to prepare the hard disk. However, as your storage needs increase, you may change the storage type, change the file system, add more partitions or volumes, or exchange hard drives.

You can configure a hard disk with two types of storage: basic or dynamic. The default storage type is basic. Basic is the storage type that previous Microsoft operating systems have used. On a basic disk, you create partitions using the unallocated disk space. This default type is adequate when a single hard drive is installed and neither fault tolerance nor striped disk access are desired. Dynamic disks were introduced in Windows 2000 Server. They are used when the simple administrative schemes of a basic disk become inadequate. Dynamic disks not only support simple volumes (which are similar to the primary partitions on a basic disk), but also include the availability of spanned volumes, striped volumes, mirrored volumes, and RAID-5 volumes.

The Disk Management MMC snap-in can be used to manage disks and partitions and optimize disk performance. In the Disk Management console, you can view disk properties and perform such functions as creating new partitions or volumes, setting an active partition, formatting drives, changing drive letters, and upgrading a disk from a conventional basic disk to a dynamic disk. You can also delete partitions or volumes and troubleshoot disk failures.

This lesson contains projects that will help you become familiar with the different storage options offered by Windows Server 2003, and that will allow you to practice customizing an MMC console for disk management, creating an additional partition, converting a basic disk to a dynamic disk, increasing the size of an existing volume, and performing routine disk defragmentation on a server hard drive.

Scenario

You have just completed installing Active Directory in the craighead.com domain (see Lesson 3). This domain controller will function primarily as a file server for the domain. You must determine the appropriate storage type and file system for your organization. In addition, you need to perform periodic maintenance on your storage hardware.

Lesson 4 Organizing a Disk for Data Storage

Project	Exam 70-290 Objective
4.1 Introducing Storage Types	Manage basic and dynamic disks.
4.2 Creating Additional Partitions	Manage basic and dynamic disks.
4.3 Converting Basic Disks to Dynamic Disks	Manage basic and dynamic disks.
4.4 Extending an Existing Volume	Manage basic and dynamic disks.
4.5 Defragmenting a Disk	Optimize server disk performance.

General Requirements

To complete the projects in this lesson, you will need administrative rights on the Windows Server 2003 computer promoted to a domain controller in Lesson 3. You will use the disk space that you left unallocated when you installed Windows Server 2003 in Project 2.2 to create additional partitions and extend the current primary partition. In addition, you will convert the existing basic disk type to dynamic. You also may find it helpful to refer to Lesson 4 in your Prentice-Hall Certification Series Exam 70-290 textbook for more information about the topics covered by the projects in this lesson.

Note: The partition and volume sizes created in this lesson are smaller than would normally exist in a production environment. This is done in the interest of hardware requirements and to reduce the lab time required.

project 4.1 Introducing Storage Types

exam objective

Manage basic and dynamic disks.

overview

You have previously created the craighead.com domain and installed Active Directory. Now you want to determine what hard drive configuration will be best suited for your organization. In order to determine the best configuration, it is necessary to have an understanding of the different storage types and file systems.

learning objective

After completing this project, you will be more familiar with the storage options available in Windows Server 2003.

specific requirements

None

estimated completion time

30 minutes

project steps

1. Prepare a table that lists the advantages and disadvantages of basic versus dynamic disks.
2. Dynamic disks support different types of volumes (**Figure 4-1**). Describe each of these types of volumes in the context of disk performance and fault tolerance.

Figure 4-1 Type of volumes available on dynamic disks

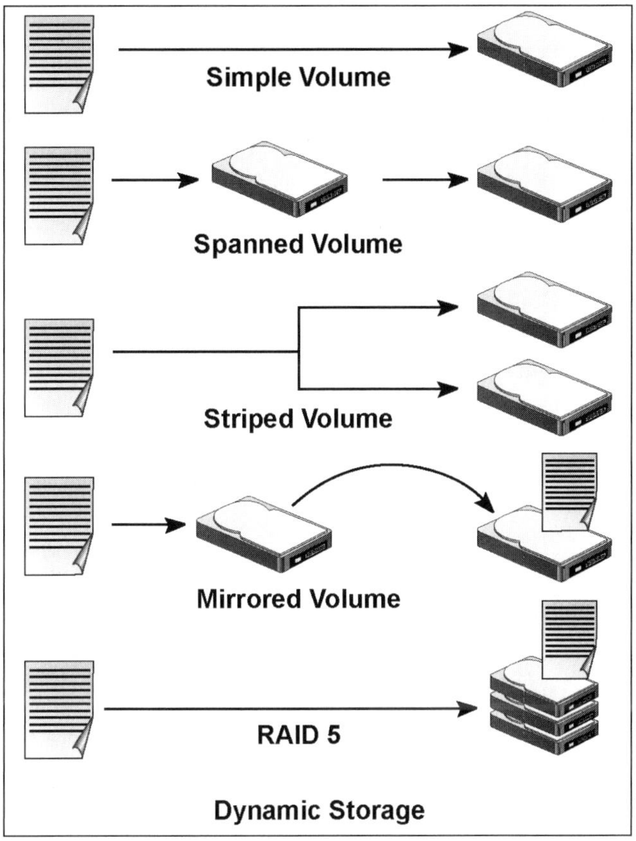

project 4.2

Creating Additional Partitions

exam objective

Manage basic and dynamic disks.

overview

You have decided to allow students and faculty to store information on the domain controller. However, you do not want them using space on the system partition that was created during installation. Microsoft recommends using the system partition only for system files. In this lesson, you will use unpartitioned disk space to create a second partition named USERS. Faculty and students will be granted the necessary access to this partition in a later lesson.

learning objective

After completing this project, you will know how to create partitions from unpartitioned disk space.

specific requirements

See general requirements.

estimated completion time

15 minutes

project steps

Customize a MMC console to administer disk management.

1. Click **Start**, click **Run**, and type **mmc** in the **Open** text box. Then click **OK** or press **[Enter]** to open an empty **Console** window.
2. Click **File** and then click **Add/Remove Snap-in (Figure 4-2)**.
3. Click **Add** in the **Add/Remove Snap-in** dialog box to open the listing of standalone snap-ins. In the **Add Standalone Snap-in** dialog box, click **Disk Management** and then click **Add (Figure 4-3)**. Ensure that the **This Computer** option button is selected and click **Finish**. Then click **Close** and then click **OK** to close the various dialog boxes.
4. To save your customized MMC to the **Administrative Tools** folder, click **File** on the Menu bar, and then click **Save**. In the **File name** text box, type **Disk Manager** and click **Save**.
5. Close all open dialog boxes and windows.

Use the Disk Manager MMC that you just saved to create an additional partition on the hard drive.

6. Click **Start**, point to **All Programs**, point to **Administrative Tools**, and then click **Disk Manager.msc**.
7. Double-click **Disk Management** in the left screen pane to open the utility.
8. In the right-hand pane, right-click the **Unallocated** disk space and click **New Partition** to start the **New Partition Wizard**.
9. Click **Next**, and in the **Select Partition Type** screen, ensure that **Primary Partition** is selected, and click **Next**.
10. In the **Specify Partition Size** screen **(Figure 4-4)**, enter **25**. In a production environment, this size would be considerably larger. Click **Next**.
11. In the **Assign Drive Letter or Path** screen, click the **Assign the following drive letter** option button and select **F** in the drop-down list box. Click **Next**.
12. In the **Format Partition** screen, select **NTFS** as the file system type and accept the default settings for **Allocation unit size** and **Volume label**. Do not place a check in the **Perform a quick format** or **Enable file and folder compression** check boxes **(Figure 4-5)**. Click **Next** and then click **Finish**. In the **Disk Management** window, you will now have a **New Volume**.
13. Close **Disk Manager** and click **Yes** to save changes.

Figure 4-2 Opening the Add/Remove Snap-in dialog box

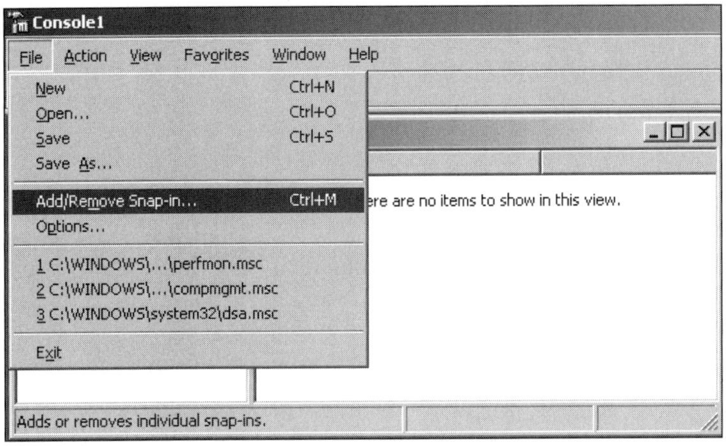

Figure 4-3 Add Standalone Snap-in dialog box

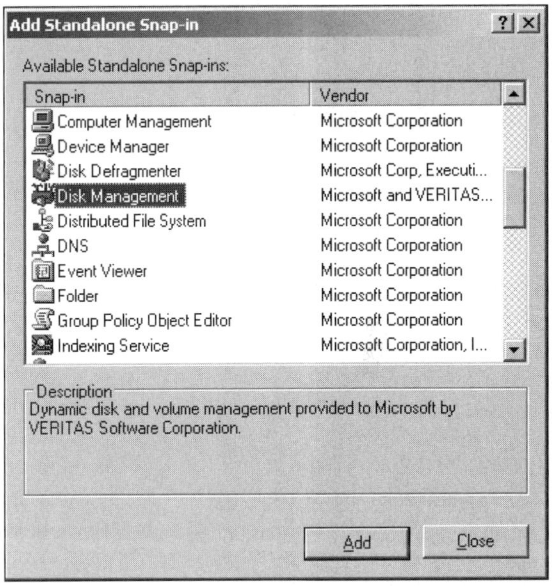

Figure 4-4 Specify Partition Size screen

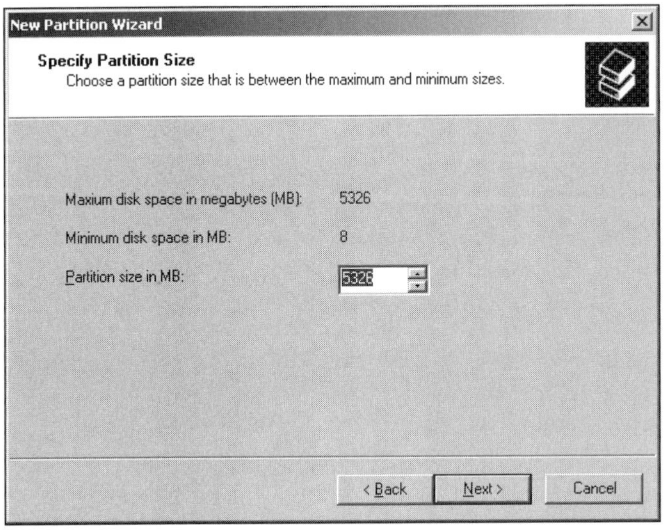

Figure 4-5 Format Partition screen

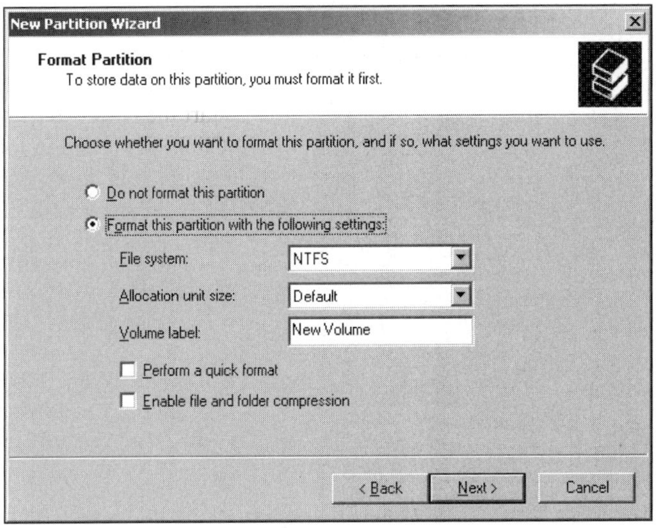

project 4.3

Converting Basic Disks to Dynamic Disks

exam objective

Manage basic and dynamic disks.

overview

Craighead College expects that it will need more hard disk space in the near future. Also, fault tolerance is needed because of the administrative data stored on the server. To enable the extension of existing partitions and to allow for the future use of fault tolerant hard drive configurations, you have decided to convert the existing hard disk to a dynamic disk.

learning objective

After completing this project, you will know how to convert a basic disk to a dynamic disk.

specific requirements

See general requirements.

estimated completion time

10 minutes

project steps

1. Click **Start**, point to **All Programs**, point to **Administrative Tools**, and then click **Disk Manager.msc**.
2. Double-click **Disk Management** in the left screen pane to open the utility, if necessary.
3. Right-click **Disk 0** and click **Convert to Dynamic Disk (Figure 4-6)**. Click **OK** in the **Convert to Dynamic Disk** dialog box.
4. The disk that will be converted is listed in the **Disks to Convert** dialog box. Click **Convert**.
5. You will see a warning indicating that dual booting from legacy operating systems will not be allowed after conversion. Click **Yes** to confirm that you want to proceed to upgrade the disk.
6. Another warning box appears, warning you that file systems on any of the disks to be converted will be dismounted. Click **Yes** again to confirm that you want to continue.
7. If you are converting a disk that includes the system volume, the boot volume or a volume which contains the paging file, the **Confirm alert** dialog box will appear, informing you that your computer will be rebooted. Click **OK** to allow the computer to restart. After it does, the disk will be upgraded from basic to dynamic.
8. If the Confirm alert dialog box does not open, the disks will automatically be converted to dynamic.

Figure 4-6 Convert to Dynamic Disk command

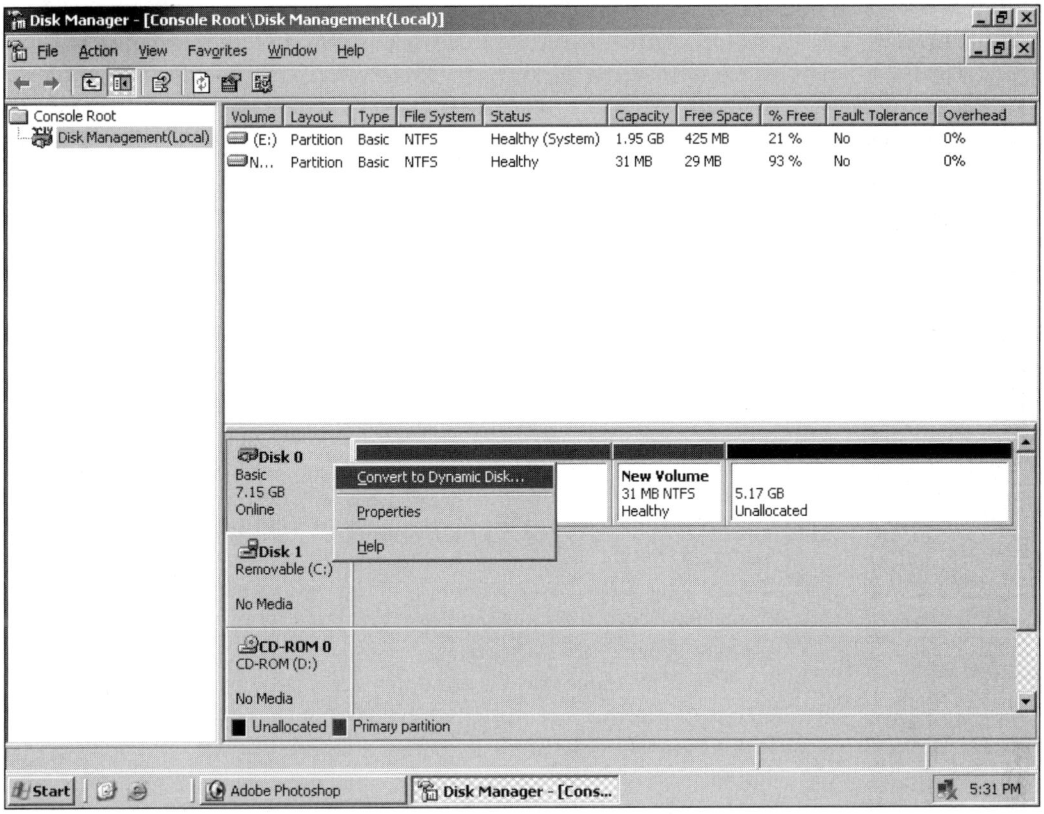

project 4.4

Extending an Existing Volume

exam objective

Manage basic and dynamic disks.

overview

In the past few months, Craighead College's storage requirements have increased faster than expected. The original 25MB volume created in the previous project is no longer adequate in size. You decide to increase the storage capacity of the new partition by utilizing unpartitioned disk space available on the existing hard drive.

learning objective

After completing this project, you will know how to increase the size of an existing volume.

specific requirements

See general requirements.

estimated completion time

10 minutes

project steps

1. Click **Start**, point to **All Programs**, point to **Administrative Tools**, and then click **Disk Manager.msc**.
2. Double-click **Disk Management** in the left screen pane to open the utility, if necessary.
3. Right-click **New Volume** and click **Extend Volume (Figure 4-7)** to start the **Extend Volume Wizard**. Click **Next**.
4. Enter **75** in the **Select the amount of space in MB** text box **(Figure 4-8)**. Click **Next** and then click **Finish**.
5. In the **Disk Manager** console, you will now notice two volume **F:** entries for a total of 100 MB.
6. Close the Disk Manager console window.

Figure 4-7 Starting the Extend Volume Wizard

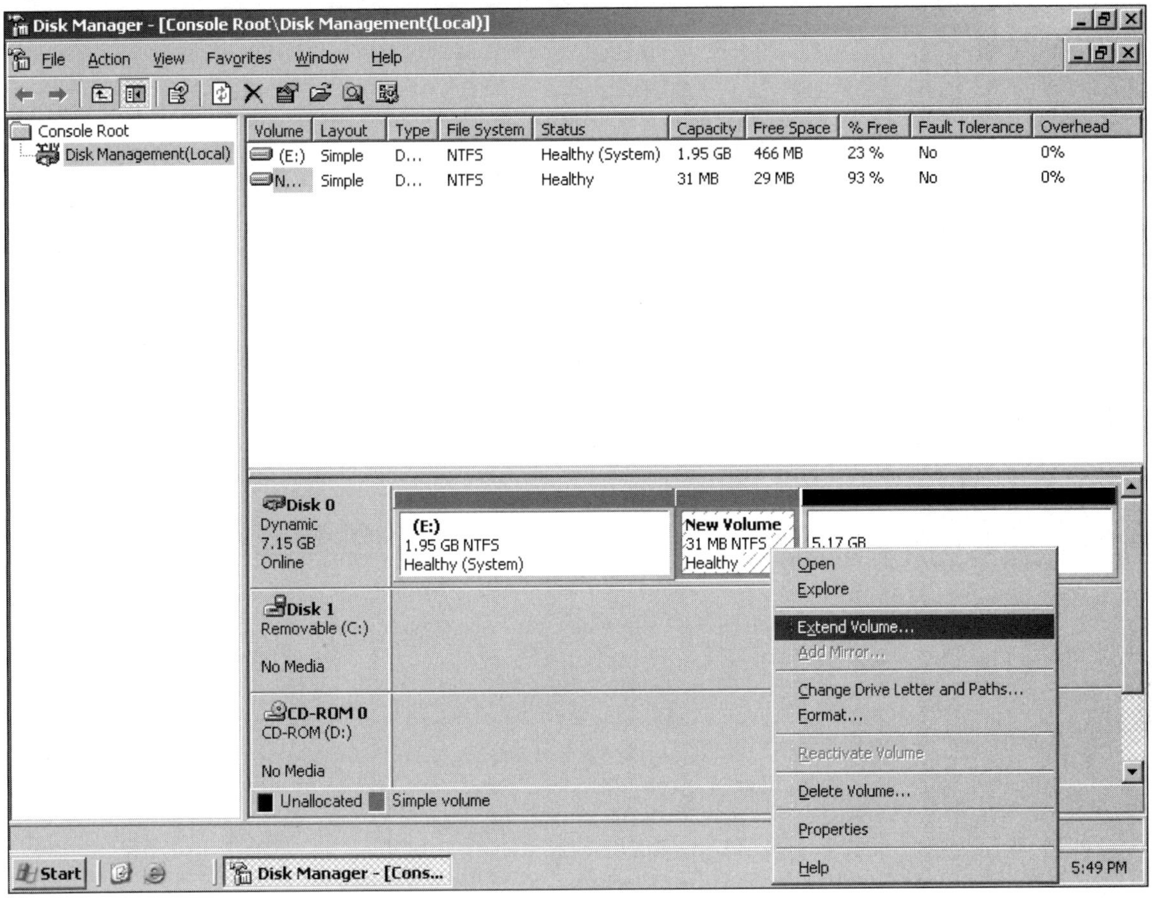

Figure 4-8 Selecting the amount of space to extend

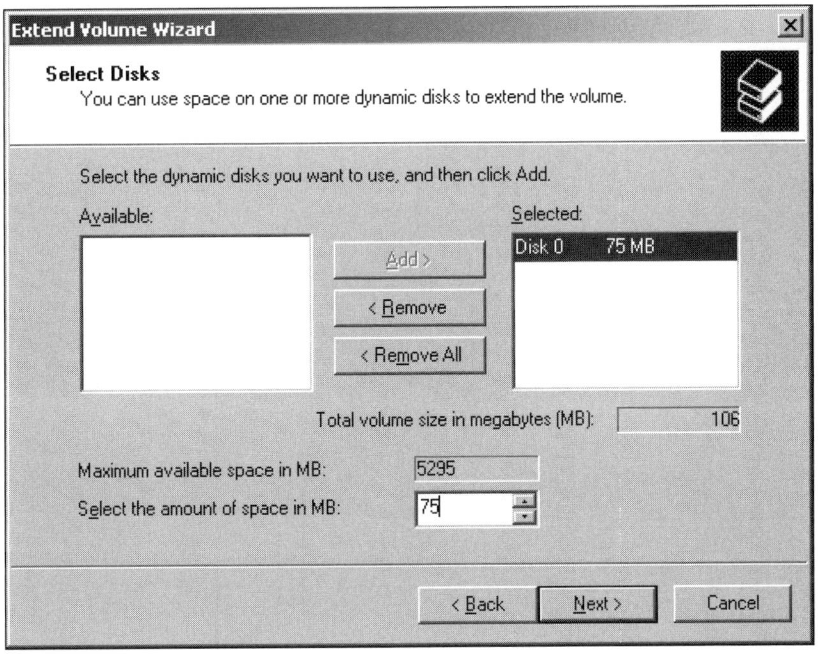

project 4.5

Defragmenting a Disk

exam objective

Optimize server disk performance.

overview

Files stored on hard drives become fragmented over time. This results in slower access time on disk reads for all users. As the network administrator for Craighead College, you want to provide optimum disk performance by performing disk defragmentation at regular intervals.

learning objective

After completing this project, you will know how to perform a routine disk defragmentation of a server hard drive.

specific requirements

See general requirements.

estimated completion time

Approximately 30–45 minutes, depending upon the speed of your computer and the size of the hard drive.

project steps

1. Click **Start**, point to **All Programs**, point to **Administrative Tools**, and then click **Disk Manager**.
2. Double-click **Disk Management** in the left screen pane to open the utility, if necessary.
3. Right-click the volume you wish to defragment and click **Properties (Figure 4-9)**.
4. Click the **Tools** tab in the **Local Disk Properties** dialog box and then click **Defragment Now**. The **Disk Defragmenter** opens **(Figure 4-10)**.
5. First, click **Analyze**. The degree of fragmentation of your drive will be analyzed. Once the analysis is complete, you will be prompted to either view a report of the drive status or defragment the drive.
6. Click **View Report** to view the report or click **Defragment** to defragment the drive (The defragmentation process could take several minutes or more.)
7. When you are finished, close all open dialog boxes and windows.

Figure 4-9 Local Disk Properties dialog box

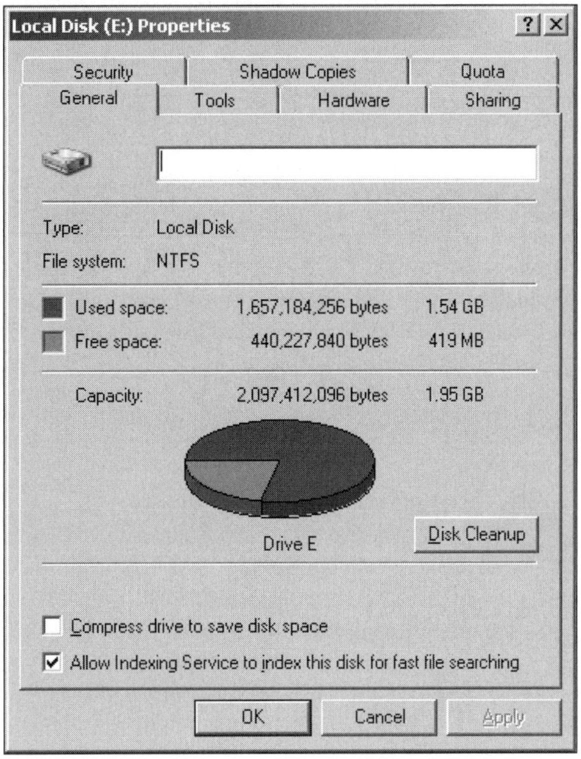

Figure 4-10 Disk Defragmenter

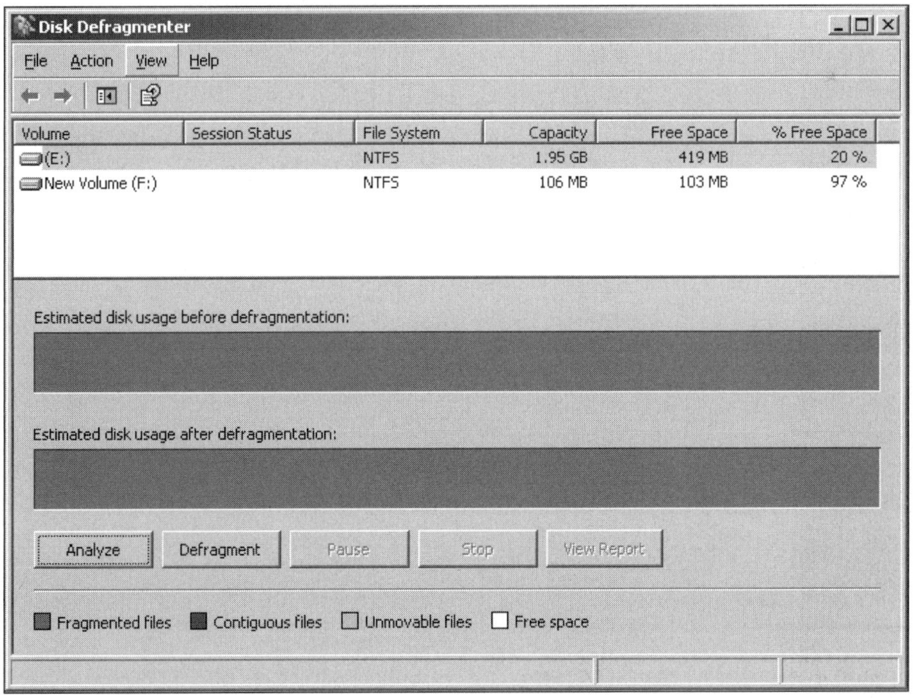

LESSON 5

Working with File Systems

After the creation of partitions or volumes on a hard disk, you must select a file system to use. The file system defines how the operating system stores files on the disk. Windows Server 2003 supports three file systems: FAT (File Allocation Table), FAT32 (the updated version of FAT), and NTFS. Each of the file systems has different security configurations and limits on the size of the volume or partition. However, FAT and FAT32 do not support the advanced security features of Windows Server 2003, such as file and folder level security. In addition, only NTFS supports disk quotas, file compression, and Encrypting File System (EFS). The main disadvantage of NTFS is incompatibility with older (pre-Windows NT 4.0) operating systems. As a guideline, use NTFS unless you need to dual-boot your computer with a non-NTFS-compatible operating system.

After you have formatted the disk with NTFS, you can store data. To improve data storage functionality on the disk, Windows Server 2003 provides data compression and encryption. Compression allows you to create additional free space by reducing the size of files on the disk. Encryption increases the security of files by only allowing authorized individuals to view their contents.

A major network security issue arises when users share files over the network. Windows Server 2003 enables you to control access to this data using shared folder permissions and NTFS permissions. Permissions can be used to specify which users can gain access and what level of access they can have to files and folders.

To simplify a user's access to shared resources over a network, you can implement Distributed file system (Dfs). Dfs organizes shared folders, regardless of their physical location, into a single logical tree that appears to users to be residing in a single location. This enables users to access resources without having to specify the exact physical location of the files.

Scenario

As network administrator for Craighead College, you have previously formatted the hard disks on the domain controller with the NTFS file system. You have determined that certain files should be compressed to better utilize disk space and you have designated files that should be encrypted for added security.

Also, you have decided to allow users to access certain folders across the network by creating shared folders. You will configure the appropriate shared folder permissions and NTFS permissions to allow proper access. After creating the shared folders, you will create a Distributed file system (Dfs) root and make Dfs links to the various shared folders.

Lesson 5 Working with File Systems

Project	Exam 70-290 Objective
5.1 Encrypting and Compressing Data on an NTFS Volume	Basic knowledge
5.2 Assigning Shared Folder Permissions	Configure access to shared folders. Verify effective permissions when granting permissions. Manage shared folder permissions.
5.3 Setting NTFS Permissions	Configure file system permissions. Configure access to shared folders. Manage shared folder permissions.
5.4 Introducing Distributed File System	Basic knowledge
5.5 Managing a Dfs Root	Basic knowledge

General Requirements

To complete the projects in this lesson, you will need administrative rights on the domain controller for Craighead College. You may also find it helpful to refer to Lesson 5 in your Prentice Hall Certification Series Exam 70-290 textbook for further information on the topics covered by the projects in this lesson.

project 5.1

Encrypting and Compressing Data on an NTFS Volume

exam objective

Basic knowledge

overview

File compression should be used when you have large amounts of data to store, but limited disk space. Some files, such as .jpg images and .zip files are already compressed, so compressing them will not create any additional free space. The files that can be more dramatically reduced in size are document files and bitmap images, which can be decreased by 50 to 90 percent. You can compress a file, folder, or the entire volume.

Compression and encryption are mutually exclusive. You cannot encrypt a compressed file or vice versa. Data encryption attempts to ensure the confidentiality of a document by scrambling the contents with secret keys. Without possession of the correct key, you cannot access the files. When accessing files, both compression and encryption are transparent to the user because they are accomplished automatically in the background without user intervention.

At Craighead College, all public memos and bulletins are stored in the folder **OldPubs** the month after their initial publication. Since all of the contents of this folder are document files that will be rarely accessed, you have decided to compress the folder. In addition, all student financial aid information is stored in the **FinAid** folder. Since federal privacy laws protect this information, you have decided to encrypt the contents of this folder.

learning objective

After completing this project, you will know how to compress and encrypt folders.

specific requirements

See general requirements.

estimated completion time

15 minutes

project steps

1. Log on to the domain controller as an **Administrator** with the appropriate password. Click **Start** and then click **Windows Explorer**.
2. Expand **My Computer** and double-click **Local Disk (C:)**. Click **File** on the Menu bar, point to **New**, and then click **Folder**. Type **OldPubs** as the name of the new folder and press **[Enter]**.
3. Right-click **OldPubs** and then click **Properties**. On the **General** tab, click **Advanced** to open the **Advanced Attributes** dialog box **(Figure 5-1)**.
4. Place a check mark in the **Compress contents to save disk space** check box, and click **OK**. Click **OK** in the **OldPubs Properties** dialog box. You will notice that the folder now appears in an alternate color (blue) in the Explorer window. This helps to identify what file and folders have been compressed.
5. Double-click the **OldPubs** folder. Click **File** on the Menu bar, point to **New**, and then click **Text Document** from the top menu. Type **Test** as the name of the document and press **[Enter]**. Notice the file is displayed in an alternate color. Since this document was created in a compressed folder, it is automatically compressed.

Figure 5-1 Advanced Attributes dialog box

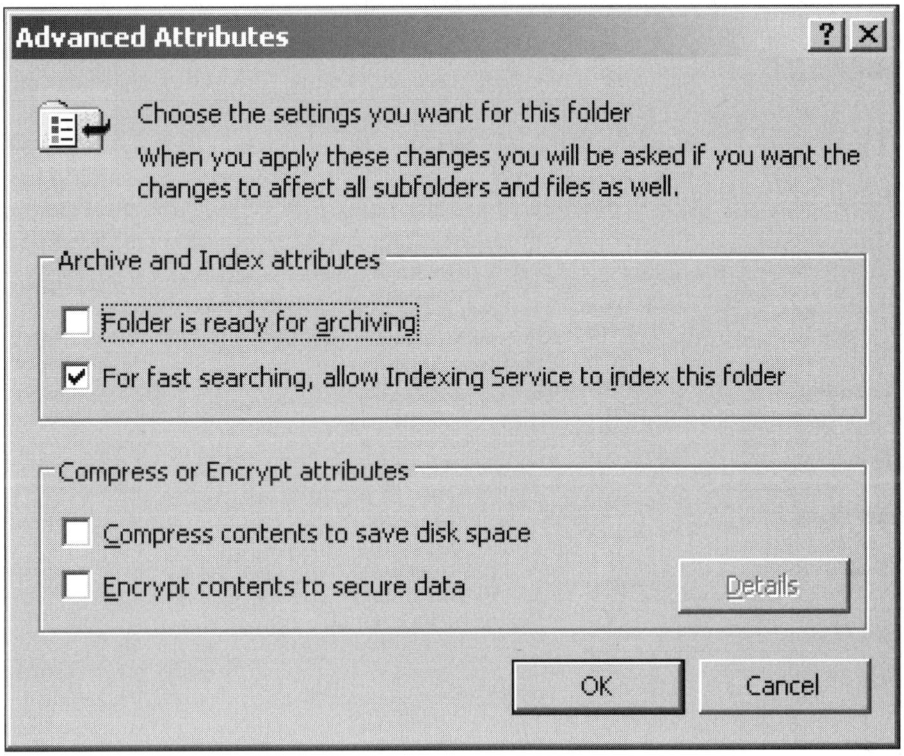

project 5.1

Encrypting and Compressing Data on an NTFS Volume *(cont'd)*

exam objective

Basic knowledge

project steps

6. Double-click the **Test** file to open **NotePad**. Cut and paste at least two pages of text from another document into the file, then close NotePad. Click **Yes** to save the changes.
7. To determine the amount of compression, right-click the **Test** file and click **Properties**. In the **Test Properties** dialog box, notice the difference between the **Size** amount and the **Size on disk** amount. This is the amount of compression for this file. Click **OK**.

Create and encrypt the **FinAid** folder.

8. Click **Local Disk (C:)** in the left pane of the Explorer window. Click **File** on the Menu bar, point to **New**, and then click **Folder**. Type **FinAid** as the name of the new folder and press **[Enter]**.
9. Right-click the **FinAid** folder and click **Properties**. On the **General** tab, click **Advanced**. Place check marks in the **Compress contents to save disk space** and the **Encrypt contents to secure data** check boxes. Notice that the check mark is automatically removed from the **Compress contents to save disk space** check box. This is because of their mutual exclusiveness **(Figure 5-2)**. Click **OK**.
10. Click **OK** in the **FinAid Properties** dialog box. Notice that the **FinAid** folder is now displayed in an alternative color (green) to identify that it is encrypted. Close all open dialog boxes and windows.

Figure 5-2 Advanced Attributes dialog box with encryption enabled

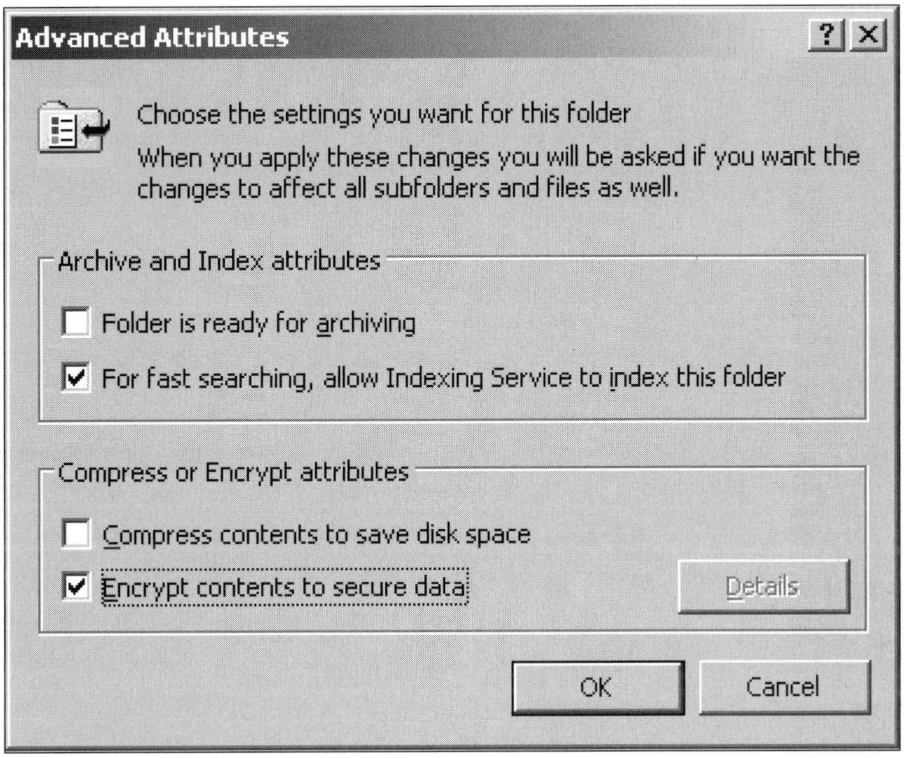

project 5.2

Assigning Shared Folder Permissions

exam objective

Configure access to shared folders. Verify effective permissions when granting permissions. Manage shared folder permissions.

overview

The ability to share files among users is one of the most important benefits of a network. However, you should prevent unauthorized access by assigning appropriate share folder permissions. With share permissions, you can assign different shared folder permissions for different types of data. The three shared folder permissions are Read, Change, and Full Control. Note that these permissions are only in effect when the folder is accessed through the share and they have no effect on a user logged on locally to that computer.

Within the craighead.com domain, all authorized users should have Read access to the OldPubs folder but only members of the Administrators group should have Full Control. You want to share the OldPubs folder with the appropriate rights.

learning objective

After completing this project, you will know how to share a folder and change the share permissions.

specific requirements

See general requirements. You also must have successfully completed Project 5.1.

estimated completion time

15 minutes

project steps

1. Click **Start** and then click **Windows Explorer**. Expand **My Computer** and **Local Disk (C:)**.
2. Right-click **OldPubs** and click **Sharing and Security** to display the **Sharing** tab of the **OldPubs Properties** dialog box **(Figure 5-3)**.
3. Click the **Share this folder** option button. Type **Public Bulletins** in the **Description** text box. Click **Permissions**.
4. In the **Permissions for OldPubs** dialog box, the default share permission **Read** is assigned to the **Everyone** group.
5. Click the **Add** button and type **Authenticated Users** in the **Enter the object names to select (examples)** text box. Click **OK**. In the **Permissions for OldPubs** dialog box, confirm that the **Authenticated Users** group has been granted only the **Read** right.
6. Remove the default **Everyone** group by clicking **Everyone** and then clicking **Remove**.
7. Click **Add** and type **Administrators** in the **Enter the object names to select (examples)** text box. Click **OK**.
8. In the **Permissions for OldPubs** dialog box, click **Administrators** and place a check mark in the **Allow** box for the **Full Control** permission **(Figure 5-4)**. Notice that when you select **Full Control**, all of the other permissions are also automatically granted. Click **OK**.
9. Click **OK** in the **OldPubs Properties** dialog box. The icon for this folder now includes a hand underneath it to indicate that it is being shared.

Figure 5-3 Sharing tab in Folder Properties dialog box

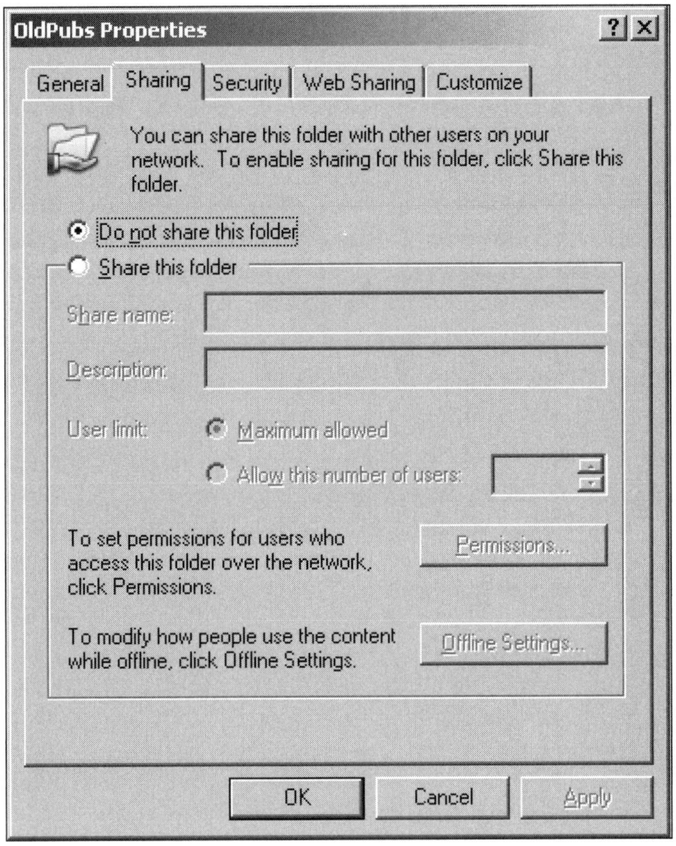

Figure 5-4 Permissions dialog box

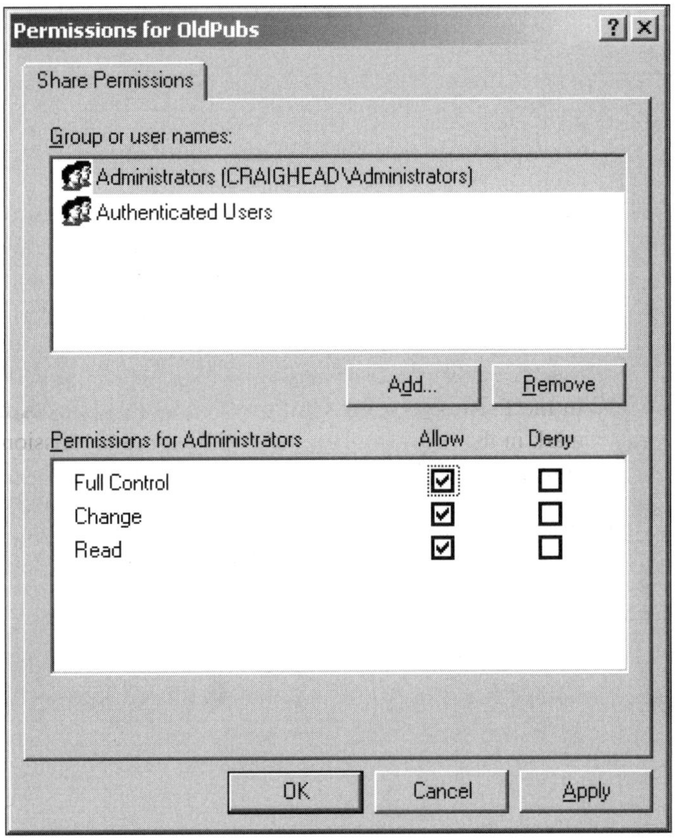

project 5.3

Setting NTFS Permissions

exam objective

Configure file system permissions. Configure access to shared folders. Manage shared folder permissions.

overview

NTFS permissions can be used to restrict unauthorized access to files and folders and control the level of access to files and folders for each user. Unlike shared folder permissions, NTFS permissions can be applied to individual files in addition to folders. Remember, by default, all NTFS permissions are inherited from parent folders to all subordinate folders.

In addition to the standard NTFS folder **(Table 5-1)** and file **(Table 5-2)** permissions, you can customize access privileges to utilize special permissions. These special permissions provide a more precise level of control over users' ability to access shared resources.

To further secure the FinAid folder at Craighead College, you want to ensure that only members of the Administrators group have any NTFS permissions. Also, you have been requested to create an SGA folder. The purpose of this folder is to allow all users free expression and exchange of ideas concerning the Student Government Association. All authenticated users should be given the rights to all tasks except the ability to delete files and folders.

learning objective

After completing this project, you will know how to grant NTFS permissions and prevent right inheritance.

specific requirements

See general requirements. You also must have successfully completed Projects 5.1 and 5.2.

estimated completion time

20 minutes

project steps

Check current NTFS permissions of the **FinAid** folder.

1. Click **Start** and then click **Windows Explorer**. Expand **My Computer** and **Local Disk (C:)**.
2. Right-click **FinAid** and click **Properties**. On the **Security** tab **(Figure 5-5)**, notice the four groups listed under **Group or user names** have inherited rights through the parent. This is indicated by the use of a gray check mark in the **Permissions for *<user-name/group>*** text box.
3. Click the **Administrators** group object and click **Remove**. A **Security** message box will appear, indicating that you cannot remove this group because this right was inherited. Click **OK**.

Remove inherited permissions and assign permissions to Administrators.

4. Click **Advanced** and then **Add**. Type **Administrators** in the **Enter the object name to select (examples)** text box and click **OK**.
5. In the **Permission Entry for FinAid** dialog box **(Figure 5-6)**, place a check mark in the **Allow** column for **Full Control** and click **OK**.
6. Remove the check mark from the **Allow inheritable permissions from the parent to propagate to this object and all child objects. Include these with entries explicitly defined here** check box and click **Remove**. Click **OK**. The only entry remaining is the **Administrators** group. Click **OK**.

Table 5-1 Standard NTFS folder permissions

NTFS Folder Permissions	Description
Read	Users can open and view the contents of files, folders, and subfolders. They can also view the ownership of objects, permissions assigned to objects, and the various folder attributes such as Read-Only, Hidden, Archive, and System.
Write	Users can create new files and subfolders in a folder. This permission also allows users to view folder ownership, the assigned permissions, and to use the Properties dialog box to change folder attributes.
List Folder Contents	Users can only view the names of subfolders and files in a folder.
Read & Execute	This permission allows users to perform the tasks permitted by the Read and List Folder Contents permissions, and also gives users the ability to navigate through folders for which they do not have permission so that they can access files and folders for which they do have permission.
Modify	Users can view, create, delete, and modify the content of folders, as well as change attributes. This permission includes all tasks permitted by the Read, Write, and Read & Execute permissions.
Full Control	Users can change permissions and take ownership of folders. This permission includes all actions that are permitted by all of the other NTFS permissions and is usually only granted to administrators.

Table 5-2 Standard NTFS file permission

NTFS File Permission	Description
Read	Users can read the file and view the file attributes, file ownership, and permissions.
Write	Users can change the file, change file attributes, and view file ownerships and permissions.
Read & Execute	Users can view the contents of files, file attributes, file ownership, and permissions, and can also run program applications.
Modify	Users can modify and delete the file, run applications, change attributes, and perform all other actions permitted by the Write and Read & Execute permissions.
Full Control	Users can change permissions, take ownership, and perform all actions permitted by the other NTFS permissions.

Figure 5-5 Security tab in the FinAid Properties dialog box

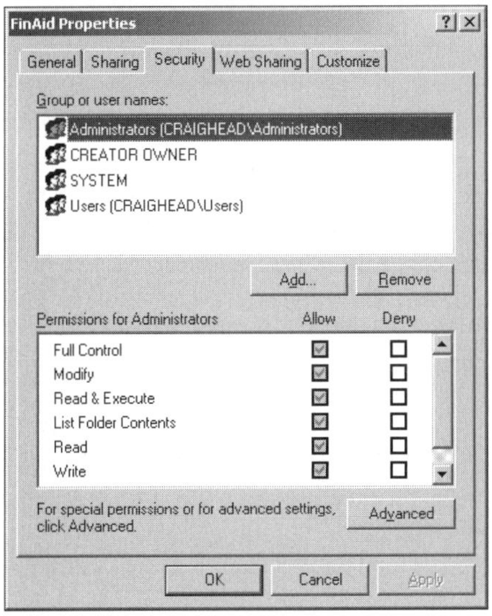

Figure 5-6 Permission Entry dialog box

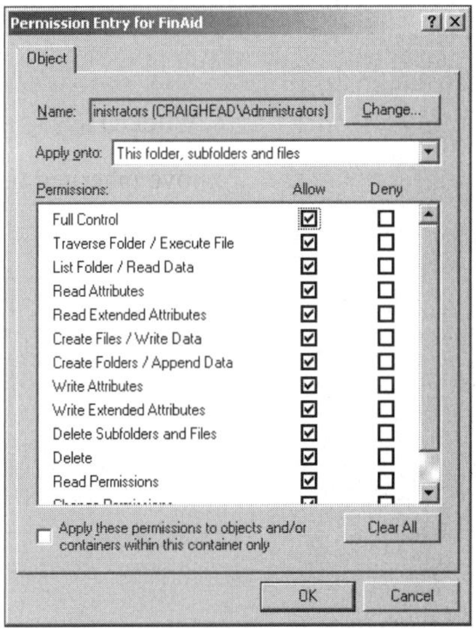

project 5.3

Setting NTFS Permissions (cont'd)

exam objective

Configure file system permissions. Configure access to shared folders. Manage shared folder permissions.

project steps

Create a **SGA** folder and assign NTFS rights.

7. Click **Local Disk (C:)** in the left pane of the Explorer screen. Click **File** on the Menu bar, point to **New**, and then click **Folder**. Type **SGA** as the name of the folder and press **[Enter]**.
8. Right-click **SGA** and click **Properties**. On the **Security** tab, click **Users** under **Group or user names**. Notice that the **Users** group currently has the **Read & Execute**, **List Folder Contents**, and **Read** permissions.
9. Click the **Full Control** permission in the **Allow** column and then click **Advanced**. Under **Permission entries**, highlight the entry with the **Name** of **Users** and the **Inherited From <not inherited> (Figure 5-7)**. Click **Edit**.
10. Under the **Deny** column in the **Permission Entry for SGA** dialog box, place check marks in the **Delete subfolders and files**, **Delete**, and **Take Ownership** check boxes. Click **OK**.
11. In the **Advanced Security Settings for SGA** dialog box, click **OK**. A security warning will appear informing you that Deny permissions entries take precedence over Allow entries. Click **Yes**.
12. To verify the NTFS rights of **Users** to the **SGA** folder, click **Advanced**. Under the **Effective Permissions** tab **(Figure 5-8)**, click **Select** and type **Users** in the **Enter the object name to select (examples)** text box. Click **OK**.
13. Scroll down the list of **Effective permissions**. You will notice that only **Full Control** and those that were denied through special permissions are not selected. Click **OK**. Close all open dialog boxes and windows.

Figure 5-7 Permissions tab in the Advanced Security Settings dialog box

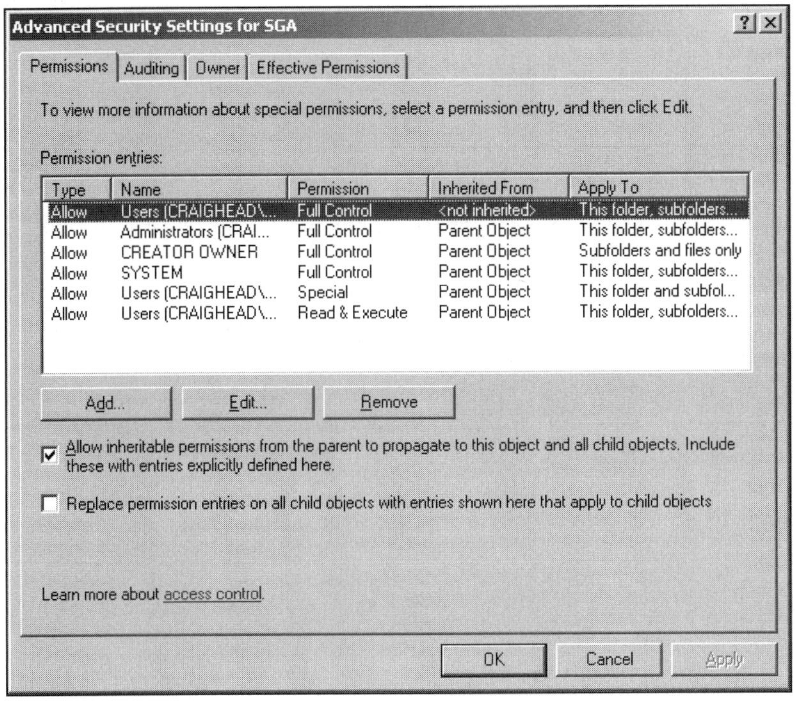

Figure 5-8 Effective Permissions tab in the Advanced Security Settings dialog box

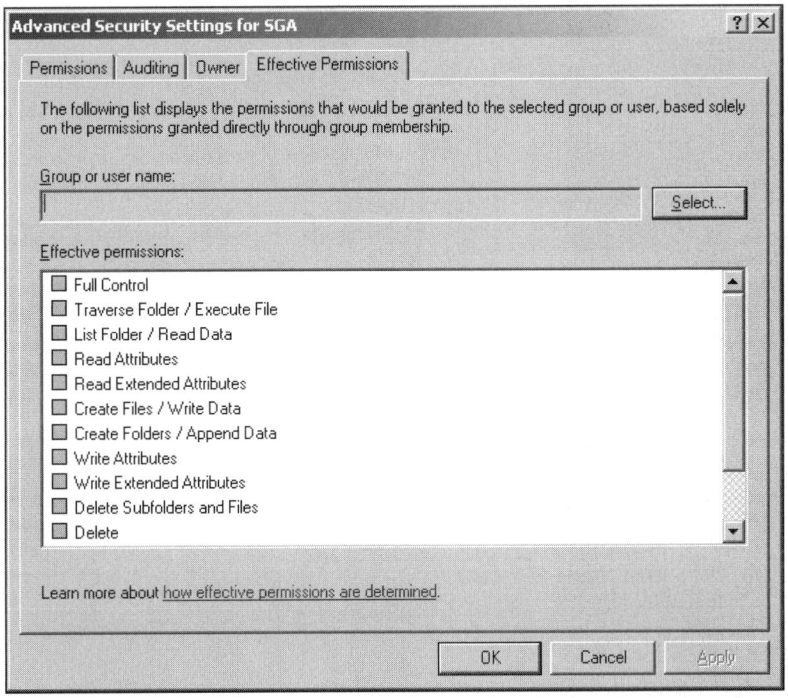

project 5.4

Introducing Distributed File System

exam objective

Basic knowledge

overview

Distributed file system (Dfs) allows users to locate files and folders on the network quickly and easily. A single Dfs shared folder, called a Dfs root, can be used to coordinate all shared folders on multiple computers in the network. Links can then be assigned to various shared folders throughout the network, regardless of location. The logical structure created by Dfs allows the user to access various shares without having to know the particular server name or physical path.

There are various shares that all users at Craighead College use on a regular basis. They are located on various drives and servers throughout the network. As network administrator, you want to simplify the users' access to these folders. For this purpose, you are going to create a Dfs root called Craighead Shares.

learning objective

After completing this project, you will know how to create a Dfs root.

specific requirements

See general requirements. You also must have successfully completed Project 5.1.

estimated completion time

10 minutes

project steps

1. Click **Start**, point to **Administrative Tools**, and then click **Distributed File System**.
2. Right-click **Distributed File System** and click **New Root (Figure 5-9)** to start the **New Root Wizard**. Click **Next**.
3. Click **Domain root** under **Select the type of root you want to create** and click **Next**.
4. The **Host Server** screen appears. Accept the **Domain name** of **craighead.com** and click **Next**.
5. The **Root Type** screen opens. Type the name of your domain controller in the **Server name** text box and click **Next**.
6. The **Root Name** screen appears. For the **Root name**, type **Dfs Root (Figure 5-10)** and click **Next**.
7. On the **Root Share** screen, click next to the **Folder to share** text box to open the **Browse for Folder** dialog box.
8. Locate the **Old Pubs** folder you created in Project 5.1, select it, and click **OK** to close the **Browse for Folder** dialog box.
9. Click **Next**. The **Completing the New Root Wizard screen** appears.
10. Click **Finish**. Close all open dialog boxes and windows.

Figure 5-9 New Root command

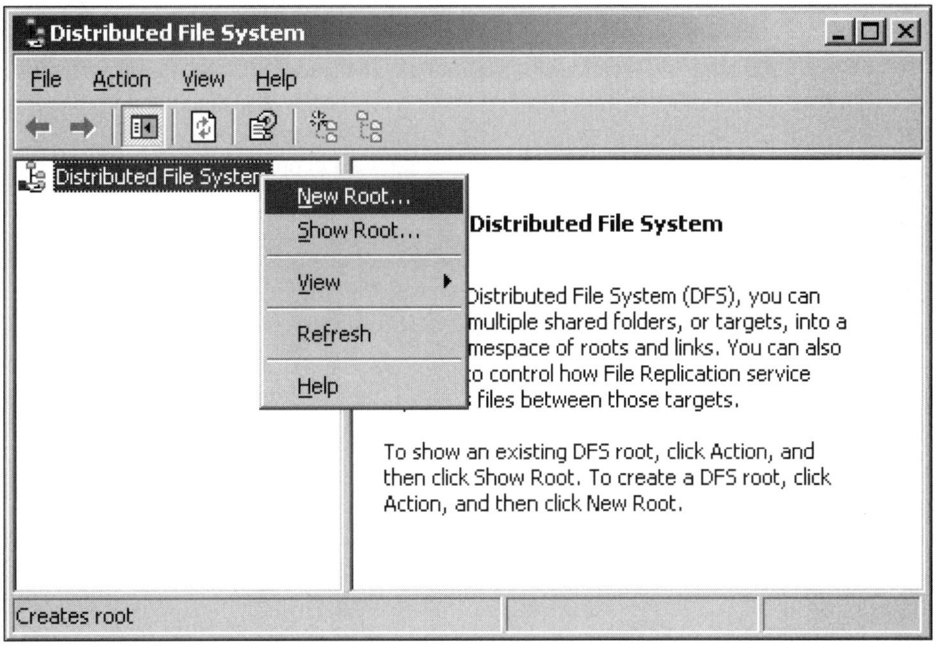

Figure 5-10 Root Name screen

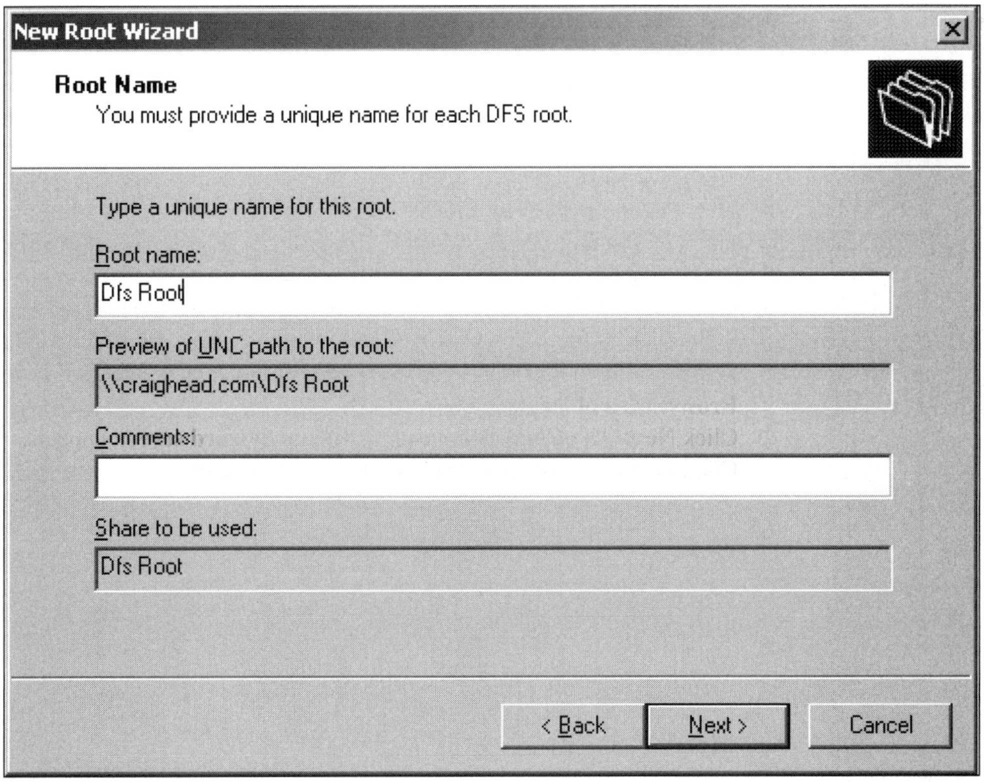

project 5.5 Managing a Dfs Root

exam objective

Basic knowledge

overview

After you have successfully created the Dfs root, you must configure links for it to have functionality. Occasionally, you may need to disable a Dfs link when you do not need it for a period of time.

At Craighead College, there are three major shares that will be accessed by all students: SGA, Schedule, and StudentNews. As network administrator, you are to create these shares and then link them to the Dfs root created in the previous project.

Note that in order not to require the use of additional computers for this project, all links will be created on the domain controller for craighead.com. However, in practice, each Dfs link can be physically located on different computers.

learning objective

After completing this project, you will know how to create Dfs links and replicas.

specific requirements

See general requirements. You also must have successfully completed Project 5.4.

estimated completion time

20 minutes

project steps

Create the shares.

1. Click **Start**, click **My Computer**, and double-click **Local Disk (C:)**.
2. Click **File** on the Menu bar, point to **New**, and then click **Folder**. Type **Schedule** as the name of the new folder and press **[Enter]**.
3. Right-click **Schedule** and click **Sharing and Security**. Click the **Share this folder** option button, and type **Class Schedule Information** in the **Description** text box **(Figure 5-11)**. Click **OK**.
4. Click **File**, point to **New**, and then click **Folder**. Type **News** as the name of the new folder and press **[Enter]**.
5. Double-click **News**. Click **File**, point to **New**, and then click **Folder**. Type **StudentNews** as the name of the new folder and press **[Enter]**.
6. Right-click **StudentNews** and click **Sharing and Security**. Share the folder by clicking the **Share this folder** option button. Type **Student Organizations and Job Openings** in the **Description** text box and click **OK**.
7. Right-click the **SGA** folder and click **Sharing and Security**. Click the **Share this folder** option button and type **Student Government News** in the **Description** text box. Click **OK**. Close all open dialog boxes and windows.

Figure 5-11 Sharing tab in Folder Properties dialog box

project 5.5

Managing a Dfs Root *(cont'd)*

exam objective

Basic knowledge

project steps

Create Dfs links for the shares.

8. Click **Start**, point to **Administrative Tools**, and then click **Distributed File System**. Right-click the **Dfs Root** in the left pane and click **New Link (Figure 5-12)**. The **New Link** dialog box opens.
9. Type **Schedule** in the **Link name** text box. Type ***server_name*\schedule** in the **Path to target (shared folder)** text box, where ***server_name*** is the name of the domain controller **(Figure 5-13)**. Then click **OK** to close the dialog box.
10. Right-click the **Dfs Root** and click **New Link**. Type **StudentNews** in the **Link name** text box and type ***server_name*\StudentNews** in the **Path to target (shared folder)** text box, where ***server_name*** is the name of the domain controller. Then click **OK** to close the dialog box.
11. Right-click the **Dfs Root** and click **New Link**. Type **SGA News** in the **Link name** text box and type ***server_name*\SGA** in the **Path to target (shared folder)** text box, where ***server_name*** is the name of the domain controller. Then click **OK** to close the dialog box.
12. To test the Dfs links, click **Start**, click **Run**, and type ***domain_name*\Dfs Root** in the **Open** text box, where ***domain_name*** is the name of your domain (in our example, craighead.com). Click **OK**. All of the links should be listed. Close all open dialog boxes and windows.

Figure 5-12 Distributed File System console

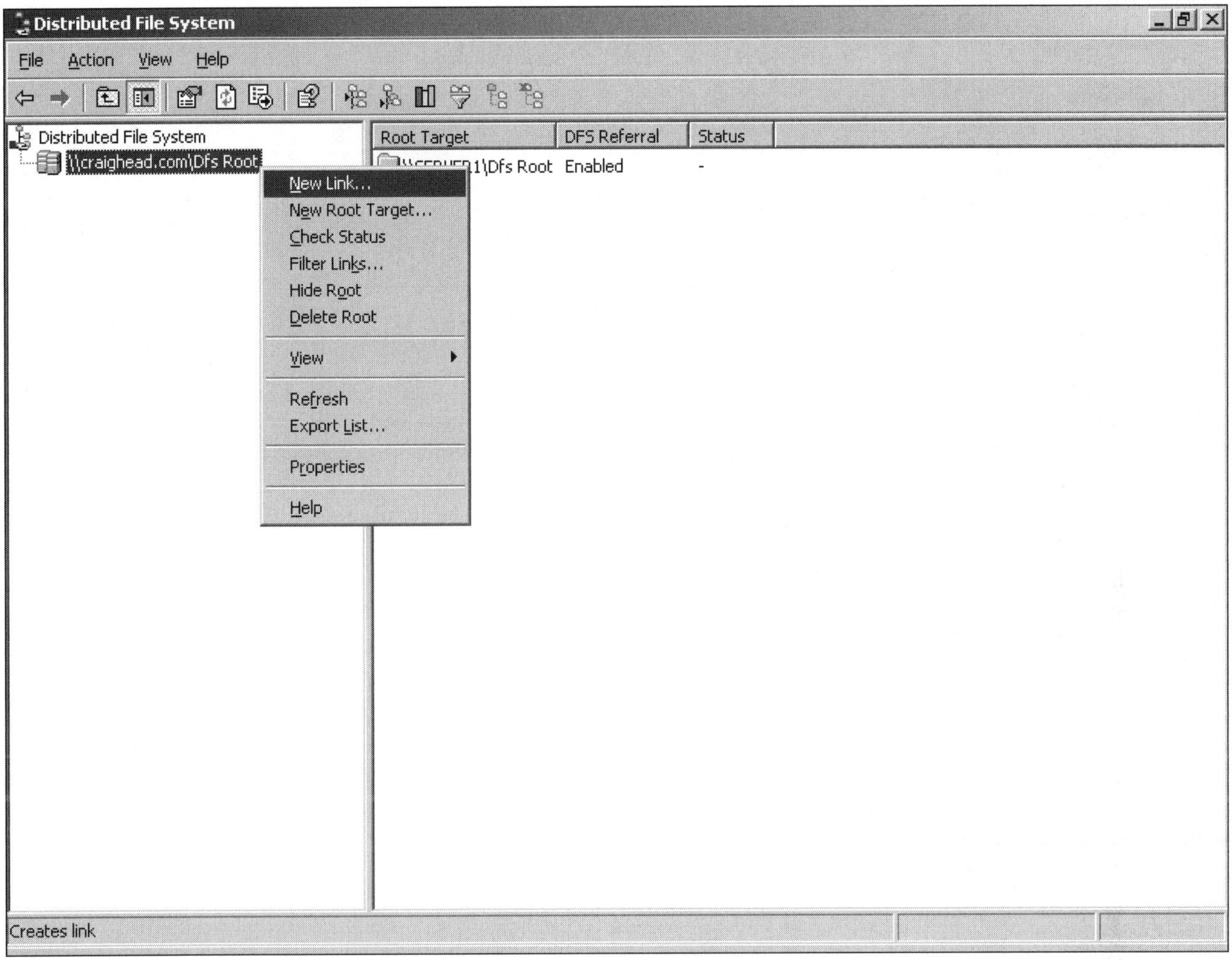

Figure 5-13 New Link dialog box

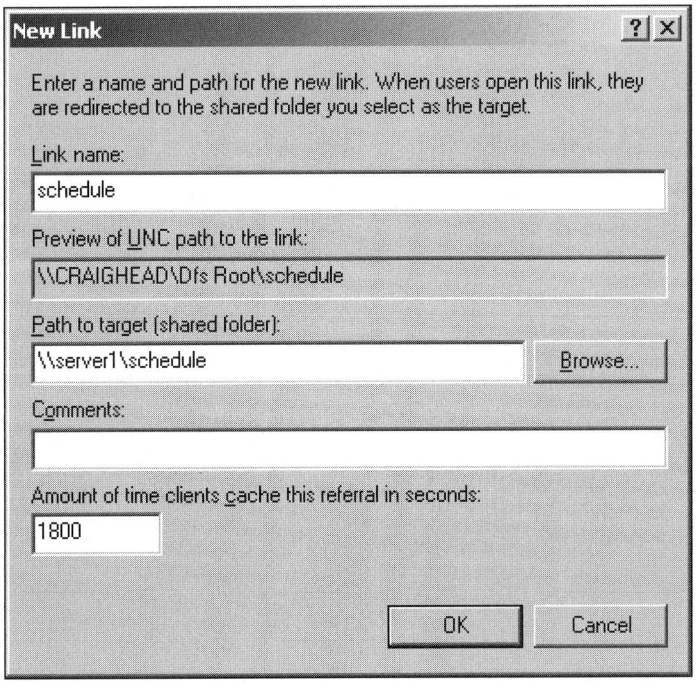

LESSON

6 Administering User Accounts

A user account represents a user on a Windows Server 2003 network. It contains information about a user, such as the user name and password. There are two types of user accounts: domain and local. A domain account allows a user to log on and gain access to domain-based resources. The domain user account is stored on a domain controller. A local account allows a user to log on only to the local computer where the account was created. When all computers are members of a domain, it is not good practice to create local user accounts because domains do not recognize local user accounts and local users will have difficulty accessing domain resources.

Windows Server 2003 automatically creates a user profile for a user account the first time an account is used to log on to a computer. User profiles contain settings that define the user environment and are applied whenever the user logs on to a system. By default, the profile is created and available only on the local computer; but, it can be stored on a network server. If the profile is stored on a network server, the user environment can follow or 'roam' with the user to any computer.

This lesson contains projects that will enable you to become more familiar with the different types of user profiles and let you practice creating domain user accounts, configuring domain user account properties, and creating a roaming profile and changing it to a mandatory profile.

Scenario

At Craighead College, all students will have an individual domain account to access the network. In addition, all members of the faculty will also be assigned domain user accounts. In a previous project, you created the Faculty and Students OUs to house the appropriate user objects.

Since students will be accessing the domain from a variety of computers, you have decided to implement roaming profiles. This will provide the user with a familiar desktop environment regardless of the access point.

Lesson 6 Administering User Accounts

Project	*Exam 70-290 Objective*
6.1 Creating a Domain User Account	Create and manage user accounts. Create and modify user accounts by using the Active Directory Users and Computers MMC snap-in.
6.2 Setting Domain User Account Properties	Create and manage user accounts. Create and modify user accounts by using the Active Directory Users and Computers MMC snap-in.
6.3 Introducing User Profiles	Basic knowledge
6.4 Creating a Mandatory User Profile	Create and manage user accounts. Manage local, roaming, and mandatory user profiles.

General Requirements

To complete the projects in this lesson, you will need administrative rights on the domain controller for the craighead.com domain used in previous lessons. You also need to have completed Projects 3.4 and 3.5 in Lesson 3. You may also find it helpful to refer to Lesson 6 in your Prentice Hall Certification Series Exam 70-290 textbook for further information about the topics covered by the projects in this lesson.

project 6.1 Creating a Domain User Account

exam objective

Create and manage user accounts. Create and modify user accounts by using the Active Directory Users and Computers MMC snap-in.

overview

During the logon process, a user provides a logon name and password. Windows Server 2003 uses this information to authenticate the user and build a ticket granting ticket that identifies the user. The purpose of a ticket granting ticket is to identify the user account in order to build session tickets, which are then used to identify the user to the domain member computers on which the user tries to access resources. An access token is then generated to allow the user specific levels of access.

Before you begin creating faculty and staff accounts, you want to create user accounts for the members of your technology staff. You will place each of these accounts in a new organizational unit named IT Staff.

learning objective

After completing this project, you will know how to create domain user accounts.

specific requirements

See general requirements.

estimated completion time

15 minutes

project steps

1. Log on as an **Administrator**.
2. Click **Start**, point to **Administrative Tools**, and then click **Active Directory Users and Computers**.
3. Right-click **craighead.com**. Click **New** and then click **Organizational Unit (Figure 6-1)**. In the **New Object — Organizational Unit** dialog box, enter **IT Staff** in the **Name** text box and click **OK**.
4. Right-click the **IT Staff** organizational unit, point to **New** and then click **User** to open the **New Object — User** dialog box **(Figure 6-2)**.
5. Enter **Kellie** in the **First name** text box and **Fisher** in the **Last name** text box. Enter **KellieF** as the **User logon name**. The pre-Windows 2000 name will automatically be completed with the **User logon name** by default. Click **Next** to continue.
6. Enter a password in both the **Password** and **Confirm password** text boxes. Be sure to remember the passwords used for each user as you will be required to log on with these accounts in later projects. Remove the check mark from the **User must change password at next logon** check box, and place a check mark in the **Password never expires** check box. Click **Next** and then **Finish** to create the user.
7. Repeat steps 4–6 for each of the following users:
   - **Farhad Morreno — FarhadM**
   - **Janet McGinnis — JanetM**
   - **Paula Laddo — PaulaL**
   - **Steven Reploga — StevenR**
8. Close all open dialog boxes and windows.

Figure 6-1 Creating a new Organizational Unit

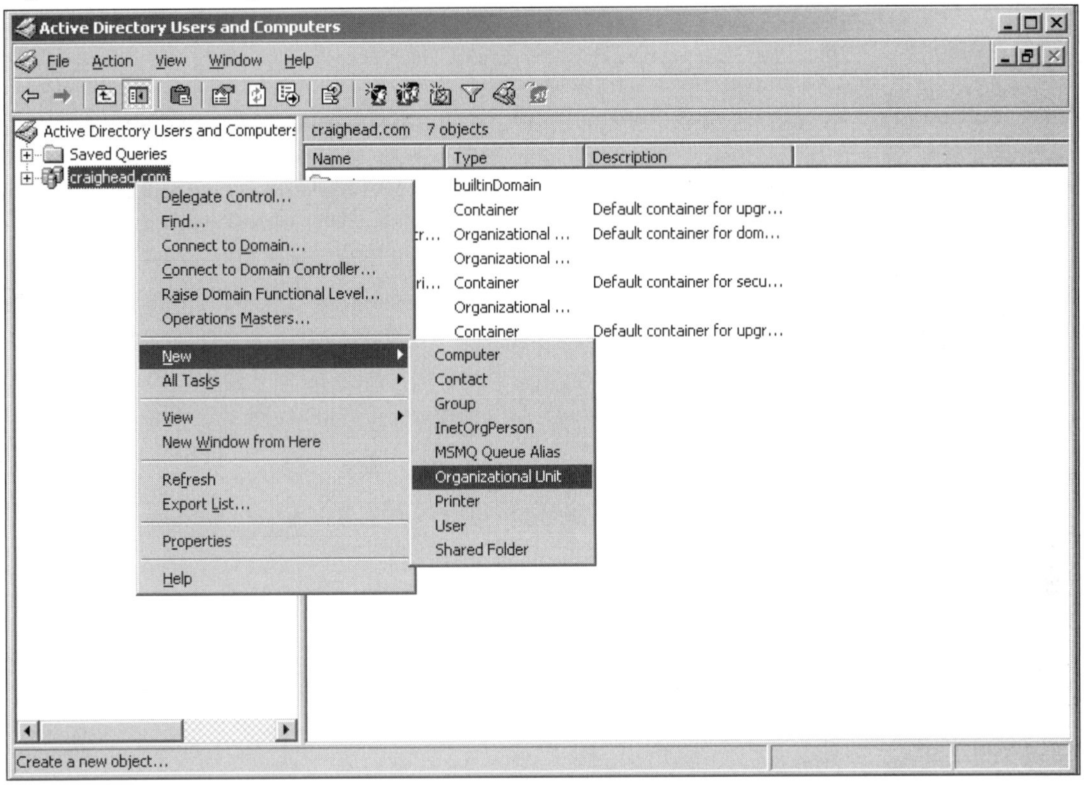

Figure 6-2 New Object — User dialog box

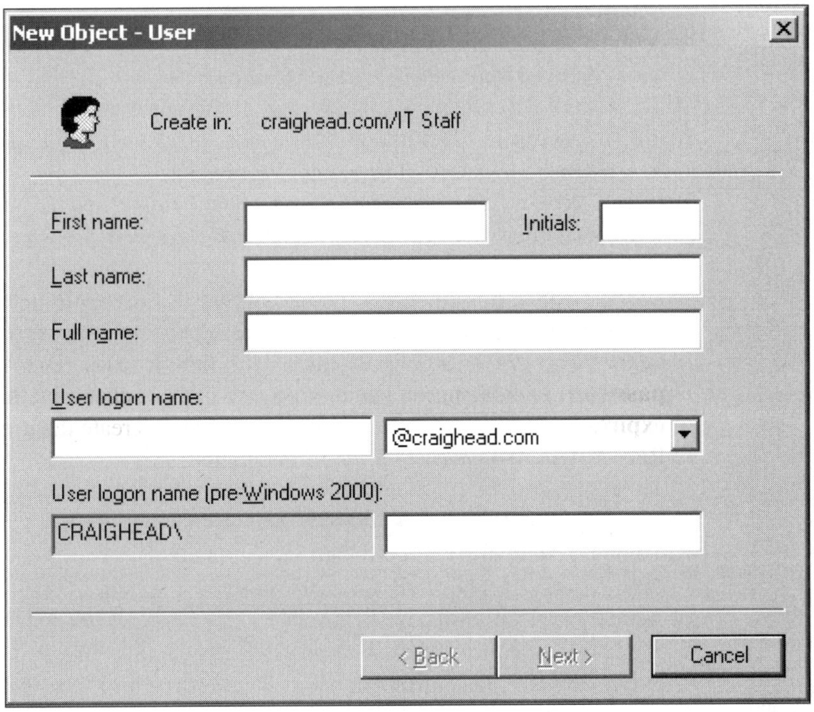

project 6.2 Setting Domain User Account Properties

exam objective

Create and manage user accounts. Create and modify user accounts by using the Active Directory Users and Computers MMC snap-in.

overview

Every user account created has a set of properties associated with the account. You can configure personal information and a variety of settings for each user by assigning values to these properties. These properties can be used to search for users within the domain. You should always provide as much detailed information for each account as possible.

You can also configure logon settings to specify the logon hours for a user. In addition, you can configure dial-in settings, Terminal Services settings, group membership, and profile settings.

The CIO of Craighead College, Chris Williamson, has decided to only allow students access to the network on weekdays. All members of the Faculty group and IT Staff will be allowed dial-up access.

learning objective

After completing this project, you will be able to configure domain user account properties to meet the needs of a particular domain environment.

specific requirements

See general requirements. You also need to have successfully completed Projects 3.4, 3.5, and 6.1.

estimated completion time

30 minutes

project steps

Change the personal information for the **IT Staff**.

1. Log on as an **Administrator** and click **Start**, point to **Administrative Tools**, and then click **Active Directory Users and Computers**.
2. Click the **IT Staff** OU in the left pane of the window. All of the user objects will appear in the right pane. Click the first user icon, hold down the **[Shift]** key and then click the last user icon to select all accounts **(Figure 6-3)**.
3. Click **Action** on the Menu bar and click **Properties**. The **Properties On Multiple Objects** dialog box will open **(Figure 6-4)**. Any changes made in this dialog box will affect all selected accounts.
4. Place a check mark in the **Description** check box and type **Information Technology Staff** in the text box. Place a check mark in the **Fax** check box and type **815-1234** in the text box. Place a check mark in the **E-mail** check box and type **Support@craighead.com** in the text box. Click **OK** to accept the changes. You can confirm that the changes were applied by right-clicking any of the user accounts within **IT Staff** and clicking **Properties**.

Restrict students logon times.

5. Click the **Students** OU in the left pane. **Nathan Swanson** will appear in the right pane. You created the **Nathan Swanson** user account in Project 3.4 and placed it in the **Students** OU in Project 3.5.
6. Right-click **Nathan Swanson** and click **Properties**. The **Properties** dialog box for the Nathan Swanson user account opens. On the **Account** tab, click **Logon Hours**.

Figure 6-3 Selecting multiple objects

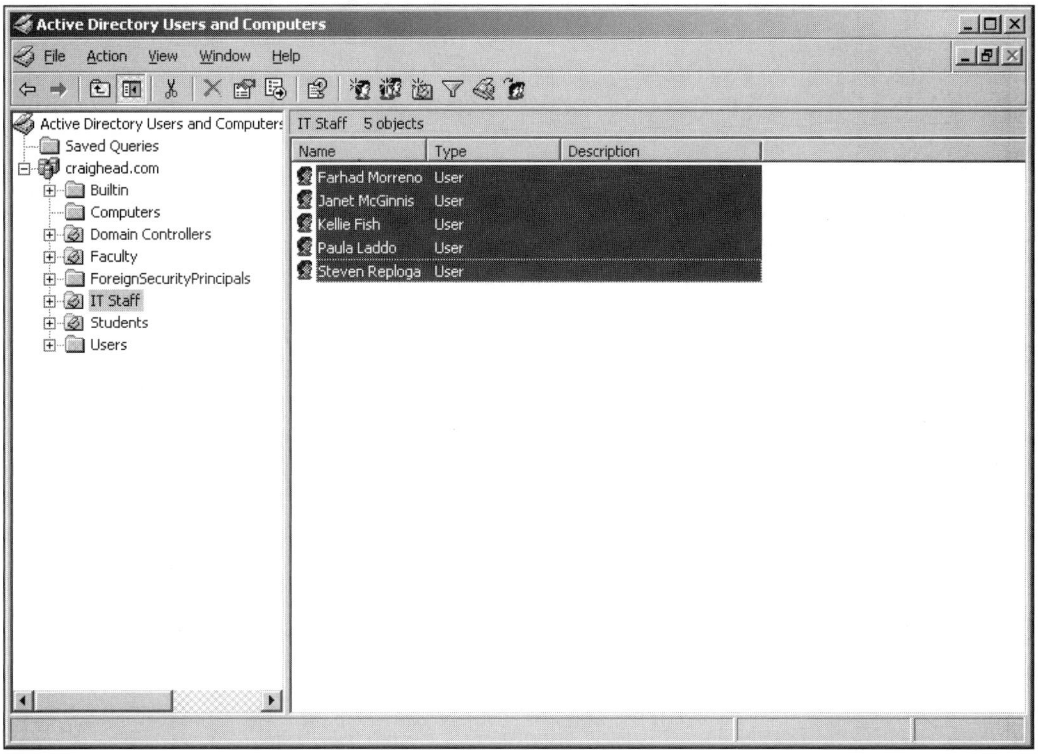

Figure 6-4 Properties On Multiple Objects dialog box

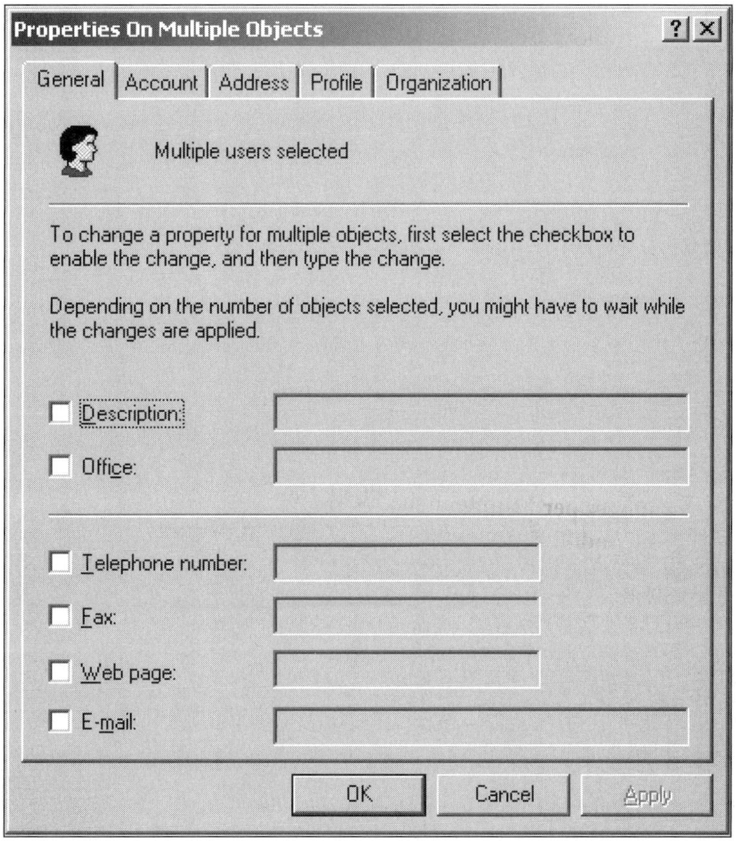

project 6.2

Setting Domain User Account Properties (cont'd)

exam objective

Create and manage user accounts. Create and modify user accounts by using the Active Directory Users and Computers MMC snap-in.

project steps

7. In the **Logon Hours for Nathan Swanson** dialog box, use your mouse to mark the entire row for **Sunday** and click **Logon Denied**. The entire row will turn from blue to white. Repeat the procedure for the **Saturday** row **(Figure 6-5)**. Click **OK** to close the **Logon Hours for Nathan Swanson** dialog box and then click **OK** again to close the **Properties** dialog box.

Allow dial-up access.

8. Click the **Faculty** OU in the left pane of the window. Right-click the **Amy Bradshaw** user account that you created in Project 3.4 in the right pane and click **Properties**.
9. On the **Dial-in** tab, click the **Allow access** option button **(Figure 6-6)** and click **OK**.
10. Click the **IT Staff** organizational unit in the left pane of the Active Directory Users and Computers console window. Right-click the **Farhad Morreno** user account and click **Properties**.
11. On the **Dial-in** tab, click the **Allow access** option button and click **OK**.
12. Repeat step #11 for each of the other four members of the **IT Staff** OU.
13. Close all open dialog boxes and windows.

Figure 6-5 Logon Hours dialog box

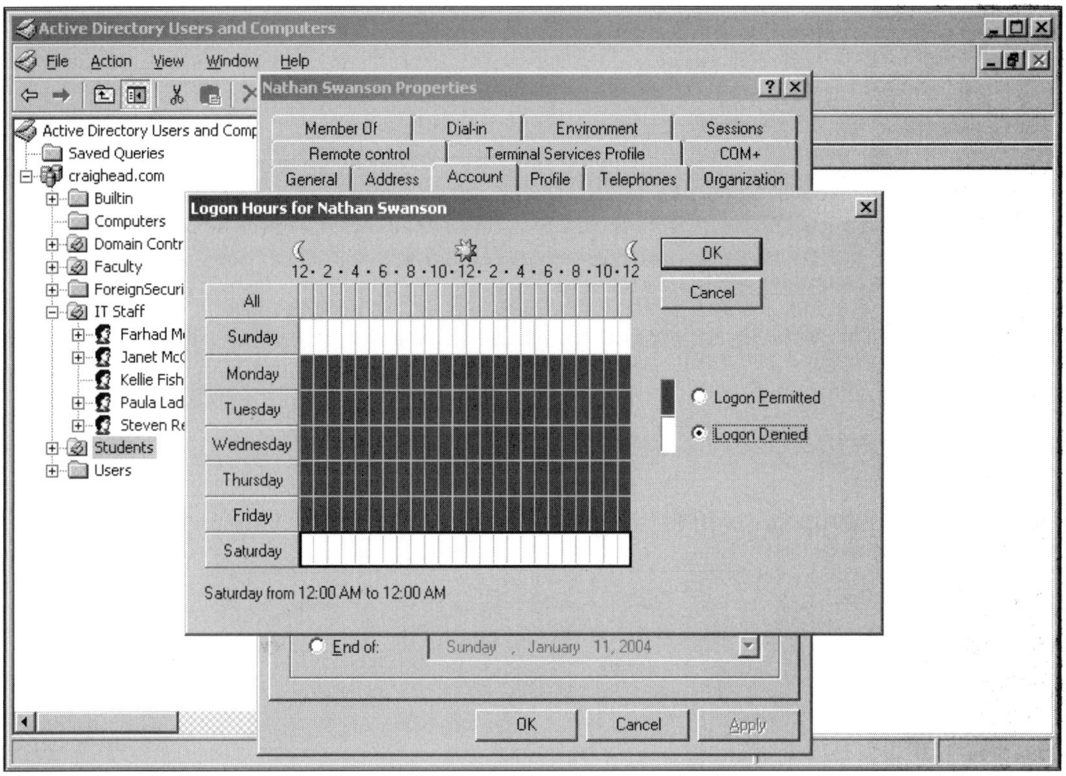

Figure 6-6 Dial-in tab in the Properties dialog box for a user account

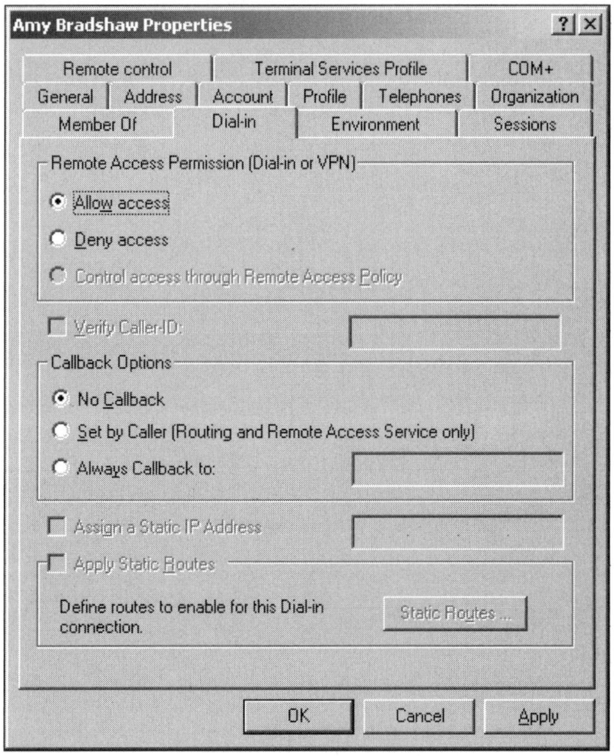

project 6.3 Introducing User Profiles

exam objective

Basic knowledge

overview

A user profile is a collection of data that includes a user's personal data, desktop settings, and other specified settings. User profiles are used to provide a consistent desktop environment each time a user logs on to a computer. There are many configurations stored in the user profile. These are explained in **Table 6-1**.

At Craighead College, there are two primary classes of users: faculty and students. Faculty primarily only log on from their office computers while students log on from a variety of computers throughout the different computer labs in various buildings. You have called a meeting of your IT staff to determine the type of user profile (local, roaming, or mandatory) to implement for each of these classes of users.

learning objective

After completing this project, you will be more familiar with the different types of user profiles.

specific requirements

None

estimated completion time

30 minutes

project steps

1. Prepare a short explanation of each of the different types of user profiles provided by Windows Server 2003. Explain the advantages and disadvantages of each.
2. Prepare a list of the folders contained in a sample user profile folder. Include a description of their contents.
3. Prepare a memo to your CIO, Chris Williamson, explaining the type of user profile you have selected for the students and why. Also, inform him of the type of profile you have selected for the faculty and why.

Table 6-1 Configuration Settings Associated with a User Profile

Configuration settings stored in the user profile	Where those settings are applied
All user-definable settings	Windows Explorer, Control Panel
All user-specific program settings affecting the user's Windows environment, such as Calculator, Notepad, Clock, and Paint	Accessories
Per-user program settings for programs written specifically for Windows Server 2003 and designed to track program settings	Windows Server 2003-based programs
Items stored on the Desktop and Shortcut elements	Desktop contents
All user-definable computer screen colors and display text settings	Display Properties
Application data and user-defined configuration settings	Application data and Registry hive
Any user-created mapped network drives	Mapped network drive
Links to other computers on the network	My Network Places
Network printer connection settings	Printer settings
Any bookmarks placed in the Windows Server 2003 Help system	Online user education bookmarks

project 6.4

Creating a Mandatory User Profile

exam objective

Create and manage user accounts. Manage local, roaming, and mandatory user profiles.

overview

If you have a user, or group of users, who access the network from a variety of computers, you can assign a standard roaming profile to that group. This provides a consistent desktop environment to these users regardless of location.

If you want this configuration to remain constant, you can change the standard roaming profile to a mandatory profile. With a mandatory profile, changes that the user makes to the desktop environment will not be saved. This is extremely useful when a user account, such as Guest, is used by a variety of individuals or if you wish to enforce a consistent desktop for different groups.

At Craighead College, you wish to create a generic account named TempStudent to be used by students that have not yet received their personal user accounts. This account should have a standardized profile that the users cannot modify. Also, for obvious reasons, the user should not be allowed to change the password.

learning objective

After completing this project, you will be able to create a roaming profile and change it to a mandatory profile.

specific requirements

See general requirements.

estimated completion time

45 minutes

project steps

Create a shared folder on the server.

1. Log on to the server as an **Administrator**. Click **Start** and then click **My Computer**. Double-click **Local Disk (C:)** to display a list of files and folders on C:.
2. Click **File** on the Menu bar, point to **New**, and click **Folder** to create a new folder on the root of the C: drive. Type **UserProfiles** as the name of the new folder and press **[Enter]**.
3. Right-click the **UserProfiles** folder and click **Sharing and Security** to display the **Sharing** tab of the **UserProfiles Properties** dialog box **(Figure 6-7)**. Click the **Share this folder** option button and accept the default share name. Type **Folder for User Profiles** in the **Description** text box.
4. Click **Permissions** to change the default share permissions. Click **Add** and type **Authenticated Users** in the **Enter the object names to select (examples)** text box and click **OK**.
5. With **Authenticated Users** highlighted in the **Permissions for UserProfiles** dialog box, place a check mark in the **Allow** box for the **Full Control** permission **(Figure 6-8)**.
6. To remove the default share right from the **Everyone** group, click the **Everyone** group and click **Remove**. Click **OK** to accept the changes. Click **OK** again to close the **UserProfile Properties** dialog box. Close all open dialog boxes and windows.

Create a generic user account.

7. Click **Start**, point to **Administrative Tools**, and then click **Active Directory Users and Computers**. Right-click the **Students** OU, point to **New** and then click **User**.
8. Type **TempStudent** in the **Last name** text box and in the **User logon name** text box. Click **Next**. Deselect **User must change password at next logon** by removing the check mark.

Figure 6-7 Sharing tab in the UserProfiles Properties dialog box

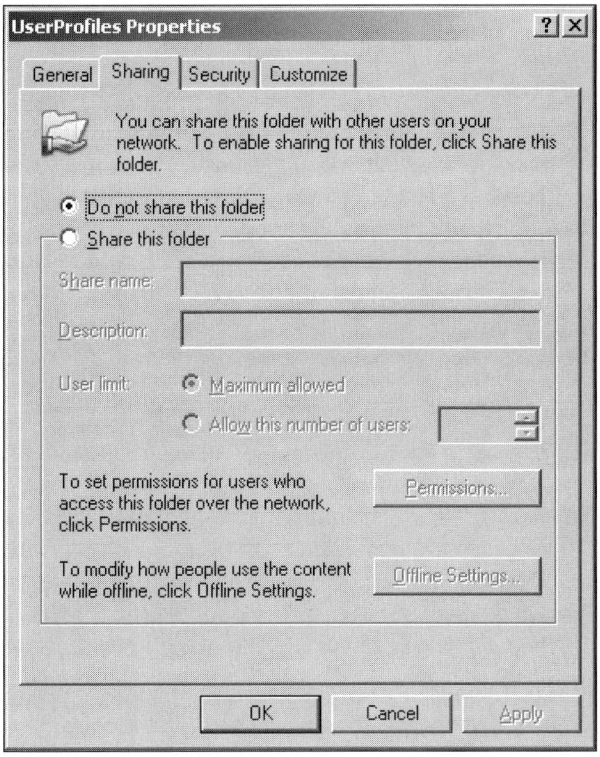

Figure 6-8 Permissions for UserProfiles dialog box

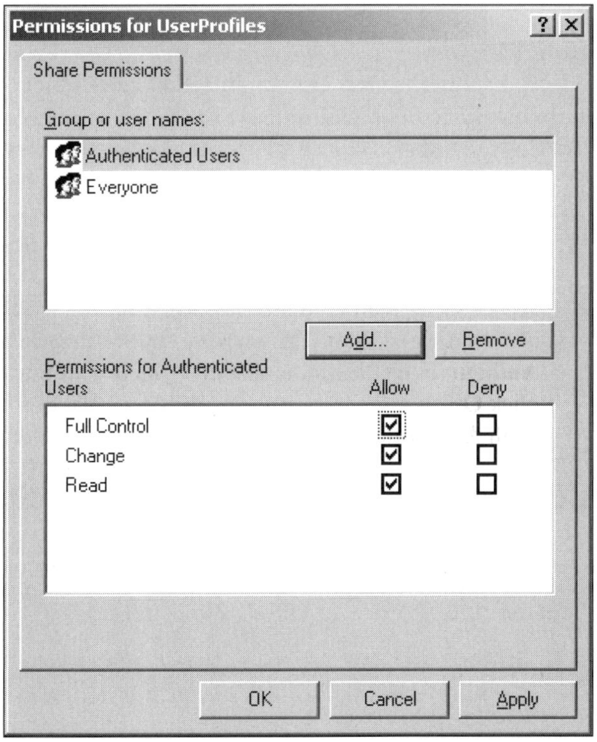

project 6.4

Creating a Mandatory User Profile

(cont'd)

exam objective

Create and manage user accounts. Manage local, roaming, and mandatory user profiles.

project steps

tip

Step 10 is needed because of the increased security of domain controllers. Since the generic user will need to log on to the domain controller to create the profile, the user must either be made a member of a built-in group that is allowed to log on locally to the domain controller or individually granted the right to log on locally. This step is not required when creating most accounts.

9. Place a check mark in the **User cannot change password** and **Password never expires** check boxes. Enter **CraigHead#1** (case sensitive) in both the **Password** and **Confirm password** text boxes. Click **Next** and **Finish** to create the user.
10. Right-click the **Student** user account in the left pane of the Active Directory Users and Computers console window and click **Add to a group**. Type **Print Operators** in the **Enter the object name to select (examples)** text box and click **OK**. Click **OK** to confirm.
11. Close all open dialog boxes and windows

Create a user profile with the appropriate configuration.

12. Log off as an **Administrator** and log on as **Student**. A local user profile is automatically created for **Student**.
13. Right-click any blank space on the desktop and click **Properties**. On the **Desktop** tab, select **Windows Server 2003** as the **Background (Figure 6-9)**. Click **Customize Desktop** and place a check mark beside **My Documents** and **My Computer**. Click **OK**.
14. On the **Screen Saver** tab, remove the check mark from the **On resume, password protect** check box and change the value in the **minutes** text box to **5.** Click **OK** to accept these changes.

Copy the user profile to the share and grant access.

15. Log off as **Student** and log on as an **Administrator**.
16. Click **Start**, right-click **My Computer**, and click **Properties** to display the **System Properties** dialog box. On the **Advanced** tab, click the **Settings** button pertaining to **User Profiles**.
17. Click **CRAIGHEAD/Student** in the **Profiles stored on this computer** section **(Figure 6-10)** and click **Copy To**.
18. Click **Browse**, drill down to and select **C:\UserProfiles** and click **OK**. Click **Change** and type **Authenticated Users** in the **Enter the object name to select (example)** text box. Click **OK**. Click **OK** to close the **Copy To** dialog box and click **Yes** in the **Confirm Copy** dialog box. Close all open dialog boxes and windows.

Specify the profile path in the user account.

19. Click **Start**, point to **Administrative Tools**, and then click **Active Directory Users and Computers**.
20. Expand **craighead.com** if necessary, and click the **Student** OU. Right-click the **Student** user object and click **Properties**. On the **Profile** tab **(Figure 6-11)**, type **\\<*server_-name*>\userprofiles** (where ***server_name*** is the name of the domain controller) in the **Profile path** text box and click **OK**. Close all open dialog boxes and windows.

Make the profile mandatory.

21. Click **Start** and then click **Windows Explorer**. Expand **My Computer** and **Local Disk (C:)**. Click **UserProfiles** in the left pane of the Explorer window.

Figure 6-9 Display Properties dialog box

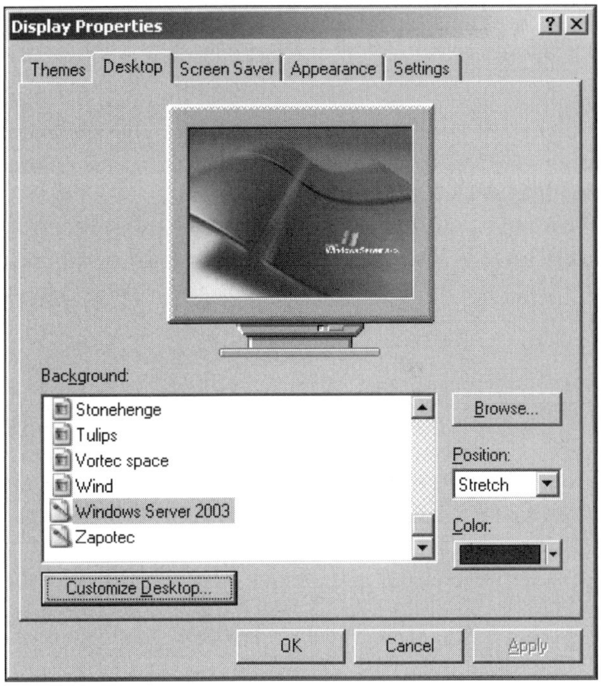

Figure 6-10 Profiles stored on this computer

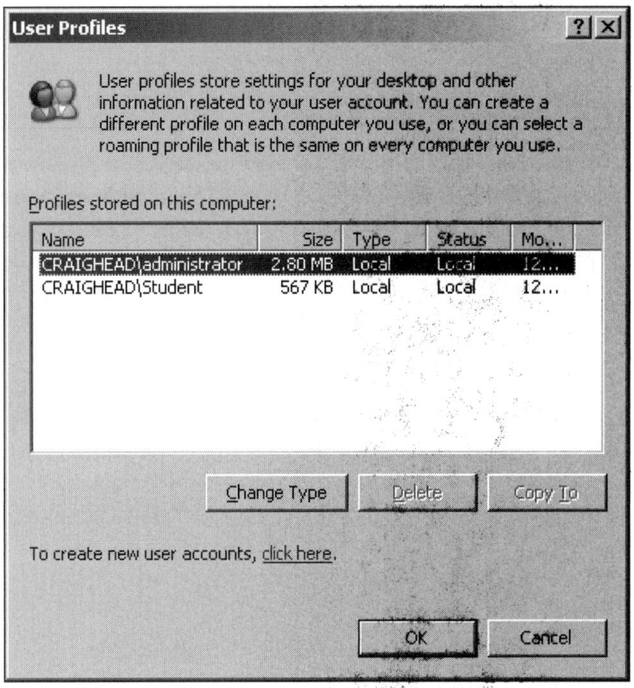

Figure 6-11 Profile tab in the Properties dialog box for a user account

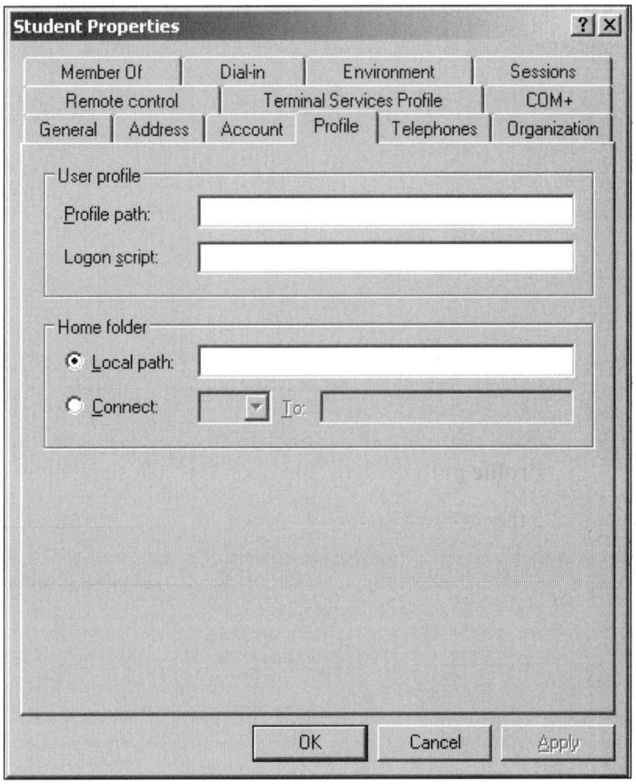

project 6.4

Creating a Mandatory User Profile

(cont'd)

exam objective

Create and manage user accounts. Manage local, roaming, and mandatory user profiles.

project steps

22. Click **Tools** on the Menu bar and then click **Folder Options**. On the **View** tab (**Figure 6-12**), select the **Show hidden files and folders** option button and remove the check mark from **Hide extensions for known file types** and click **OK**.
23. Right-click the file **ntuser.dat** in the right pane and click **Rename**. Type **ntuser.man** as the new name of the file and press **[Enter]** to save the changed file name. Close all open dialog boxes and windows.

Test the profile.

24. Log off as an **Administrator** and log on as **Student**. Right-click the **My Documents** icon on the desktop and click **Delete**. Click **Yes** to confirm the deletion. The icon will be removed from the desktop.
25. Log off and back on as **Student**. You will notice that the **My Documents** icon will appear on the desktop because you have employed a mandatory user profile.

Figure 6-12 View tab in the Folder Options dialog box

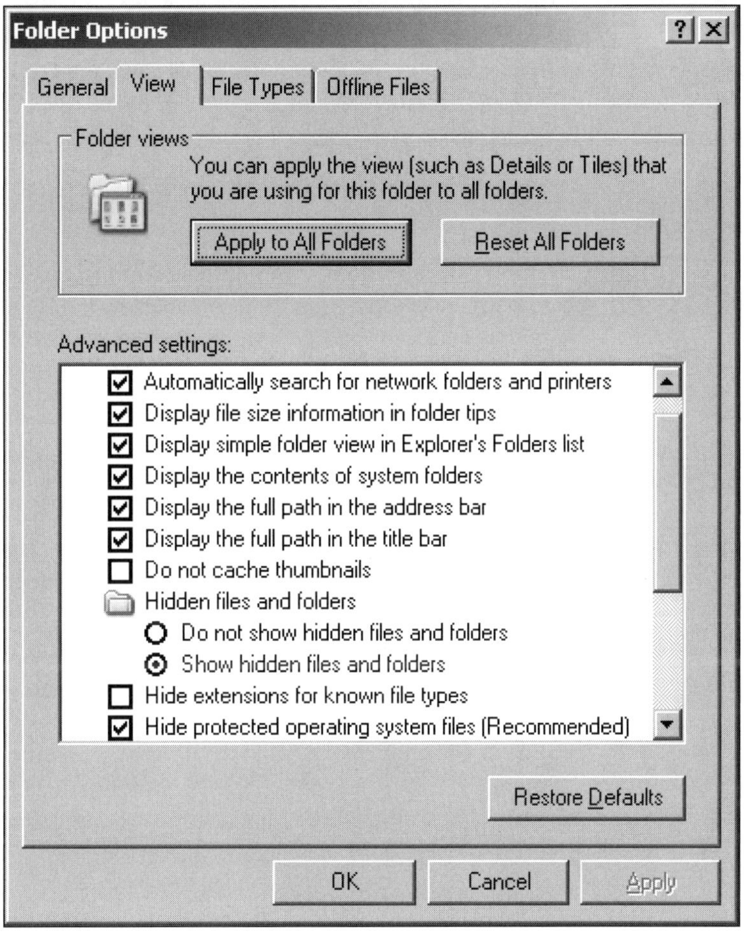

LESSON

7 Introducing Group Accounts

A group is a collection of user accounts that require similar rights and permissions. Groups are used to simplify the management of multiple user accounts because it is much easier to assign permissions and rights to a single group of users rather than to many users individually.

In the Windows Server 2003 environment, there are various types of groups. Within the domain, a Domain Local Group is used to assign permissions in order to access resources and a Global Group is used to organize domain user accounts. A Global Group is made a member of a Domain Local Group to allow users to access resources. When Active Directory has been placed in either Windows 2000 native mode or Windows Server 2003 mode, you can also create Universal Groups. Global Groups can be members of Universal Groups, and Universal Groups can be members of Domain Local groups.

Windows Server 2003 also includes built-in groups to manage the accessibility of various resources. They are predefined groups that have a set of rights and permissions.

Scenario

For easier management of the Craighead College network, you will implement rights and permissions to various resources by utilizing the different types of groups available in Windows Server 2003. You will also create Group Policy Objects for the purpose of folder redirection, software installation settings, and to secure the work environment for users.

Lesson 7 Introducing Group Accounts

Project	Exam 70-290 Objective
7.1 Introducing Built-in Groups	Create and manage groups.
7.2 Creating and Modifying Groups	Create and manage groups. Manage group membership. Identify and modify the scope of a group.
7.3 Creating Group Policy Objects	Basic knowledge
7.4 Modifying the Software Settings Using GPO Software Policies	Basic knowledge
7.5 Redirecting Folders Using GPOs	Basic knowledge

General Requirements

To complete the projects in this lesson, you will need administrative rights on the domain controller for craighead.com and the Windows Server 2003 installation CD-ROM. You will also need to create a folder on the local drive C: named AutoCAD. You may also find it helpful to refer to Lesson 7 of your Prentice Hall Certification Series Exam 70-290 textbook for further information about the topics covered by the projects in this lesson.

project 7.1

Introducing Built-in Groups

exam objective

Create and manage groups.

overview

Built-in groups have a preset collection of rights and permissions and are used to manage common tasks performed by users. Built-in groups can save you time because you can assign user accounts to the appropriate built-in group instead of having to create a group with the appropriate rights and permissions. Members are automatically added to some of the built-in global groups.

At Craighead College, all members of your IT Staff should be familiar with built-in group accounts. You will prepare a summary of the types of built-in accounts available on Windows Server 2003. In addition, you will add them to the appropriate group to enable them to administer domain user and group accounts.

learning objective

After completing this project, you will be more familiar with the various types of built-in groups. You will also know how to add a user to a built-in group.

specific requirements

None

estimated completion time

45 minutes

project steps

1. Prepare a description of the rights and permissions assigned to the following Built-in Local Groups located in the Builtin folder in the Active Directory Users and Computers console **(Figure 7-1)**:
   - Account Operators
   - Administrators
   - Backup Operators
   - Print Operators
   - Users
2. Prepare a description of the rights and permissions assigned to the following Built-in Domain Local Groups located in the Users folder in Active Directory Users and Computer **(Figure 7-2)**:
   - DHCP Administrators
   - Cert Publishers
   - DHCP Users

tip

Refer to your Prentice Hall Certification Series Exam 70-290 textbook for further information on these rights and permissions.

Figure 7-1 Builtin folder in the Active Directory Users and Computers console

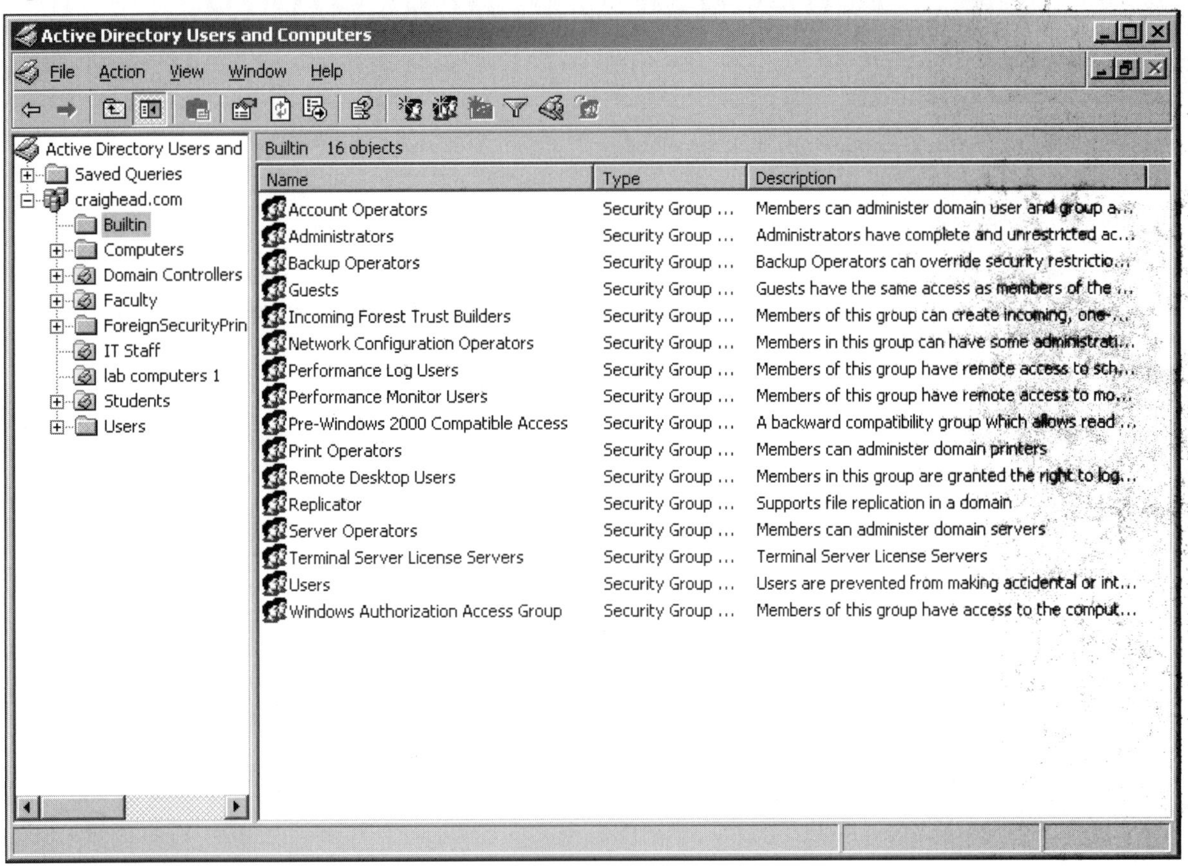

Figure 7-2 Users folder in the Active Directory Users and Computers console

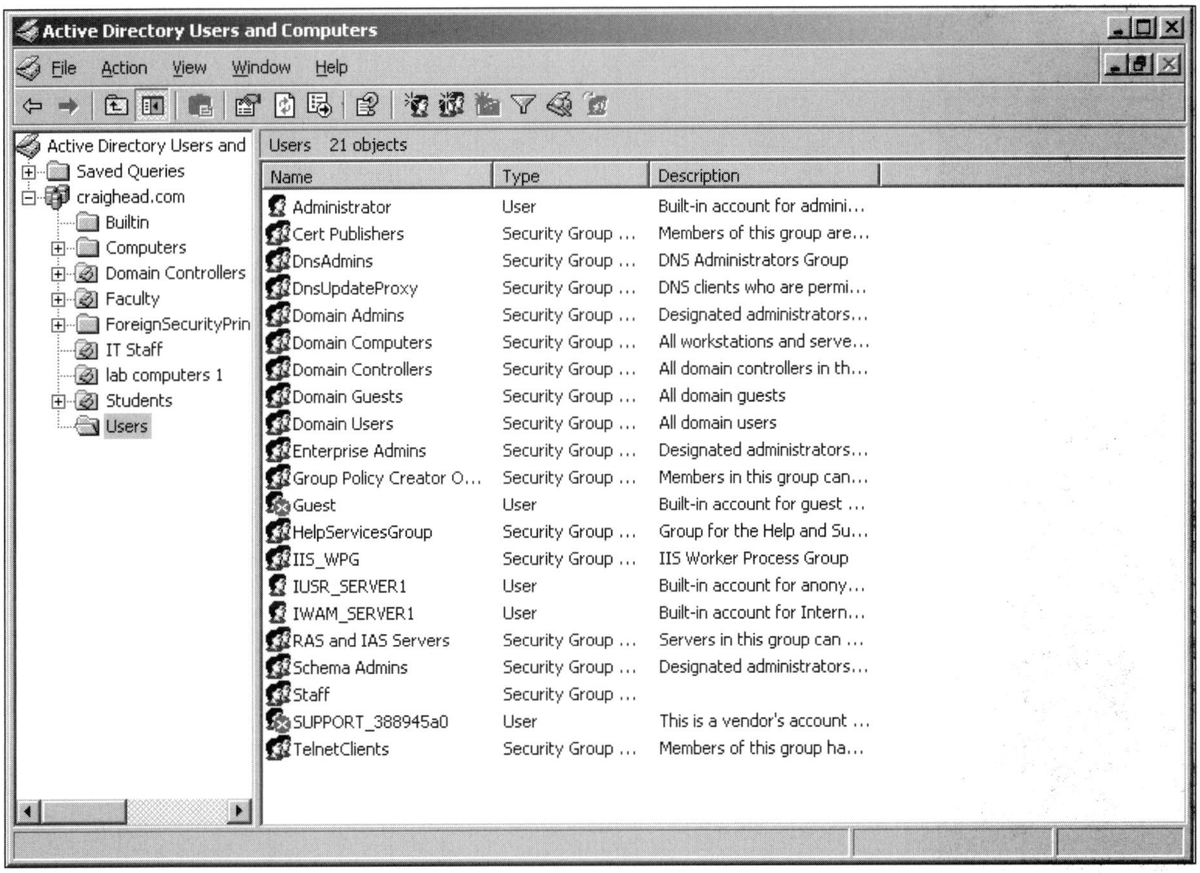

project 7.1

Introducing Built-in Groups (cont'd)

exam objective

Create and manage groups.

project steps

3. Built-in System Groups are populated with users based upon how they access a computer or a resource. You cannot add, delete, or modify the membership of these groups. Prepare a description of the following types of Built-in System Groups:
   - Authenticated Users
   - Creator Owner
   - Everyone
   - Interactive
   - Dial-up

4. To allow your IT Staff to manage user and group accounts, click **Start**, point to **Administrative Tools**, and click **Active Directory Users and Computers**. Expand the **craighead.com** domain and click the **IT Staff** OU.
5. Highlight all five members of the OU by clicking on each user in the right pane of the window and holding down the **Ctrl** button. Right-click and select **Add to a group**.
6. In the **Select Group** dialog box, type **Account Operators (Figure 7-3)** and click **OK**. Click **OK** to close the confirmation screen. Close all open windows.

Figure 7-3 Select Group dialog box

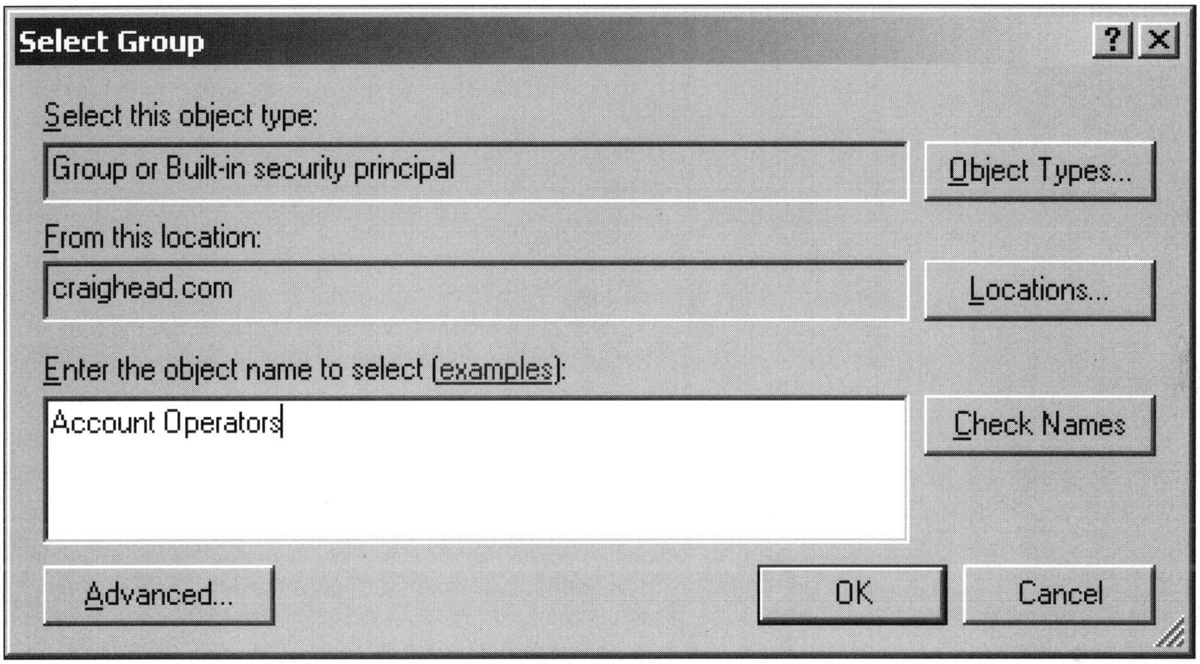

project 7.2 Creating and Modifying Groups

exam objective

Create and manage groups. Manage group membership. Identify and modify the scope of a group.

overview

Groups can be used effectively to manage large numbers of users and resources. It is advised that you follow the Microsoft rule for creating groups and assigning permissions. While it takes more work, in the long run it reduces effort to such a large degree that the extra time is worth it.

The Microsoft rule is to use domain local and global groups following what is referred to as the A-G-DL-P strategy. You put user (A)ccounts into (G)lobal groups, put the global groups into domain local (DL) groups, and grant (P)ermissions to the domain local group. In native or Windows Server 2003 mode, universal groups can be used to organize global groups from multiple domains. When used, they fit between global and domain local group in the strategy, i.e. A-G-U-DL-P.

Because the network requirements will differ for students at Craighead College depending upon their major, you will create a group for each of the five degree programs on campus. As each student is created, they will be made a member of the appropriate group. Also, each member of your IT Staff has been assigned primary management responsibility for a particular degree program.

To allow for full functionally of all types of groups, you have decided to raise the domain functional level of craighead.com to Windows Server 2003. This is possible because no legacy servers are in use on campus.

Craighead College has just installed the newest version of AutoCAD software on the C: drive under the Program Files folder in a folder named AutoCAD. Only members of the Administrators group and the Art group should have access to this folder. You need to create the necessary type of groups to control this access.

learning objective

After completing this project, you will know how to create groups and raise the domain functional level.

specific requirements

Administrative rights on the domain controller for the craighead.com domain.

estimated completion time

15 minutes

project steps

1. Click **Start**, point to **Administrative Tools**, and click **Active Directory Users and Computers**.
2. Right-click the **craighead.com** domain and click **Raise Domain Functional Level**. In the drop-down list, click **Windows Server 2003 (Figure 7-4)** and then click **Raise**. You will receive a warning that this procedure is irreversible. Click **OK**. Click **OK** again to confirm.
3. Click **Users** in the left pane of the window. Right-click **Users**, point **New** and then click **Group**. In the **New Object — Group** dialog box **(Figure 7-5)**, type **Business** in the **Group name** text box. Ensure that the **Global** and **Security** option buttons have been selected. Click **OK**.
4. Repeat Step #3 to create the following groups: **Education**, **Art**, **Agri**, and **Science**.

Figure 7-4 Raise Domain Functional Level dialog box

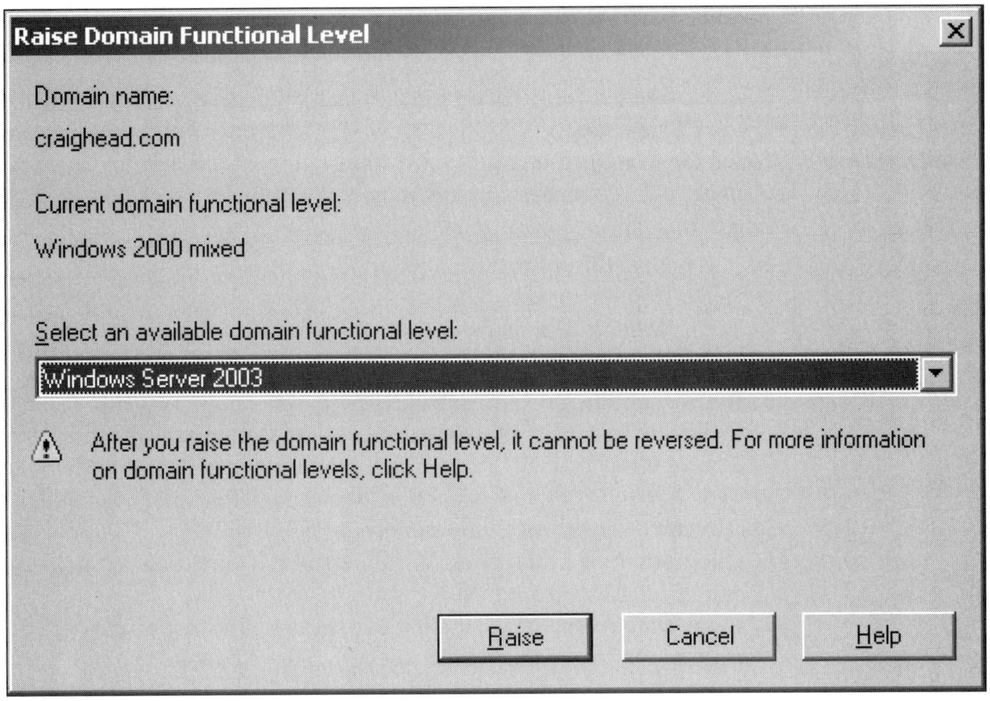

Figure 7-5 New Object — Group dialog box

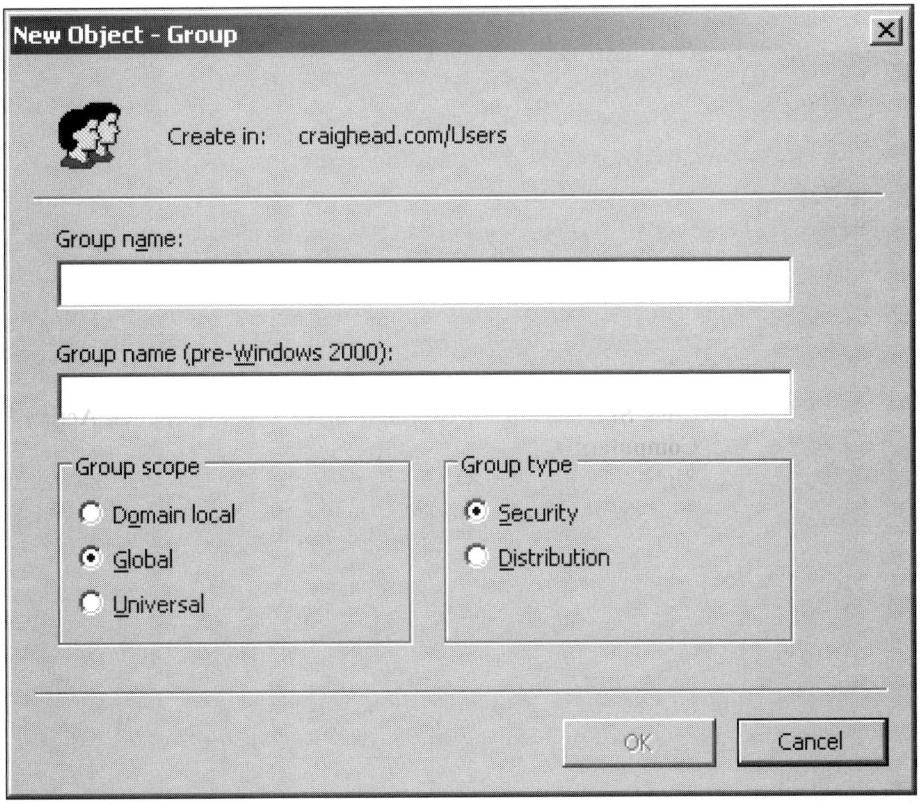

project 7.2

Creating and Modifying Groups

(cont'd)

exam objective

Create and manage groups. Manage group membership. Identify and modify the scope of a group.

project steps

5. Click **Users** in the left pane. Right-click the **Business** security group in the right pane and click **Properties**.
6. On the **Managed by** tab, click **Change**. Type **FarhadM** and click **OK**. Place a check mark in the **Manager can update membership list** check box and click **OK**.
7. Repeat Step #5 and assign the following managers:
   - **JanetM** to **Education** group
   - **KellieF** to **Art** group
   - **PaulaL** to **Agri** group
   - **StevenR** to **Science** group
8. Right-click the **Users** folder in the left pane, click **New** and then click **Group**. Type **CadUsers** as the **Group name** and click the **Domain local** option button. Click **OK**.
9. Double-click the **CadUsers** group in the right pane. On the **Members** tab, click **Add**. Type **Art** and click **OK**. Click **OK** to close the Properties dialog box. Close the **Active Directory Users and Computers** console.
10. Click **Start**, and then click **My Computer**. Double-click **Local Disk (C:)** and then double-click **Program Files**.
11. Right-click **AutoCAD** and click **Properties**. On the **Security** tab **(Figure 7-6)**, click **Advanced**. Remove the check mark from the **Allow inheritable permissions from the parent to propagate to this object and all child objects** check box and click **Remove**.
12. Click **Add** and type **Administrators** in the **Enter the object name to select (examples)** text box. Place a check mark in the **Allow** box for the **Full Control** permission, and click **OK**.
13. Click **Add** and type **CadUsers** in the **Enter the object name to select (examples)** text box. Place a check mark in the **Allow** box for the following permissions:
    - **Traverse Folder/Execute File**
    - **List Folder/Read Data**
    - **Read Attributes**
    - **Create Files/Write Data**
    - **Create Folders/Append Data**
    - **Read Permissions**

    Click OK. Close all open dialog boxes, saving changes as necessary.

As students are made members of the **Art** group, they will receive rights to the **AutoCad** folder through the **A-G-DL-P** strategy. For example, user **John** (an Account) will be made a member of **Art** (a Global Group). **Art** is a member of **CadUsers** (a Domain Local Group). **CadUsers** has been granted permissions to the **AutoCad** folder.

Figure 7-6 Security tab in Folder Properties dialog box

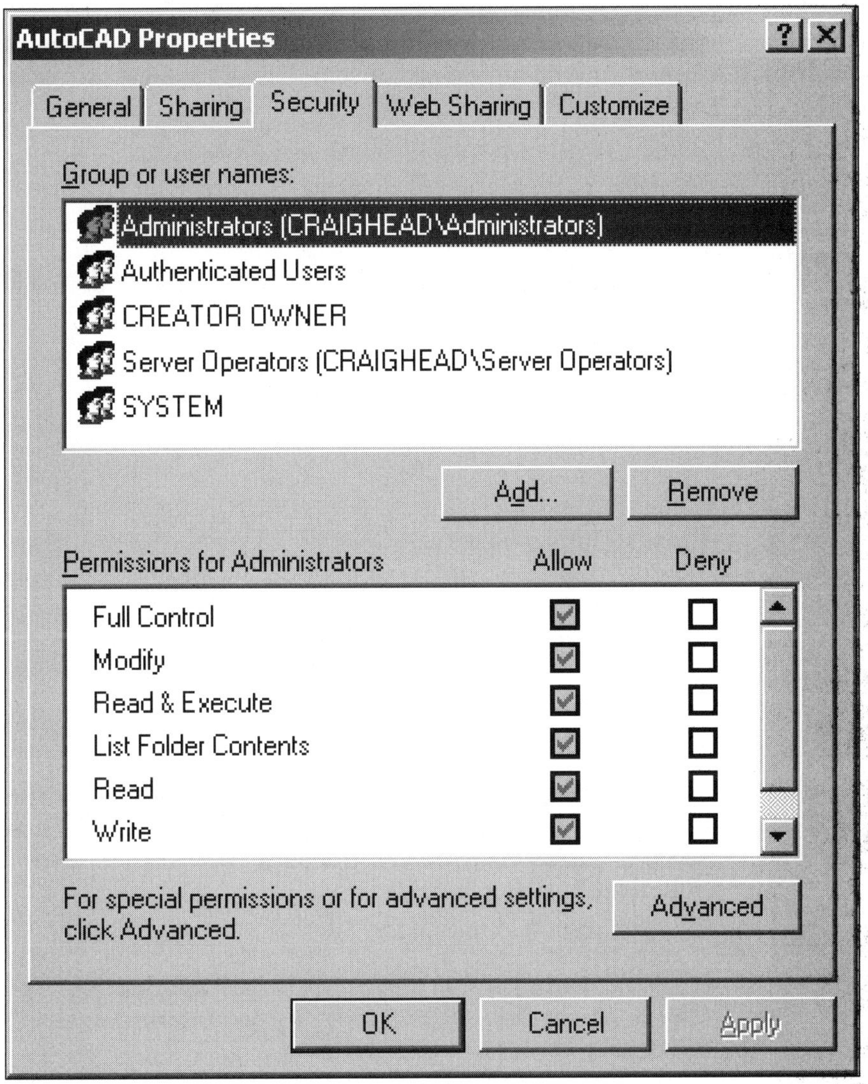

project 7.3

Creating Group Policy Objects

exam objective

Basic knowledge

overview

Group Policies are used to control computer configurations, user environments, and account policies. Network administrators usually apply these policies to centrally manage configuration settings for an organizational unit or a domain. They can also be used to control the distribution of software applications. The idea is to enforce uniform policies on the entire network or portions of the network.

Students at Craighead College should not be able to change the display settings or lock the computer. You have decided to create a Group Policy Object for the Students OU to accomplish these requirements.

learning objective

After completing this project, you will know how to create Group Policy Objects.

specific requirements

Administrative rights on the domain controller for the craighhead.com domain.

estimated completion time

15 minutes

project steps

1. Click **Start**, point to **Administrative Tools**, and then click **Active Directory Users and Computers**.
2. Expand the **craighead.com** domain, if necessary. Right-click the **Students** OU and click **Properties**.
3. On the **Group Policy** tab, click **Edit** to open the **Group Policy Object Editor (Figure 7-7)**.
4. Under **User Configuration**, expand **Administrative Templates** and then expand **System**. Click **Ctrl+Alt+Del Options** in the left pane. In the right pane, double-click **Remove Lock Computer**.
5. In the **Remove Lock Computer Properties** dialog box, click **Enabled (Figure 7-8)** and then click **OK**.
6. Click **Control Panel** in the left pane of the window. Double-click **Display** in the right pane. Double-click **Remove Display in Control Panel** and click **Enabled** in the **Properties** dialog box. Click **OK**.
7. Close the **Group Policy Object Editor** console. Click **OK** in the **Students Properties** dialog box. Close the **Active Directory Users and Computers** console.
8. Log off as an **Administrator** and log on as NathanS with the password **p@$$w0rd**, to test the configuration. NathanS is member of the **Students** OU and has been given permission to log on locally to the server in a previous lesson.

Figure 7-7 Group Policy Object Editor

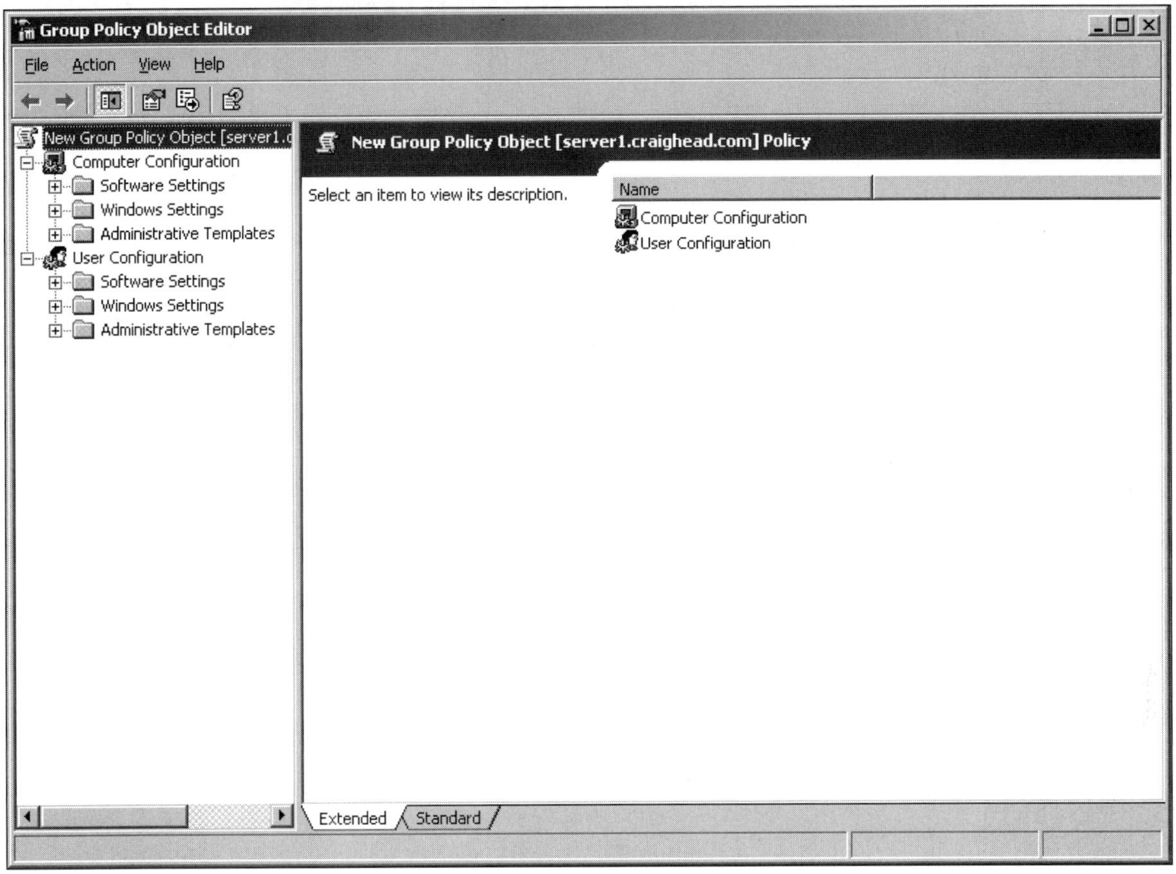

Figure 7-8 Remove Lock Computer Properties dialog box

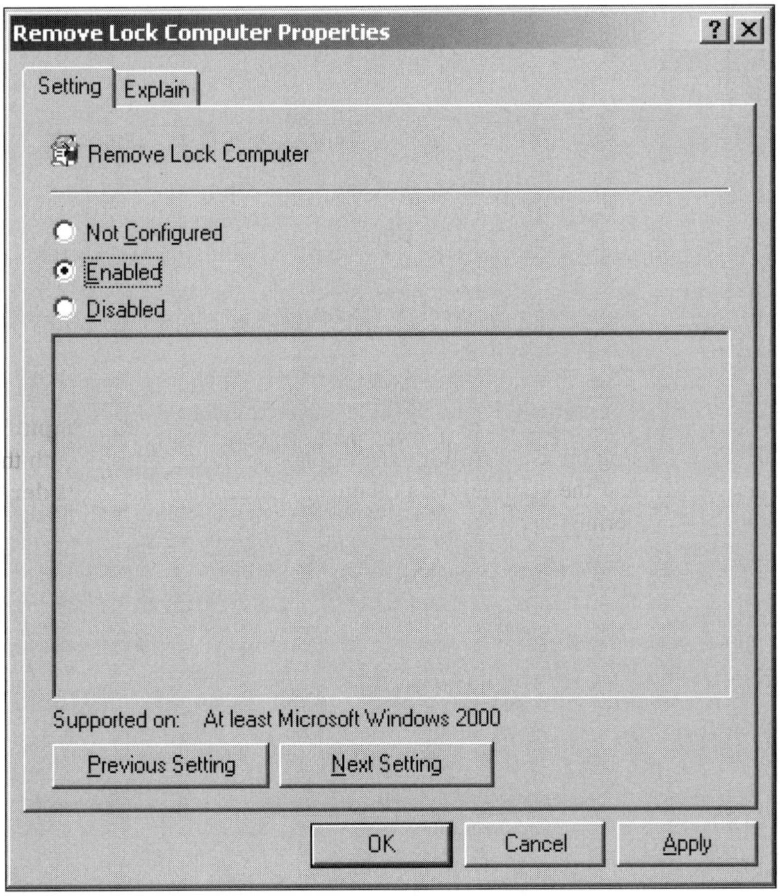

project 7.4

Modifying the Software Settings Using GPO Software Policies

exam objective

Basic knowledge

overview

Group Policies can be used to assign and publish applications to users or computers. Applications can be assigned to either users or computers, but they can be published only to users. When an application is assigned to a user, it will automatically display in the Start menu, but will not actually be installed until the user selects it on the menu or tries to open a document created with the program (known as document invocation). When the application is assigned to a computer, it is immediately installed when the computer boots. If a part of the program is deleted, it will automatically reinstall the next time it is activated.

When an application is published for users in the site, domain, or OU, it is listed as being available to install in Add or Remove Programs. The user can install the application using the applet or by document invocation.

As network administrator, you want the Windows Server 2003 Support Tools installed automatically on all computers within the craighead.com domain. You have decided to assign the software through GPO software policies.

learning objective

After completing this project, you will know how to assign software for distribution through GPO policies.

specific requirements

Administrative rights on the domain controller for the craighead.com domain.

estimated completion time

30 minutes

project steps

1. Click **Start** and then click **My Computer**. Double-click **Local Disk (C:)** and then double-click **Support**. (*Note:* If the **Support** folder is not found, copy the folder and its contents from the Windows Server 2003 installation CD-ROM.)
2. Right-click the **Tools** folder and click **Sharing and Security**. Click the **Share this folder** option button. Click **Permissions**. Click **Add** and type **Administrators** in the **Enter the object names to select (examples)** text box. Click **OK**. Click **OK** to close the **Tools Properties** dialog box.
3. Click **Start**, point to **Administrative Tools**, and then click **Active Directory Users and Computers**. Right-click the **craighead.com** domain and click **Properties**.
4. On the **Group Policy** tab, click **Edit** to open the **Group Policy Object Editor**. Double-click **Software Settings** under **Computer Configuration**.
5. Right-click **Software Installation**, point to **New** and then click **Package**. In the **Open** dialog box, type ***server_name*** in the **File name** text box and click **Open**. From the list of shares, double-click **Tools**.
6. Double-click the **2000RKST** or **SUPTOOLS** file, whichever is present, to open the **Deploy Software** dialog box **(Figure 7-9)**. Ensure that **Assigned** is selected and click **OK**.
7. Close the **Group Policy Object Editor**. Click **OK** to close the **craighead.com Properties** dialog box. Close all open dialog boxes and windows.
8. Reboot your machine. During the reboot process, you will receive a message in the splash screen, **Installing managed software Windows Support Tools**. Since the software was assigned, installation did not require any user intervention.

Figure 7-9 Deploy Software dialog box

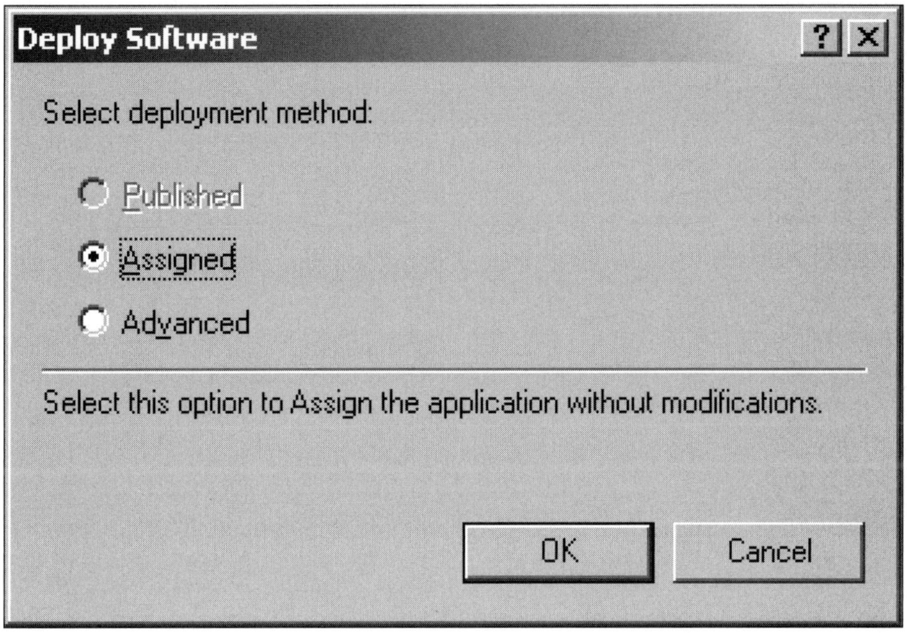

project 7.5

Redirecting Folders Using GPOs

exam objective

Basic knowledge

overview

Group Policies can be used to redirect folders, normally found on local computers, to a server on the network. For example, the network administrator can redirect the My Documents folder to a location on the server. This provides the user access to documents regardless of the computer the user logs on to, as long as the user is connected to the network. Since all user documents are stored centrally on the server, backup of individual files becomes easier and workstation failure does not mean losing access to important data.

To provide more reliable access to documents and easier backup of user files, you have decided to redirect the My Documents folders of all users to the domain controller for Craighead College.

learning objective

After completing this project, you will know how to redirect folders using GPOs.

specific requirements

Administrative rights on the domain controller for the craighead.com domain.

estimated completion time

15 minutes

project steps

1. Click **Start** and then click **Windows Explorer**. Double-click **My Computer** and click **Local Disk (C:)**.
2. Click **File**, point to **New**, and then click **Folder**. Type **HomeDirs** as the name of the new folder, and press **[Enter]**. Right-click **HomeDirs** and click **Properties**.
3. On the **Sharing** tab, click the **Share this folder** option button and click **OK**.
4. Click **Start**, point to **Administrative Tools**, and then click **Active Directory Users and Computers**.
5. Right-click the **craighead.com** domain and click **Properties**. On the **Group Policy** tab, click **Edit**.
6. Expand **Windows Settings** under **User Configuration** and click **Folder Redirection**. In the right-pane, right-click **My Documents**, and click **Properties** to open the **My Documents Properties** dialog box **(Figure 7-10)**.
7. In the **Setting** drop-down list box, select **Basic – Redirect everyone's folder to the same location**. Ensure that **Create a folder for each user under the root path** is selected in the **Target folder location** drop-down box.
8. Type ***\\server_name\homedirs*** in the **Root Path** text box. On the **Settings** tab **(Figure 7-11)**, make sure that the **Grant the user exclusive rights to My Documents** and **Move the contents of My Documents to the new location** check boxes, and the **Leave the folder in the new location when policy is removed** option button are selected. Click **OK**.
9. Close all open dialog boxes and windows.

Figure 7-10 My Documents Properties dialog box

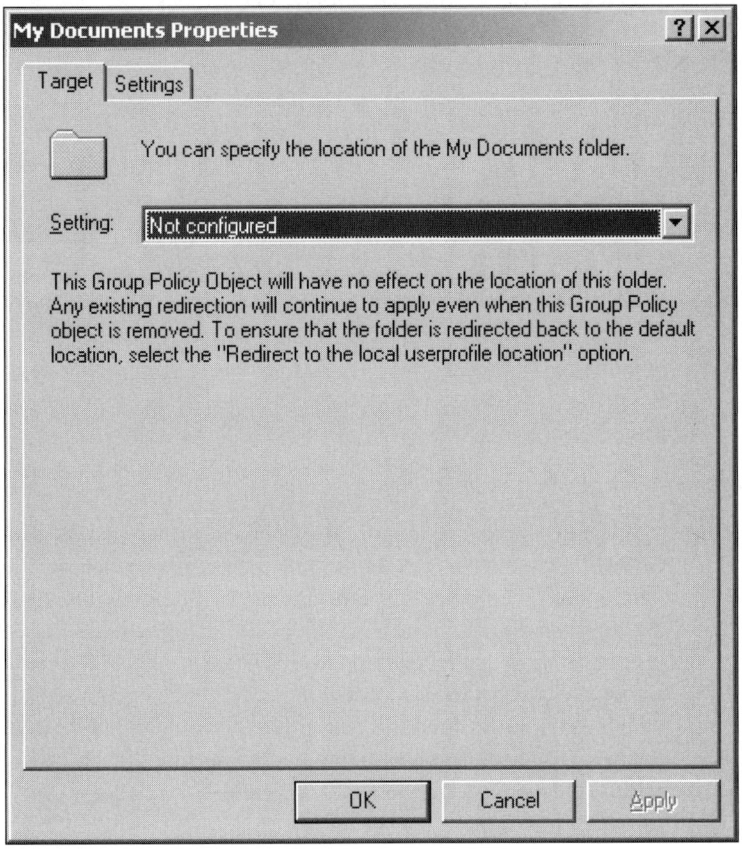

Figure 7-11 Settings tab in My Documents Properties dialog box

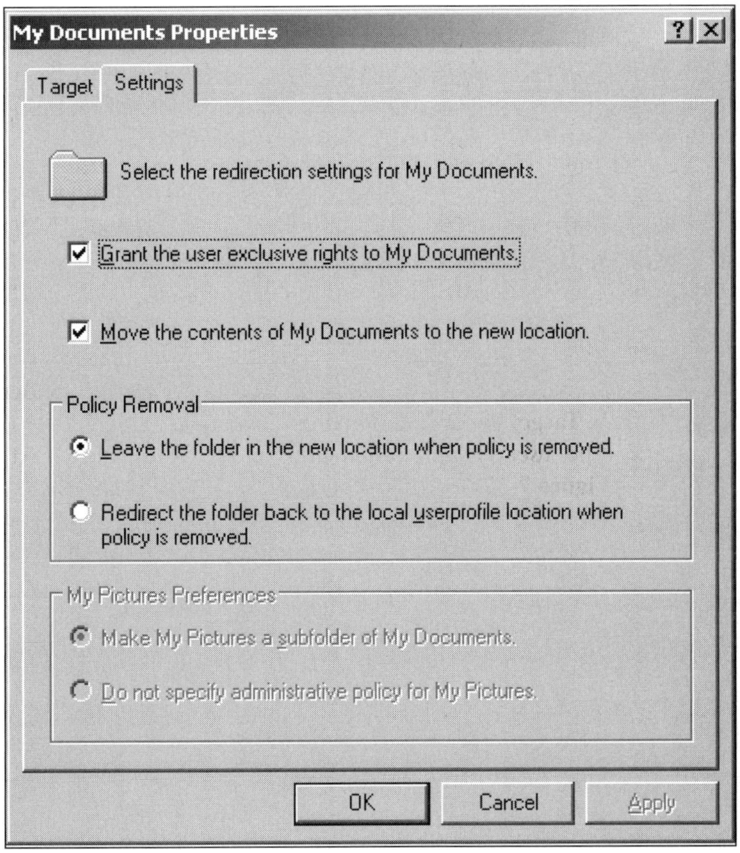

LESSON

8 Introducing Computer Accounts

Just as user accounts are used to identify users, computer accounts are used to identify computers. They are also security principals. As a security principal, a computer account has a SID, which means it can be used to grant access to resources. Additionally, computer accounts can be used to apply Group Policies. When Group Policies are configured through the Computer Configuration node, these settings apply to all users logging on to those computers, regardless of the user account. This is an easy way to ensure that a computer, such as those located in public areas, have specific settings, regardless of the user who logs on. Each Windows Server 2003, Windows 2000 Server, and Windows NT Server in your environment must be given a computer account in order to belong to a domain. Also, each Windows XP, Windows 2000 Professional, and Windows NT client must be given a computer account.

Scenario

When users log on to computers in the public areas of the library, the desktop should be controlled by a Group Policy to ensure specific settings, regardless of the user. This policy should restrict access to certain functions within the desktop environment.

Lesson 8 Introducing Computer Accounts

Project	Exam 70-290 Objective
8.1 Creating Computer Accounts	Create and manage computer accounts in an Active Directory environment.
8.2 Managing Computer Accounts	Create and manage computer accounts in an Active Directory environment.
8.3 Troubleshooting Computer Accounts	Create and manage computer accounts in an Active Directory environment. Troubleshoot computer accounts. Diagnose and resolve issues related to computer accounts by using the Active Directory Users and Computers MMC snap-in. Reset computer accounts.

General Requirements

To complete the projects in this lesson, you will need administrative rights on the domain controller for the Craighead College domain. You may also find it helpful to refer to Lesson 8 in your Prentice Hall Certification Series Exam 70-290 textbook for further information about the topics covered by the projects in this lesson.

project 8.1

Creating Computer Accounts

exam objective

Create and manage computer accounts in an Active Directory environment.

overview

As noted in the introduction, computer accounts are required for computers running the Windows Server 2003, Windows 2000 Server, Windows XP, and Windows NT operating systems to operate within a domain. Computer accounts can be created before the computer is added to the domain by using the Active Directory Users and Computers console. Alternatively, joining a client or member server to a domain will automatically create computer accounts. Furthermore, the Dcpromo utility will automatically create a computer account for the new domain controller.

As network administrator for Craighead College, you want to create computer accounts in advance for all computers that will be located in the public area of the library.

caution

A computer running the DOS, Windows 9.x, Windows Me, or Windows XP Home operating system cannot have a computer account.

learning objective

After completing this project, you will know how to create computer accounts through the Active Directory Users and Computers console.

specific requirements

Administrative rights on the domain controller for craighead.com.

estimated completion time

10 minutes

project steps

1. Click **Start**, point to **Administrative Tools**, and then click **Active Directory Users and Computers**.
2. Right-click the **craighead.com** domain, point to **New**, and then click **Organizational Unit**. Type **Lab Computers** in the **Name** text box and click **OK**.
3. Right-click the new **Lab Computers** OU, click **New**, and then click **Computer**.
4. In the **New Object — Computer** dialog box **(Figure 8-1)**, type **LIB-WS1** in the **Computer name** text box. Notice that this name will automatically be entered as the pre-Windows 2000 computer name. Make sure that there is not a check mark in either of the check boxes and click **Next**.
5. In the **Managed** dialog box, make sure that the **This is a managed computer** check box is not selected, click **Next**, and then click **Finish**.
6. Repeat steps 4 and 5 for computers **LIB-WS2**, **LIB-WS3**, and **LIB-WS4**. Leave all windows open for the next project.

Figure 8-1 New Object — Computer dialog box

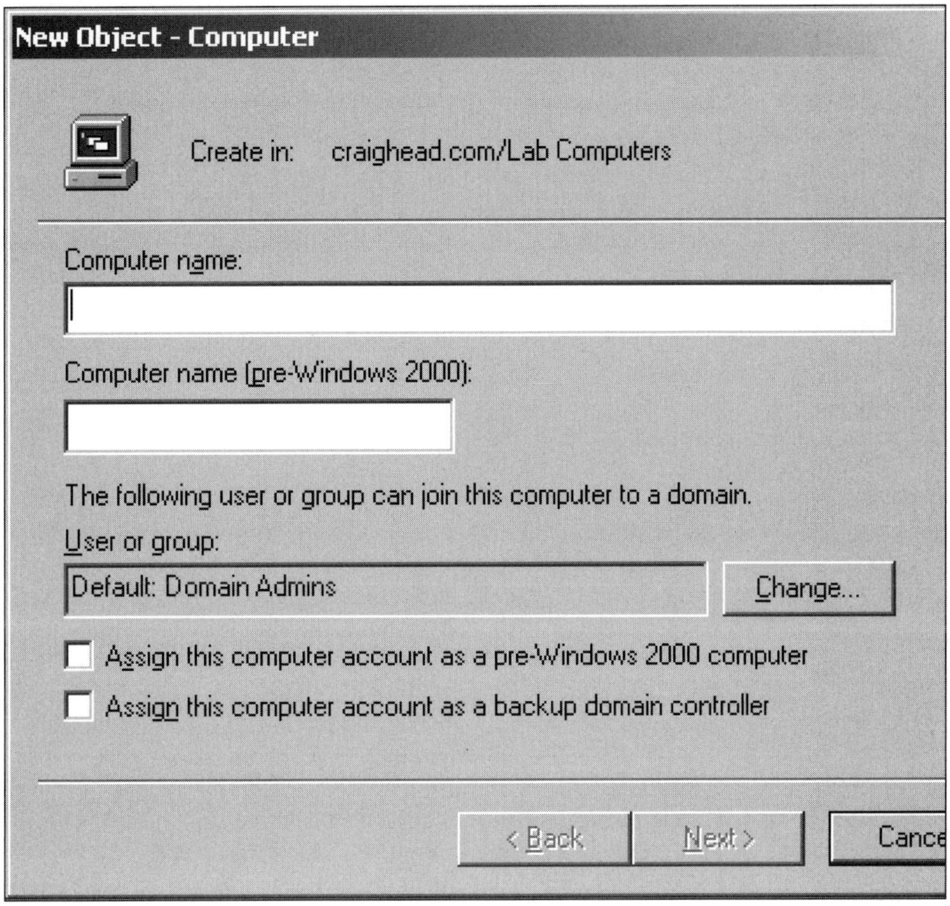

project 8.2 Managing Computer Accounts

exam objective

Create and manage computer accounts in an Active Directory environment.

overview

After you create computer accounts, you will be able to modify the properties of those accounts. When a Group Policy is configured for an OU containing computer accounts, that policy is effective for all computers in that OU regardless of the user that logs on.

As network administrator, you want to modify the description property of the computer accounts within the Lab Computers OU. In addition, you want to configure a default Group Policy for the OU.

learning objective

After completing this project, you will know how to modify the properties of computer accounts and configure Group Policy configurations for computer accounts.

specific requirements

Administrative rights on the domain controller for craighead.com.

estimated completion time

20 minutes

project steps

1. Highlight all of the computer accounts in the right pane of the **Active Directory Users and Computers** console. Right-click the highlighted area and then click **Properties**.
2. In the **Properties On Multiple Objects** dialog box **(Figure 8-2)**, place a check mark in the **Change the description text for all selected objects** check box and type **Library public access computers** in the **Description** text box. Click **OK**.
3. Right-click the **Lab Computers** OU in the left pane of the console window and click **Properties**.
4. On the **Group Policy** tab, click **New** and then click **Edit**. This will open the **Group Policy Object Editor**.
5. Under **Computer Configuration**, expand **Administrative Templates** and **Windows Components**. Then click **Internet Explorer (Figure 8-3)**.
6. Double-click **Security Zones: Do not allow users to change policies** in the right pane and click **Enabled**. Click **OK**.
7. Double-click **Security Zones: Do not allow users to add/delete sites** and click **Enabled**. Click **OK**.
8. Click **Task Scheduler** in the left pane. Double-click **Hide Property Pages** in the right pane and click **Enabled**. Click **OK**.
9. Click **Windows Installer** in the left pane. Double-click **Prohibit User Installs** in the right pane and click **Enabled**. Select **Prohibit User Installs** from the **User Install Behavior** drop-down list **(Figure 8-4)**. Click **OK**.
10. Close the **Group Policy Object Editor**. Click **Close** in the **Lab Computers Properties** dialog box. Close the **Active Directory Users and Computers** console.

Figure 8-2 Properties On Multiple Users dialog box

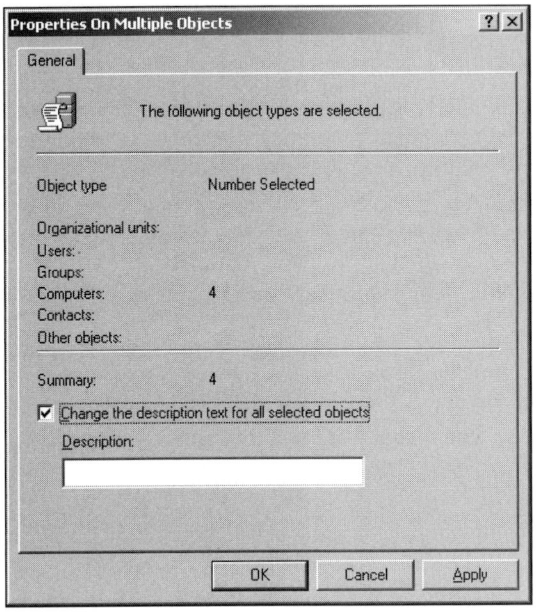

Figure 8-3 Group Policy Object Editor

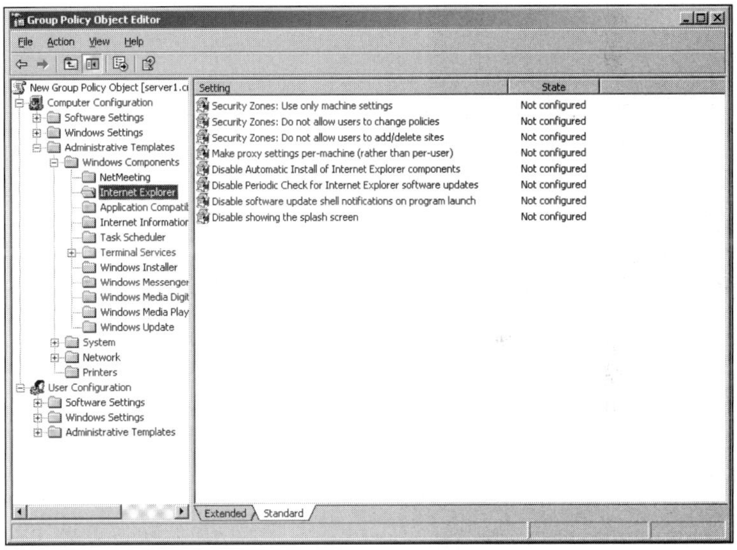

Figure 8-4 Prohibiting User installs

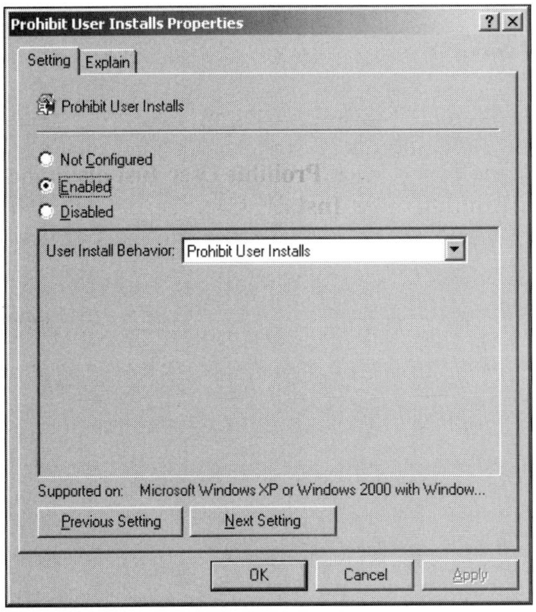

project 8.3

Troubleshooting Computer Accounts

exam objective

Create and manage computer accounts in an Active Directory environment. Troubleshoot computer accounts. Diagnose and resolve issues related to computer accounts by using the Active Directory Users and Computers MMC snap-in. Reset computer accounts.

overview

Computer accounts, like user accounts, can be disabled and enabled through the Active Directory Users and Computers console. When a computer account is disabled, the computer is prevented from participating in the domain, which prevents users from accessing the domain on that computer.

The CIO has loaned two of the computers in the public area of the library to a student organization that will be offering a tutoring session for Microsoft Office 2003. While these two computers are being used for this purpose, you do not want to allow users to log on to the domain.

learning objective

After completing this project, you will know how to disable and enable computer accounts.

specific requirements

Administrative rights on the domain controller for craighead.com.

estimated completion time

10 minutes

project steps

1. Click **Start**, point to **Administrative Tools**, and then click **Active Directory Users and Computers**.
2. Expand the **craighead.com** domain, if necessary. Click the **Lab Computers** OU.
3. While holding down the **[Ctrl]** key, click **LIB-WS1** and **LIB-WS4**. Right-click to open the shortcut menu **(Figure 8-5)**. Click **Disable Account**. Click **Yes** to confirm. Click **OK** when informed that **All of the selected objects have been disabled**. Notice the red X over both of the selected computer accounts.
4. The student organization has informed you that they will only be needing **LIB-WS4**. To enable the other computer, click **LIB-WS1**. Right-click LIB-WS1 and select **Enable Account**. Click **OK** to confirm. You will notice that a red X appears over only **LIB-WS4** **(Figure 8-6)**.
5. Close all open dialog boxes and windows.

Figure 8-5 Computer Account short-cut menu

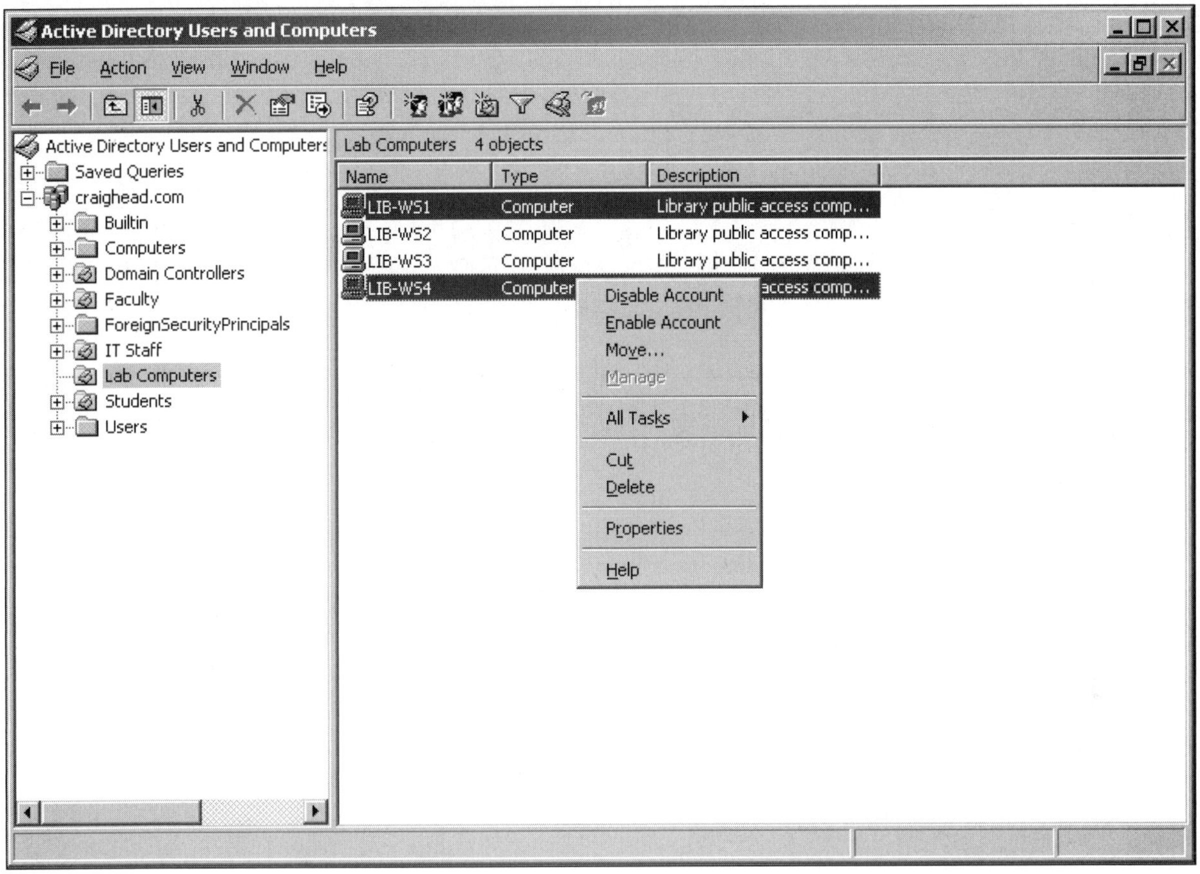

Figure 8-6 Computer Account listing

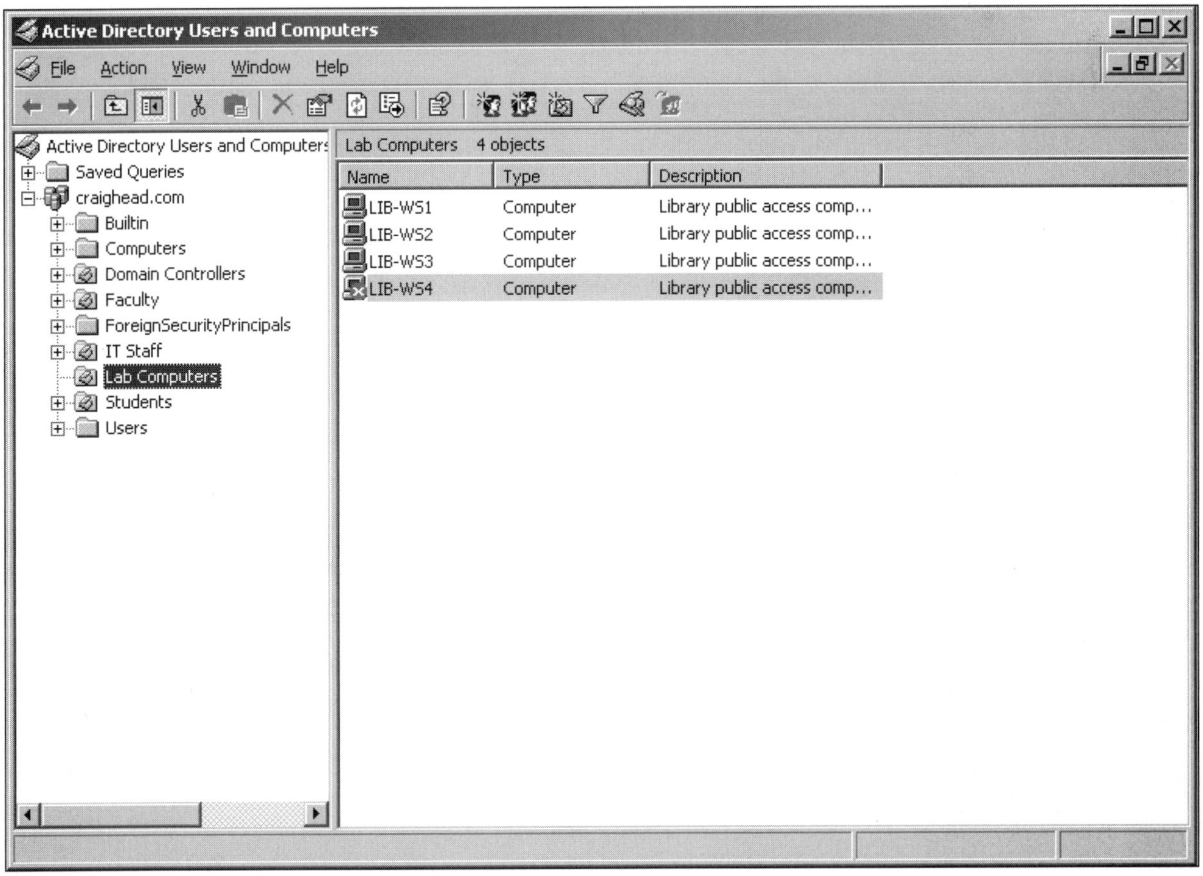

LESSON

9

Installing and Configuring Network Printers

One of the most important, cost-saving advantages of a network is that it enables you to share print resources among multiple users. Shared print devices allow users on a network to print documents to the shared print device from their own computers, even though they are not physically connected to the printers.

There are several ways you can connect to a network printer. You could use the Add Printer Wizard or browse My Network Places to locate the printer on the print server. The print server is simply a computer running Windows Server 2003 that controls printing functions. Window Server 2003 can also be configured to include the printer driver for several different versions of Windows that can be downloaded automatically across the network.

This lesson contains projects that will help you practice planning a network printing environment, installing a local printer, and sharing it for use across a network. You will also be able to practice facilitating priority printing, enabling printing pooling on a network, and searching for printers within a domain.

Scenario

You plan to take advantage of the ability to share print resources among multiple users. The use of shared print devices allows all users on a network to print documents from their own computers without the need of being physically connected to a print device.

At Craighead College, faculty and staff will primarily use local print devices located in department offices and in their own office. Both students and staff will be allowed to print in the computer labs. As network administrator, you need to design the most efficient configuration of computer lab printers.

Lesson 9 Installing and Configuring Network Printers

Project	Exam 70-290 Objective
9.1 Planning the Printing Environment	Basic knowledge
9.2 Installing and Sharing a Local Printer	Basic knowledge
9.3 Setting Printer Priorities	Basic knowledge
9.4 Creating Printer Pools	Troubleshoot print queues.
9.5 Searching for Publishing Domain Printers	Basic knowledge

General Requirements

To complete the projects in this lessons, you will need administrative rights on the domain controller for craighead.com and the Windows Server 2003 installation CD-ROM. No print devices are required. You may also find it helpful to refer to Lesson 9 in your Prentice Hall Certification Series Exam 70-290 textbook for further information about the topics covered by the projects in this lesson.

project 9.1

Planning the Printing Environment

exam objective

Basic knowledge

overview

When you plan the configuration of your network printing, you should attempt to provide all users with fast, convenient printing while using the fewest number of print devices. Two of the major criteria for determining the number and placement of network printers are number of users and location of print devices.

In this project, you will plan the number and location of print devices to be purchased and the number of printers to be configured **(Table 9-1)** at Craighead College. Since every faculty and staff member has their own local printer, you will only be concerned with printers in computer labs.

learning objective

After completing this project, you will know how to determine the number of printers and print devices needed in a given situation.

specific requirements

None

estimated completion time

30 minutes

project steps

The following computer labs exist, primarily for use by students, on the campus of Craighead College.

LAB01 — Arts Building, 1st Floor — HP LaserJet 6Si
LAB02 — Arts Building, 3rd Floor — HP LaserJet 5Si and a Panasonic 24-pin Dot Matrix
LAB03 — Education Building, 1st Floor — HP LaserJet 6Si
LAB04 — Administration, 1st & 2nd Floors — HP Color LaserJet 5000s
LAB05 — Engineering, 1st Floor — HP DesignJet 1050

The volume of printing in each of the labs is as follows:

LAB01 — Medium Volume
LAB02 — High Volume (Laser) & Low Volume (Dot-Matrix)
LAB03 — Very High Volume
LAB04 — High Volume (1st Floor) & Low Volume (3rd Floor)
LAB05 — Low Volume

Given the above scenario, determine how many print devices need to be purchased and how many network printers should be defined.

Table 9-1 Windows Printing Environment

Printer	A printer is the software interface that delivers the requests for service from the operating system to the physical print device.
Print Device	The term print device refers to the physical hardware that actually prints data.
Print Server	A print server is a computer that runs server software, such as Windows Server 2003, that is connected to one or more print devices. It is used to print documents and to manage the printers on a network. The performance of your network printing depends mainly on the print server. Therefore, it is essential that print servers satisfy memory and disk space requirements.
Printer driver	A printer driver is the software that contains the information used by the operating system to convert the print commands for a particular model of print device into a printer language such as PostScript. The driver translates a high-level view of the printed document, called a metafile, into the printer language understood by the print device. It tells the operating system what attributes the print device has and what print commands it follows so that documents can be properly printed.
Print Queue	A print queue resides on the print server, where most of the spooling and management of documents occurs. You can observe the status of the print queue by double-clicking the printer icon in the Printers and Faxes window or by clicking the printer icon that may appear in the system tray when you send a print command from your workstation. The printer window displays the print queue for a single printer only.

project 9.2

Installing and Sharing a Local Printer

exam objective

Basic knowledge

overview

In this project, you will install the Hewlett-Packard HP LaserJet 5Si printer to be located in LAB04 on the 1st floor of the Administration building. For the purpose of this project, we will assume that the domain controller will provide the print server function for this printer. This printer will be directly connected to the network media instead of attached to the LPT port of the server.

To create a network printer, you must first install the printer locally on the computer that is to become the print server. Once installed, you will share the printer to make it accessible to users over the network.

learning objective

After completing this project, you will know how to install a local printer and share it for use across the network.

specific requirements

Administrative rights on the craighead.com domain controller and your Windows Server 2003 installation CD.

estimated completion time

30 minutes

project steps

1. Click **Start** and then click **Printers and Faxes**. Double-click the **Add Printer** icon.
2. The **Add Printer Wizard** opens. Click **Next**. In the **Local or Network Printer** screen **(Figure 9-1)**, select the **Local printer attached to this computer** option button and remove the check mark in the **Automatically detect and install my Plug and Play printer** check box. Click **Next**.
3. On the **Select a Printer Port** screen, make sure that the **Use the following port: LPT1: (Recommended Printer Port)** option is selected and click **Next**.
4. On the **Install Printer Software** screen **(Figure 9-2)**, select **HP** as the manufacturer and **HP LaserJet 5Si** as the printer type. Click **Next**.
5. On the **Name Your Printer** screen, type **AD1-HP5Si** in the **Printer name** text box. This will identify the printer's location and model. Always use descriptive names for objects such as printers. Click **Next**.
6. In the **Printer Sharing** screen, select the **Share name** option button and type **AD1-HP5Si** as the share name. Click **Next**.
7. In the **Location and Comment** screen, enter the **Location** as **Administration Building**. In the **Comment** text box, enter **High-speed laser printer for LAB04**. Click **Next**.
8. Choose the **No** option button when prompted to print a test page. Click **Next** and then **Finish**. The shared printer icon for **AD1-HP5Si** will now appear in the **Printer and Faxes** window. Close all open windows.

Figure 9-1 Local or Network Printer screen

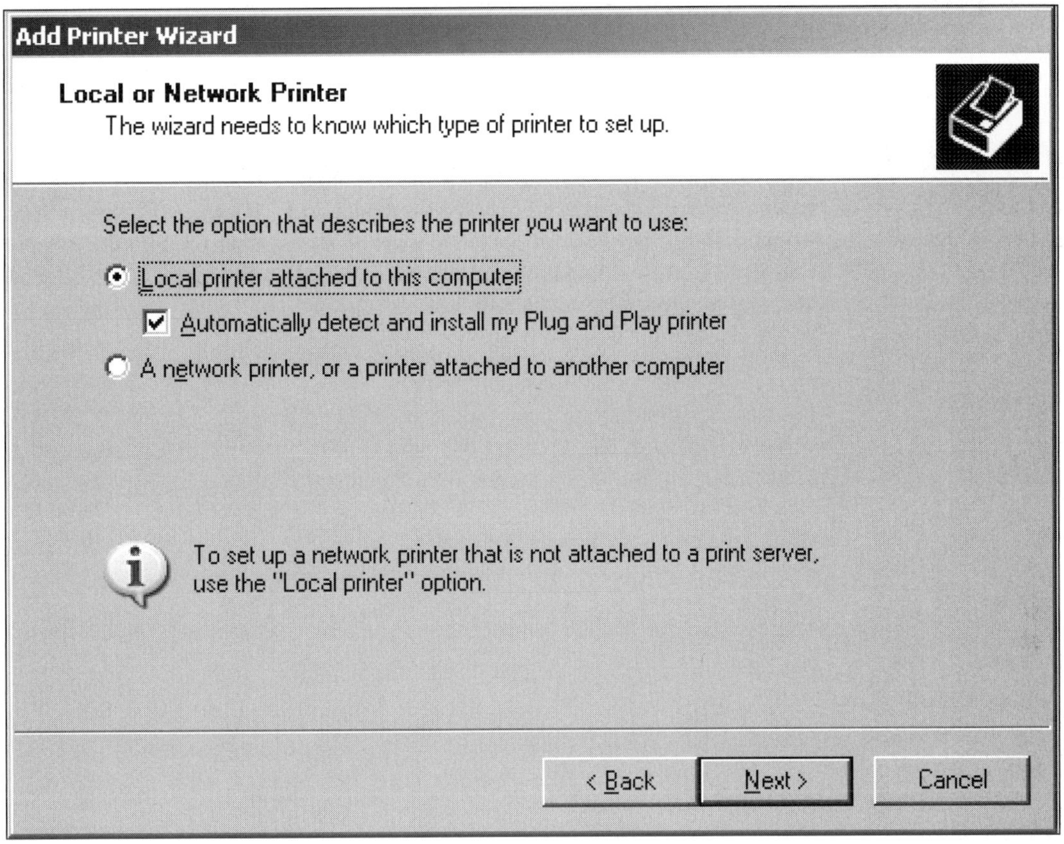

Figure 9-2 Install Printer Software screen

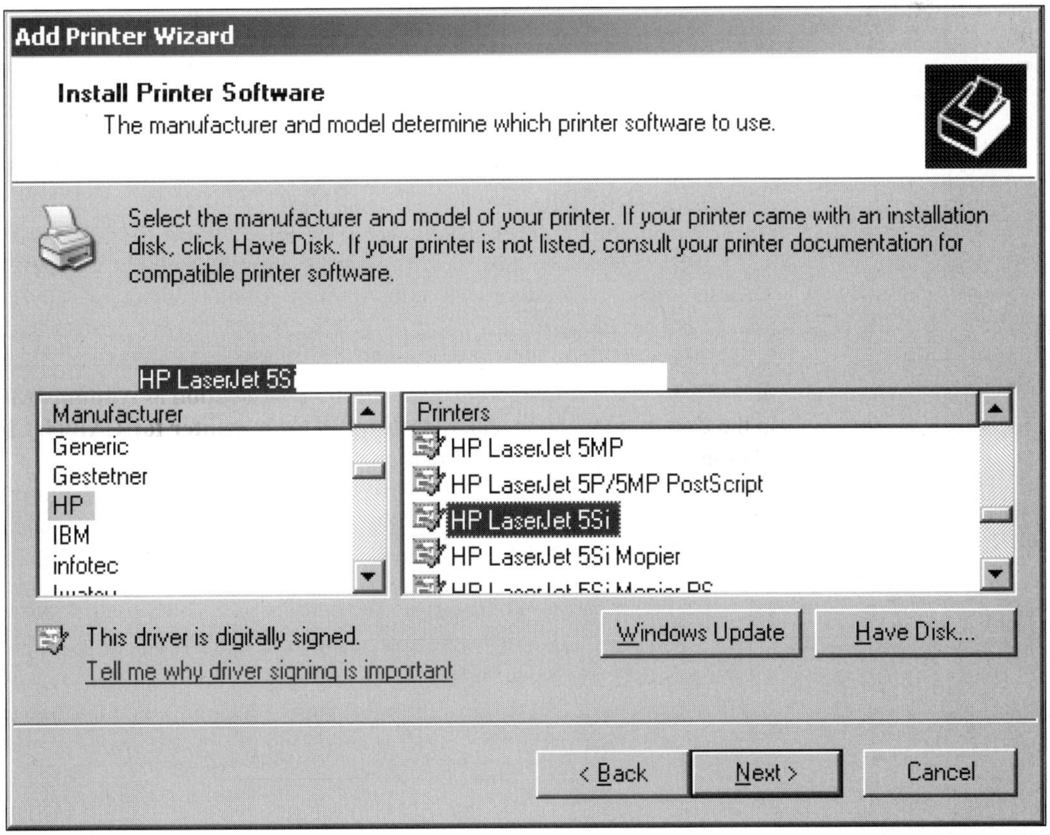

project 9.3

Setting Printer Priorities

exam objective

Basic knowledge

overview

Although print devices can have a one-to-one relationship with printers, in a business environment, it sometimes becomes necessary to prioritize access to the print device. The network administrator can facilitate this by defining multiple printers assigned to the same print device, but with different priorities. Print jobs sent by higher priority printers bypass other documents in the queue with lower priorities. The highest priority for printing is 99 and the lowest, also the default, is 1.

Since the HP Laserjet 5Si installed in Project 9.2 is currently heavily used both by faculty and students, the administration has requested that another printer be installed and assigned to the current HP Laserjet 5Si. Only members of the Staff group will be allowed to print to the new printer and the priority is to be set to the highest available.

learning objective

After completing this project, you will know how to assign multiple printers to a print device to facilitate priority printing.

specific requirements

Administrative rights on the craighead.com domain controller.

estimated completion time

15 minutes

project steps

1. Click **Start**, click **Printers and Faxes**, and then double-click the **Add Printer** icon to start the **Add Printer Wizard**.
2. Click **Next**. Make sure that the **Local Printer** option button is selected and remove the check mark in the **Automatically detect and install my Plug and Play printer** check box. Click **Next**.
3. In the **Select a Printer Port** screen, ensure that **LPT1: (Recommended Printer Port)** has been selected and click **Next**. In the **Install Printer Software** screen, select **HP** as the manufacturer and **HP LaserJet 5Si** as the appropriate model. Click **Next**.
4. Click **Next** to keep the existing driver that has already been installed. In the **Name Your Printer** screen, type **Admin5Si** in the **Printer Name** field and click **Next** to accept this printer as your new default.
5. Click **Next** to share the printers with the name **Admin5Si**. In the **Location and Comment** screen **(Figure 9-3)**, type **Administration Building** in the **Location** text box. Enter **Priority Access Printing for Staff Use** in the **Comment** text box. Click **Next**.
6. Make sure that the **No** option is selected so that you do not request a test page to be printed and click **Next** and then **Finish**. The printer will now appear in your **Printers and Faxes** window. Close all open windows.
7. You need to create a new group that will be given printing privileges to the newly installed printer. Click **Start**, point to **Administrative Tools**, and then click **Active Directory Users and Computers**.
8. Expand **craighead.com**, if necessary, and then right-click **Users**. Point to **New** and then click **Group**. In the **New Object — Group** dialog box **(Figure 9-4)**, enter **Staff** as the name of the group and make sure that **Group Scope** is set to **Global** and that **Group Type** is set to **Security**. Click **OK** to create the group and close the **Active Directory Users and Computers** console window.

Figure 9-3 Location and Comment screen

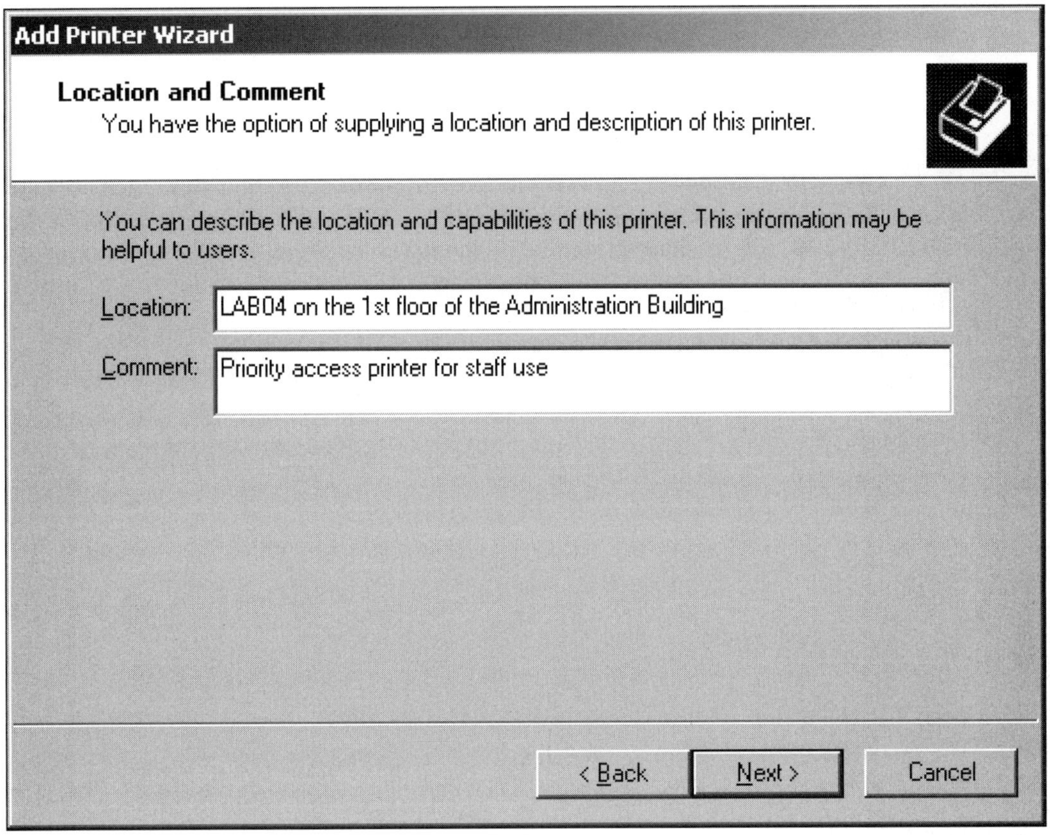

Figure 9-4 New Object — Group dialog box

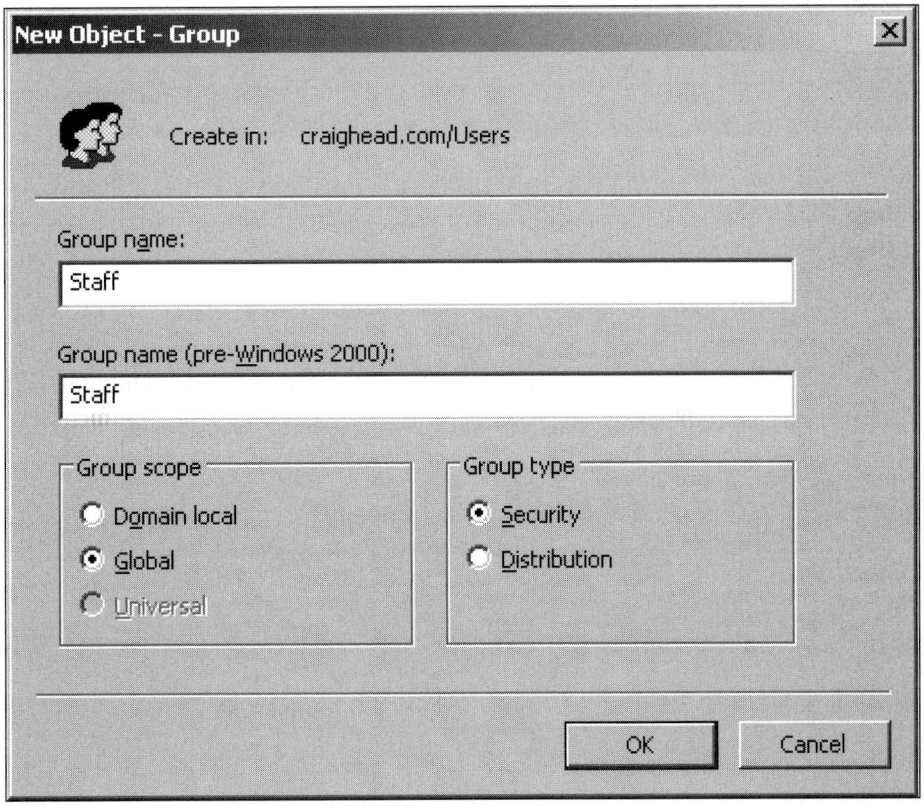

project 9.3

Setting Printer Priorities (cont'd)

exam objective

Basic knowledge

project steps

9. Click **Start** and then click **Printers and Faxes**. Right-click **Admin5Si** and select **Properties**. On the **Security** tab, click the group **Everyone** and select **Remove**.
10. Click **Add** and type **Staff** in the **Enter the object names to select** text box. Click **OK**. In the **Admin5Si Properties** dialog box **(Figure 9-5)**, highlight the **Staff** group and ensure that only the **Print** right has been assigned.
11. Click the **Advanced** tab in the **Admin5si Properties** dialog box **(Figure 9-6)**. Change the **Priority** spin box value to **99** and click **OK**. Close all open dialog boxes and windows.

Figure 9-5 Print permission assigned to Staff group

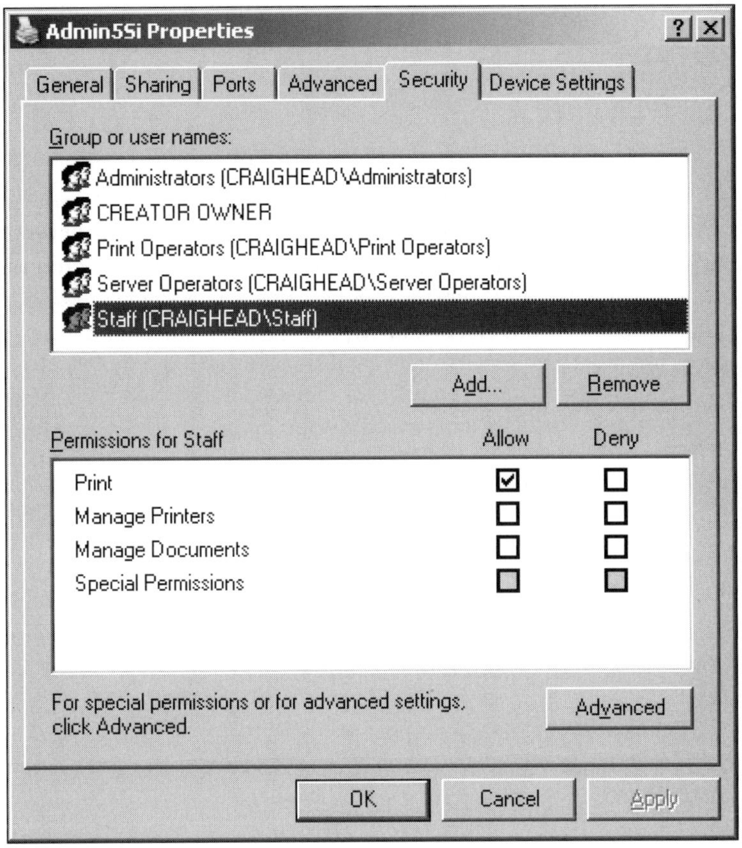

Figure 9-6 Advanced tab in the Printer Properties dialog box

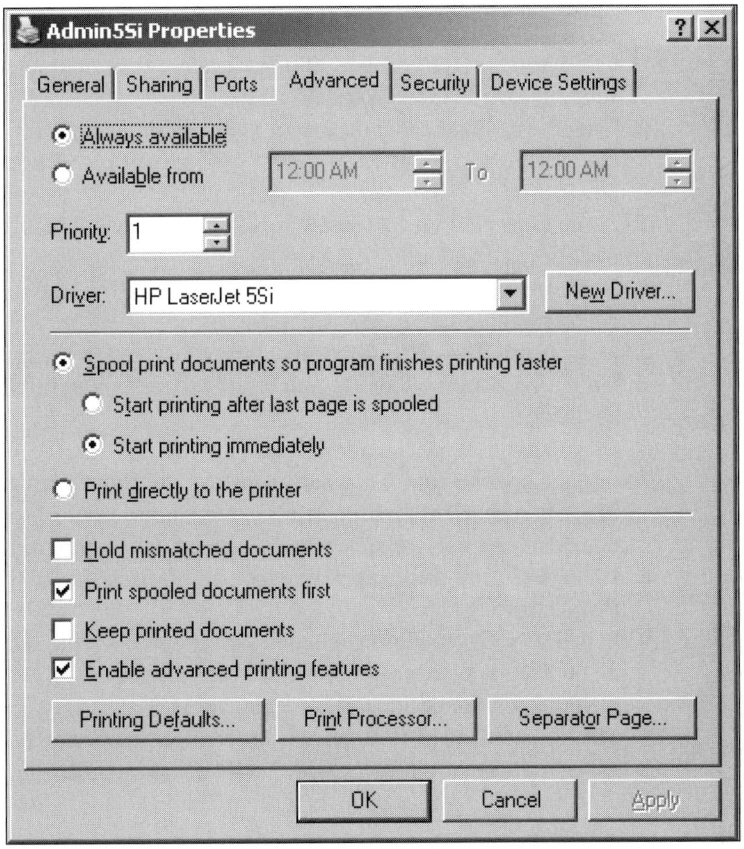

project 9.4 Creating Printer Pools

exam objective

Troubleshoot print queues.

overview

Sometimes it will be desirable to connect multiple print devices to one printer. This allows the print server to distribute print jobs automatically to the several print devices so that no single device becomes overloaded. A printer pool is for this purpose. You can use printer pooling when you have a number of print devices in a single location and desire your print job to be serviced by the first available print device in the pool. However, all print devices must be of the same type because they use a single printer driver. Printer pooling decreases the amount of time spent by users waiting for their documents and users need not be aware of the available print devices. It is the job of the print server, not the user, to find an available port and send the documents it receives to that port.

At Craighead College, LAB03 in the Education Building has two HP LaserJet 5 print devices for student use. As network administrator, you wish to create a printer pool for access to these printers to facilitate a faster printing time for the students.

learning objective

After completing this project, you will know how to enable printer pooling on the network.

specific requirements

Administrative rights on the craighead.com domain controller

estimated completion time

30 minutes

project steps

1. Click **Start**, click **Printers and Faxes**, and then double-click the **Add Printer** icon to start the **Add Printer Wizard**.
2. Click **Next**. Ensure that the **Local Printer** option button is selected and there is no check mark in the **Automatically detect and install my Plug and Play printer** box. Click **Next**.
3. In the **Select a Printer Port** screen, ensure that **LPT1**: **(Recommended Printer Port)** has been selected and click **Next**.
4. In the **Install Printer Software** screen, select **HP** as the manufacturer and **HP LaserJet 5** as the appropriate model. Click **Next**.
5. In the **Name Your Printer** screen, type **ED1-HP5** in the **Printer name** text box, click the **No** option button under **Do you want to use this printer as the default printer**, and click **Next**.
6. Click **Next** to share the printers with the name **ED1-HP5**.
7. In the **Location and Comment** screen, type **Education Building** in the **Location** text box. Enter **Student Lab Printing** in the **Comment** text box. Click **Next**. Make sure that you do not request a test page to be printed. Click **Next** and then **Finish**.
8. In the **Printers and Faxes** window, right-click the **ED1-HP5** printer icon and click **Properties**.
9. In the ***<Printer_name>*Properties** dialog box, click the **Ports** tab and place a check mark in the **Enable printer pooling** check box **(Figure 9-7)**. Place a check mark in the box in the **Port** column beside **LPT2**. Then click **OK**.
10. The last step would be to physically connect the print devices to ports LPT1 and LPT2. When a document is sent to the **ED1-HP5** printer, the print server will search the ports until it finds an idle print device to send the job. Close all open dialog boxes and windows.

Figure 9-7 Ports tab in the Printer Properties dialog box

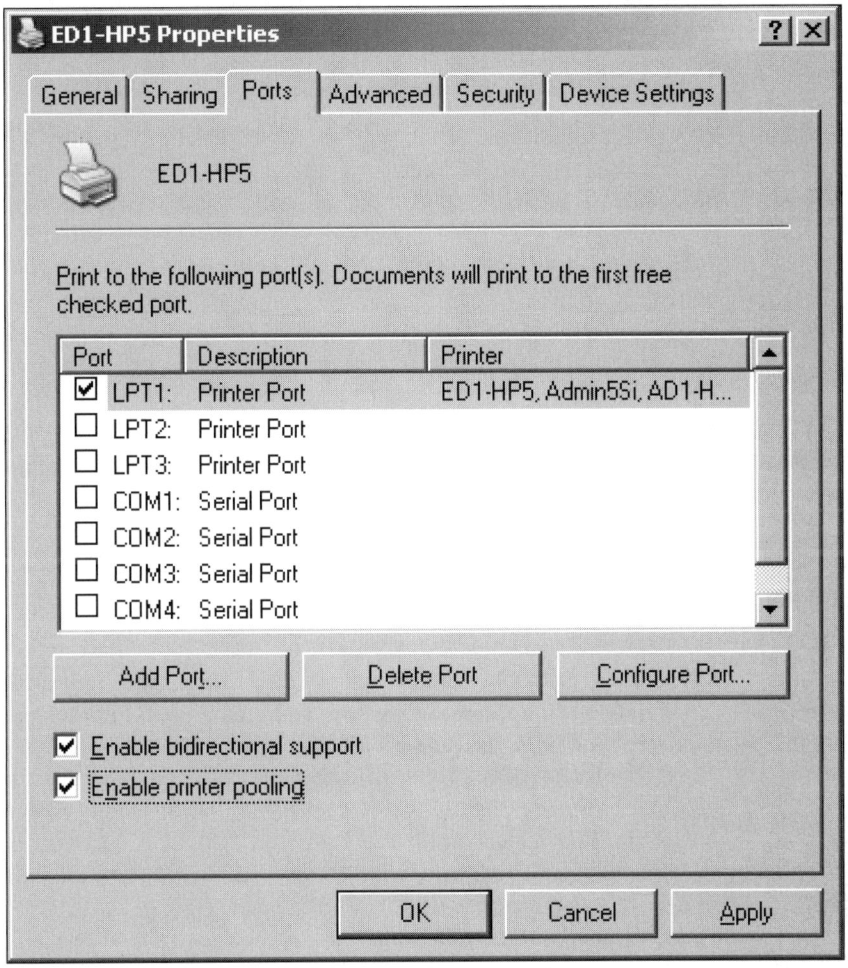

project 9.5

Searching for Published Domain Printers

exam objective

Monitor file and print services.

overview

With Active Directory, all domain controllers can access and share printer information to allow users across the domain to easily locate a network printer. Active Directory automatically publishes any printers that are installed on a domain print server by default. Since the printers you installed in the previous projects were located on the domain controller, all of these printers are available through Active Directory. By default, all printers are published because a check mark is placed in the List in Directory check box in the Sharing tab in the Properties dialog box for the printer.

At Craighead College, all printers should be easily located by anyone in the domain. All students and staff should receive training on how to locate printers by their name, properties, or location. You have developed the following exercise to assist users in locating printers.

learning objective

After completing this project, you will know how to search for printers throughout the domain.

specific requirements

Administrative rights on the craighead.com domain controller.

estimated completion time

15 minutes

project steps

1. Click **Start** and then select **Search**.
2. In the **Search Companion** pane, scroll if necessary, click **Other search options**, click **Printers, computers, or people**, and then click **A printer on the network**. This will open the **Find Printers** dialog box **(Figure 9-8)**.
3. On the **Printers** tab, type **Education** in the **Location** text box and click **Find Now**.
4. In the **Search results** window, the **ED1-HP5** printer will appear due to the string **Education** appearing in the **Location** text. You can then attach to that printer by double-clicking the icon in the **Search Results** window. Click **Clear All** and then **OK** to begin a new search.
5. Click the **Features** tab, then place a check mark next to **Can print double-sided** and click **Find Now**.
6. In the **Search results** window, all three of the HP printers will appear. HP LaserJet printers have the default property of being able to print double-sided. Click **Clear All** and then **OK**.
7. Click the **Advanced** tab, and then select **Pages per Minute** in the **Field** drop-down box. Select **Greater than or equal to** in the **Condition** box and type **15** in the **Value** box. Click the **Add** button and then click **Find Now**.
8. The two HP LaserJet 5Si printers will appear but the HP LaserJet 5 printer **(ED1-HP5)** will not be in the **Search results** window. The speed of the HP LaserJet 5, according to the printer driver information, is only 12 ppm. The speed of the HP LaserJet 5Si is 24 ppm. To confirm this information, right-click either of the two printers in the **Search results** window and select **Properties**. On the **General** tab, you will see that the speed is listed as 24 ppm. Close all open dialog boxes and windows.

Figure 9-8 Find Printers dialog box

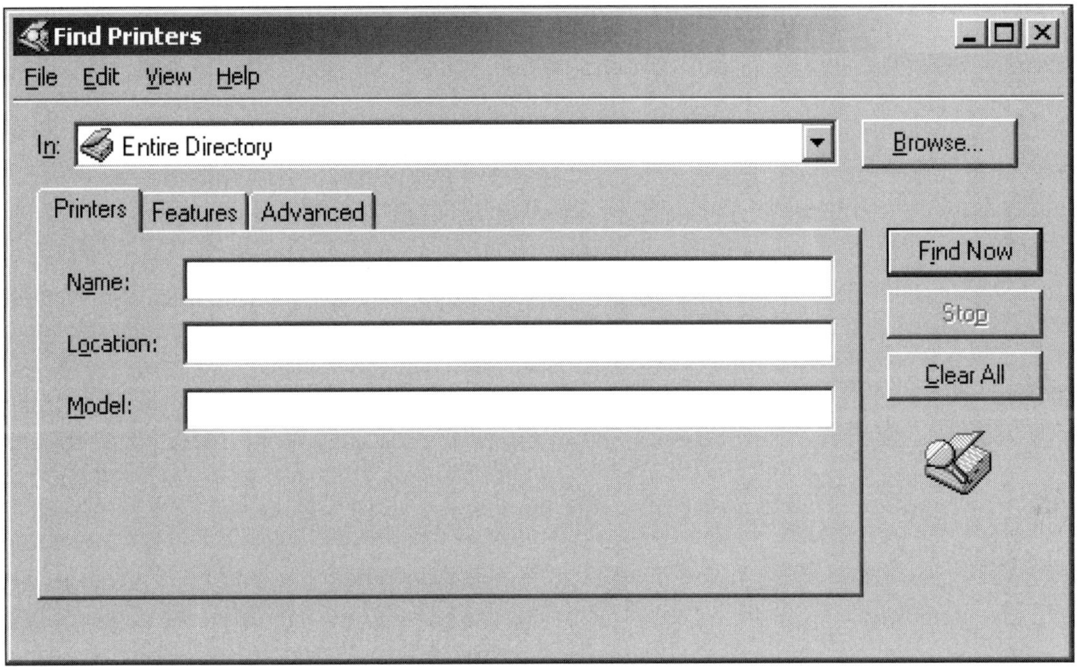

LESSON

10 Exploring TCP/IP and DHCP

The main protocol, or set of rules, used to send information over a network is TCP/IP (Transmission Control Protocol/Internet Protocol). TCP/IP can be used for both large and small networks, and data can be transferred across networks and between computers using different operating systems and with various structural designs. TCP/IP is also the core protocol of the Internet. It provides reliable and routable data transfer over Local Area Networks (LANs) or Wide Area Networks (WANs).

In addition to TCP/IP, Windows Server 2003 supports several other protocols, including AppleTalk and NWLink (a protocol that emulates the IPX/SPX protocol within the Microsoft network architecture). NWLink enables computers running Microsoft operating systems to access resources on servers running a version of Novell Netware that predates Netware 4.0. Netware 4.0 servers and above support TCP/IP, while Netware 5.0 and above run TCP/IP as the native protocol suite.

A computer using TCP/IP must have a unique IP address that identifies the computer on the network. This address can be obtained either manually (through editing the properties of TCP/IP on each computer) or the process can be automated by using the Dynamic Host Configuration Protocol (DHCP) Server service. The DHCP Server service dynamically assigns IP addresses from a range of IP addresses to computers as they boot. This simplifies the administration of TCP/IP configuration because it automates the process of assigning IP addresses to the clients.

This lesson contains projects that will help you become more familiar with the TCP/IP suite of protocols, various TCP/IP troubleshooting utilities, and the DHCP Server service. You will also be able to practice configuring TCP/IP, using the Ping, Ipconfig, and Route print utilities to troubleshoot TCP/IP problems, and installing and configuring the DCHP Server service.

Scenario

As network administrator for Craighead College, you have decided to dynamically assign IP addresses to each of the workstations in your domain. Initially, the domain controller for craighead.com will provide DHCP services. The network will be using the network address 192.168.100.0. Since this is a Class C address, you have 254 IP addresses that can be assigned to hosts.

Note: The network address of 192.168.100.0 is a reserved address for internal use only and cannot be routed. It is used in this Project Lab Manual for demonstration use only and to ensure no conflict with other existing networks in case the classroom network is connected to other networks or the Internet.

Lesson 10 Exploring TCP/IP and DHCP

Project	Exam 70-290 Objective
10.1 Identifying the Fundamentals of TCP/IP	Basic knowledge
10.2 Configuring TCP/IP	Basic knowledge
10.3 Troubleshooting TCP/IP	Basic knowledge
10.4 Installing and Configuring DHCP	Basic knowledge

General Requirements

To complete the projects in this lesson, you will need administrative rights on the domain controller for craighead.com and the Windows Server 2003 installation CD-ROM. You may also find it helpful to refer to Lesson 10 in your Prentice Hall Certification Series Exam 70-290 textbook for further information about the topics covered by the projects in this lesson.

project 10.1 Identifying the Fundamentals of TCP/IP

exam objective

Basic knowledge

overview

Before installation and configuration of DHCP, it is necessary for each of your computer services staff to have a basic understanding of the TCP/IP suite of protocols. You will develop and present a presentation of the fundamentals of the TCP/IP suite of protocols.

learning objective

After completing this lesson, you will have a better understanding of the fundamentals of the TCP/IP suite of protocols.

specific requirements

None

estimated completion time

45 minutes

project steps

1. The TCP/IP suite of protocols can be mapped to a four-layered conceptual model called the DOD Model (**Figure 10-1**). Prepare a chart that identifies the four layers of the model and a synopsis of the functions of each of the layers.
2. There are four protocols within the TCP/IP suite that function primarily at the Internet Layer. Identify and describe each of these protocols.
3. At the Transport Layer, there are three protocols that provide the Application Layer with session and datagram communication services: TCP, PGM, and UDP. Describe the differences between these three protocols.
4. The Application Layer enables applications to access the services of the other layers and defines the protocols that applications must use to exchange data. The most common are HTTP, FTP, SMTP, and Telnet. What is the primary purpose of each of these protocols?

Figure 10-1 The Department of Defense (DOD) Model

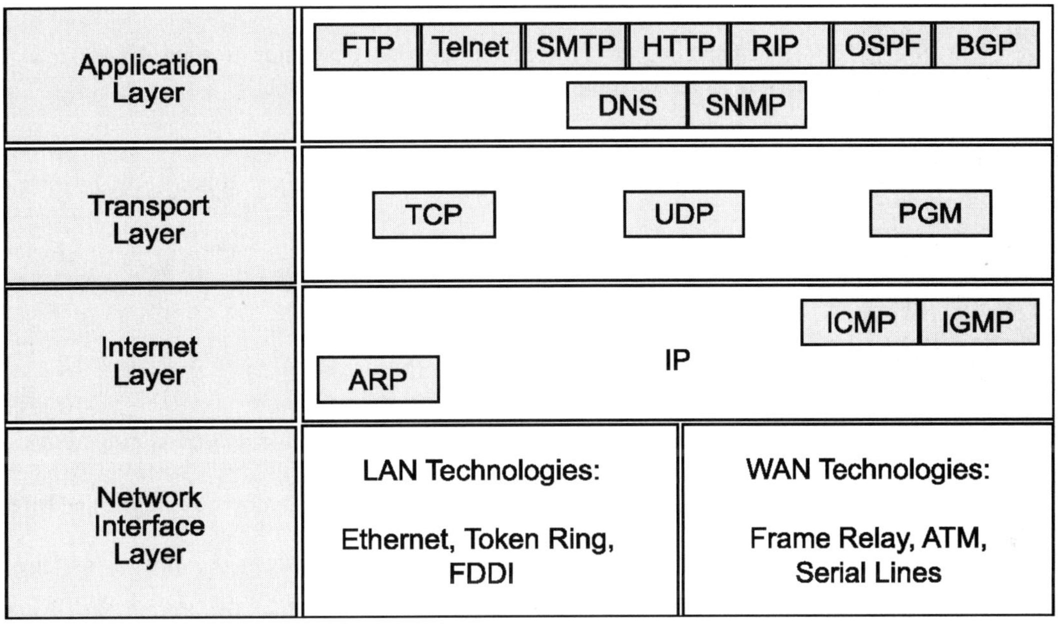

project 10.2 Configuring TCP/IP

exam objective

Basic knowledge

overview

The TCP/IP protocol is required by Windows Server 2003 and is installed during installation. In addition, when the craighead.com domain controller was promoted from a member server to a domain controller in Lesson 3, it was given a static IP address. This was necessary for DNS to function correctly. At that time, you assigned the domain controller an IP address of 10.1.1.1. You now need to assign it an IP address from the address range 192.168.100.0 – 192.168.100.255. The network also has a Windows Server 2003 computer with an IP address of 192.168.100.250. That server will function as the gateway, or connection, to the Internet.

learning objective

After completing this project, you will understand how to statically assign an IP address and gateway address to a Windows Server 2003 computer.

specific requirements

Administrative rights on the craighead.com domain controller.

estimated completion time

15 minutes

project steps

1. Click **Start**, point to **Control Panel**, point to **Network Connections**, and right-click **Local Area Connection**.
2. In the **Local Area Connection Properties** dialog box, highlight **Internet Protocol (TCP/IP) (Figure 10-2)** and click **Properties**.
3. Replace the current IP address with the new address of **192.168.100.1**. Replace the current subnet mask with the default subnet mask for a Class C network: **255.255.255.0**.
4. Enter the default gateway IP address as **192.168.100.250** and replace the current preferred DNS server IP address with the domain controller's new IP address. **192.168.100.1**. Click **OK** and then **Close**. Close all open dialog boxes and windows.

Figure 10-2 Local Area Connection Properties dialog box

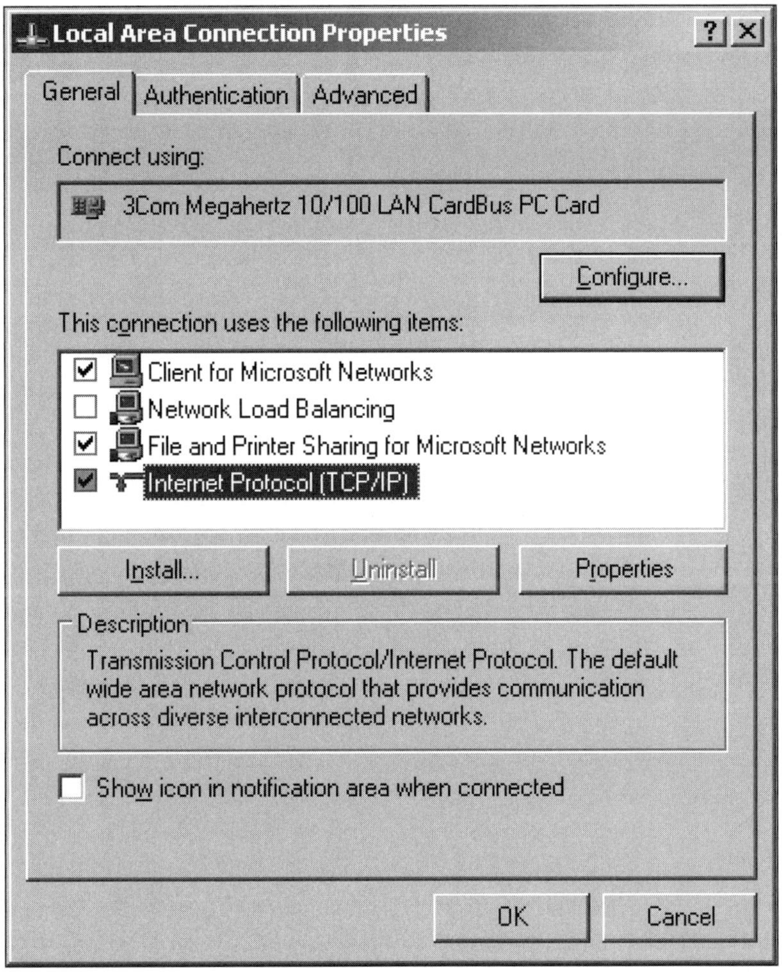

project 10.3 Troubleshooting TCP/IP

exam objective

Basic knowledge

overview

Despite the precautions that you have taken in the configuration of TCP/IP services, Craighead College may still encounter communication problems. Windows Server 2003 includes utilities to troubleshoot such problems. These utilities are executed from the command prompt.

You have decided to have a training session on the use of these utilities for any users that wish to attend. During the session, you will present a slide, or handout, describing the functions and options of each of these commands. In addition, you will demonstrate several of the commands on the domain controller.

learning objective

After completing this project, you will better understand the functions of each of the TCP/IP troubleshooting utilities.

specific requirements

Administrative rights on the craighead.com domain controller.

estimated completion time

45 minutes

project steps

1. Prepare a handout or PowerPoint slide that describes the primary purpose of each of the following utilities (include the primary switches that are available in each, when applicable):
   - Ping
   - Arp
   - Ipconfig
   - Tracert
   - Pathping
   - Route
2. Click **Start**, click **Run**, and type **cmd** in the **Open** text box. Click **OK**. At the command prompt, type **Ping 192.168.100.1** and press **[Enter]**. Since this is the domain controller's IP address, this command will ping your local network card. You will receive four replies with a reply time of less than 1 millisecond **(Figure 10-3)**.
3. At the command prompt, type **ipconfig /all** and then press **[Enter]**. This will display the IP configuration and Ethernet adapter settings for the domain controller **(Figure 10-4)**. Notice that DHCP is NOT enabled and the IP settings entered in the previous project are displayed.
4. At the command prompt, type **route print** and then press **[Enter]**. This will display the current routing table **(Figure 10-5)**. Since the domain controller is the only host available on the network, only loopback addresses (127.0.0.1), broadcast addresses (255.255.255.255), and the local IP address of 192.168.100.1 are available. Type **Exit** and then press **[Enter]** to close the command prompt window.

Figure 10-3 Ping results

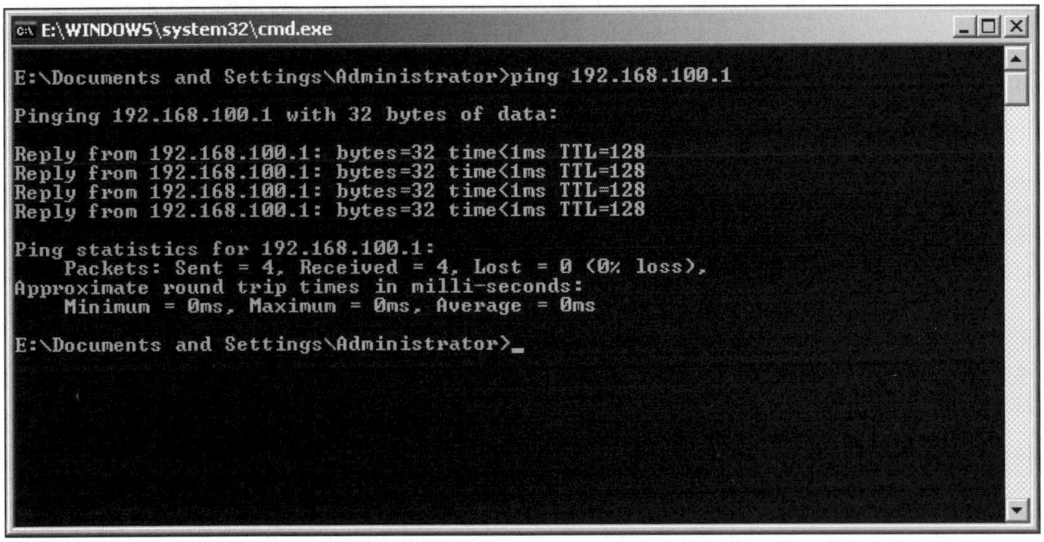

```
E:\WINDOWS\system32\cmd.exe

E:\Documents and Settings\Administrator>ping 192.168.100.1

Pinging 192.168.100.1 with 32 bytes of data:

Reply from 192.168.100.1: bytes=32 time<1ms TTL=128
Reply from 192.168.100.1: bytes=32 time<1ms TTL=128
Reply from 192.168.100.1: bytes=32 time<1ms TTL=128
Reply from 192.168.100.1: bytes=32 time<1ms TTL=128

Ping statistics for 192.168.100.1:
    Packets: Sent = 4, Received = 4, Lost = 0 (0% loss),
Approximate round trip times in milli-seconds:
    Minimum = 0ms, Maximum = 0ms, Average = 0ms

E:\Documents and Settings\Administrator>_
```

Figure 10-4 Ipconfig results

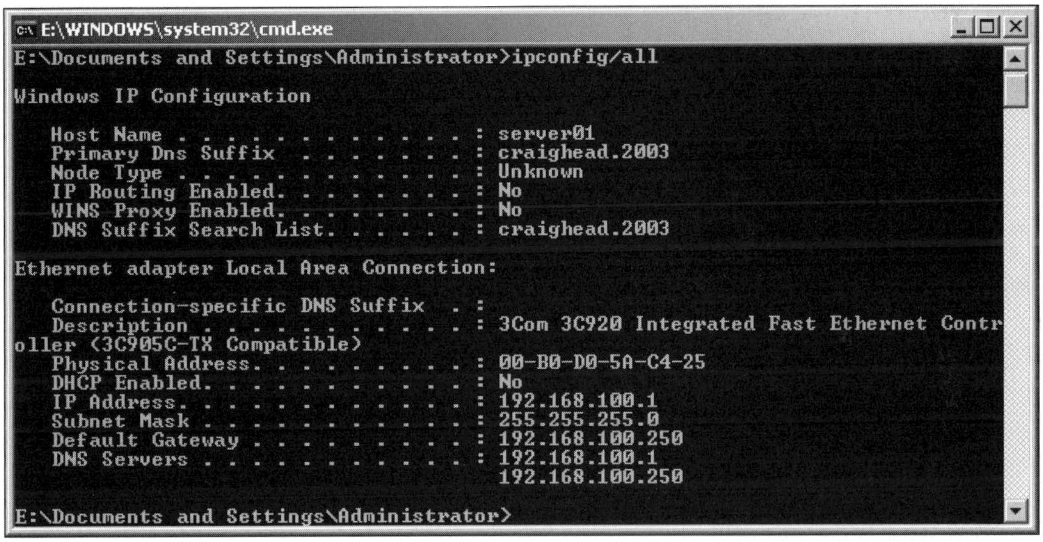

```
E:\WINDOWS\system32\cmd.exe
E:\Documents and Settings\Administrator>ipconfig/all

Windows IP Configuration

   Host Name . . . . . . . . . . . . : server01
   Primary Dns Suffix  . . . . . . . : craighead.2003
   Node Type . . . . . . . . . . . . : Unknown
   IP Routing Enabled. . . . . . . . : No
   WINS Proxy Enabled. . . . . . . . : No
   DNS Suffix Search List. . . . . . : craighead.2003

Ethernet adapter Local Area Connection:

   Connection-specific DNS Suffix  . :
   Description . . . . . . . . . . . : 3Com 3C920 Integrated Fast Ethernet Contr
oller (3C905C-TX Compatible)
   Physical Address. . . . . . . . . : 00-B0-D0-5A-C4-25
   DHCP Enabled. . . . . . . . . . . : No
   IP Address. . . . . . . . . . . . : 192.168.100.1
   Subnet Mask . . . . . . . . . . . : 255.255.255.0
   Default Gateway . . . . . . . . . : 192.168.100.250
   DNS Servers . . . . . . . . . . . : 192.168.100.1
                                       192.168.100.250

E:\Documents and Settings\Administrator>
```

Figure 10-5 Route print results

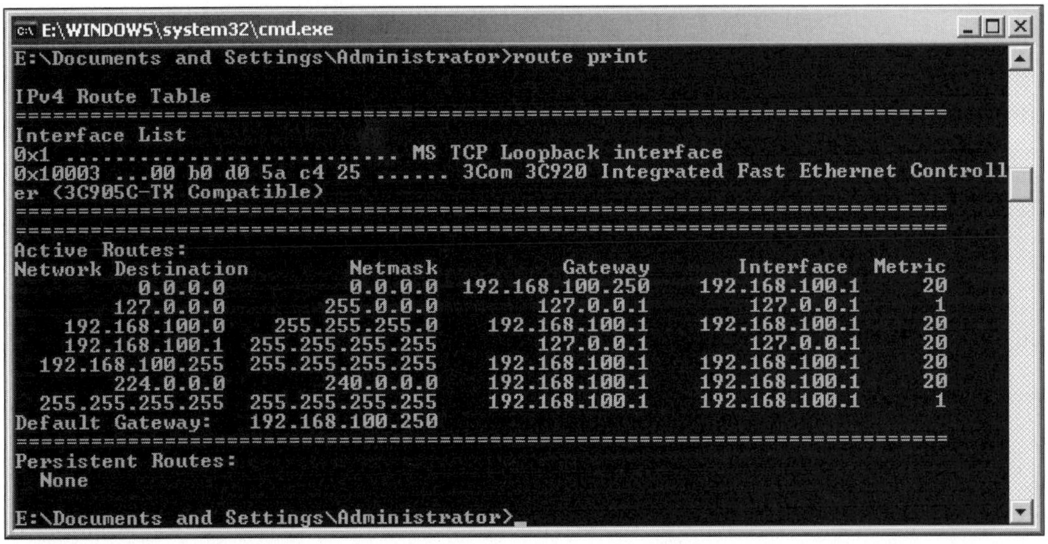

```
E:\WINDOWS\system32\cmd.exe
E:\Documents and Settings\Administrator>route print

IPv4 Route Table
===========================================================================
Interface List
0x1 ........................... MS TCP Loopback interface
0x10003 ...00 b0 d0 5a c4 25 ...... 3Com 3C920 Integrated Fast Ethernet Controll
er (3C905C-TX Compatible)
===========================================================================
===========================================================================
Active Routes:
Network Destination        Netmask          Gateway       Interface  Metric
          0.0.0.0          0.0.0.0  192.168.100.250    192.168.100.1     20
        127.0.0.0        255.0.0.0        127.0.0.1        127.0.0.1      1
    192.168.100.0    255.255.255.0    192.168.100.1    192.168.100.1     20
    192.168.100.1  255.255.255.255        127.0.0.1        127.0.0.1     20
  192.168.100.255  255.255.255.255    192.168.100.1    192.168.100.1     20
        224.0.0.0        240.0.0.0    192.168.100.1    192.168.100.1     20
  255.255.255.255  255.255.255.255    192.168.100.1    192.168.100.1      1
Default Gateway:     192.168.100.250
===========================================================================
Persistent Routes:
  None

E:\Documents and Settings\Administrator>_
```

project 10.4

Installing and Configuring DHCP

exam objective

Basic knowledge

overview

You are now ready to install and configure the DHCP Server service on the domain controller. After installation of DHCP, you will need to define the scope of addresses allocated to Craighead College. In addition, you will need to reserve addresses for network servers/printers and configure other DHCP options.

learning objective

After completing this project, you will know how to install and configure the DHCP Server service in a Windows Server 2003 environment.

specific requirements

The Windows Server 2003 installation CD-ROM and administrative rights on the domain controller for craighead.com.

estimated completion time

45 Minutes

project steps

1. Click **Start**, point to **Control Panel**, and then click **Add or Remove Programs**.
2. In the **Add or Remove Programs** dialog box, click **Add/Remove Windows Components** along the left side of the dialog box.
3. The **Windows Components Wizard** opens. Highlight **Networking Services** and click **Details**. Mark the check box associated with **Dynamic Host Configuration Protocol (DHCP) (Figure 10-6)** and click **OK** and then **Next**.
4. The **Configuration** screen will now appear. After components are configured, the **Completing the Windows Components Wizard** screen appears. Click **Finish**. Close all open dialog boxes and windows.
5. Click **Start**, point to **Administrative Tools**, and then click **DHCP**. Expand the domain controller to display **Server Options** in the left pane. Right-click the domain controller and click **New Scope (Figure 10-7)**.
6. When the **New Scope Wizard** begins, click **Next**. In the **Name** text box, type **Network IP Addresses** and, in the **Description** text box, type **Class C Addresses for Distribution**. Click **Next**.

Figure 10-6 Networking Services screen

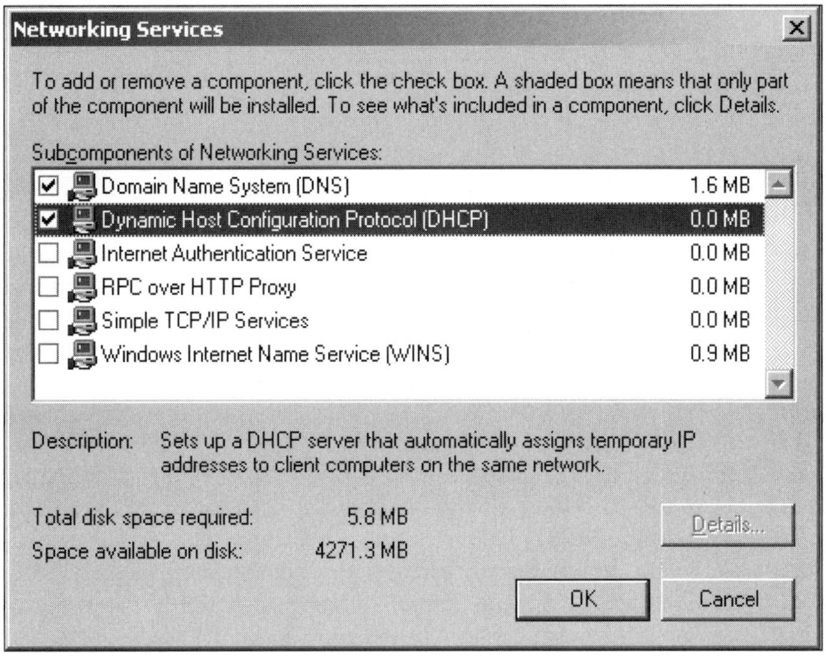

Figure 10-7 New Scope command

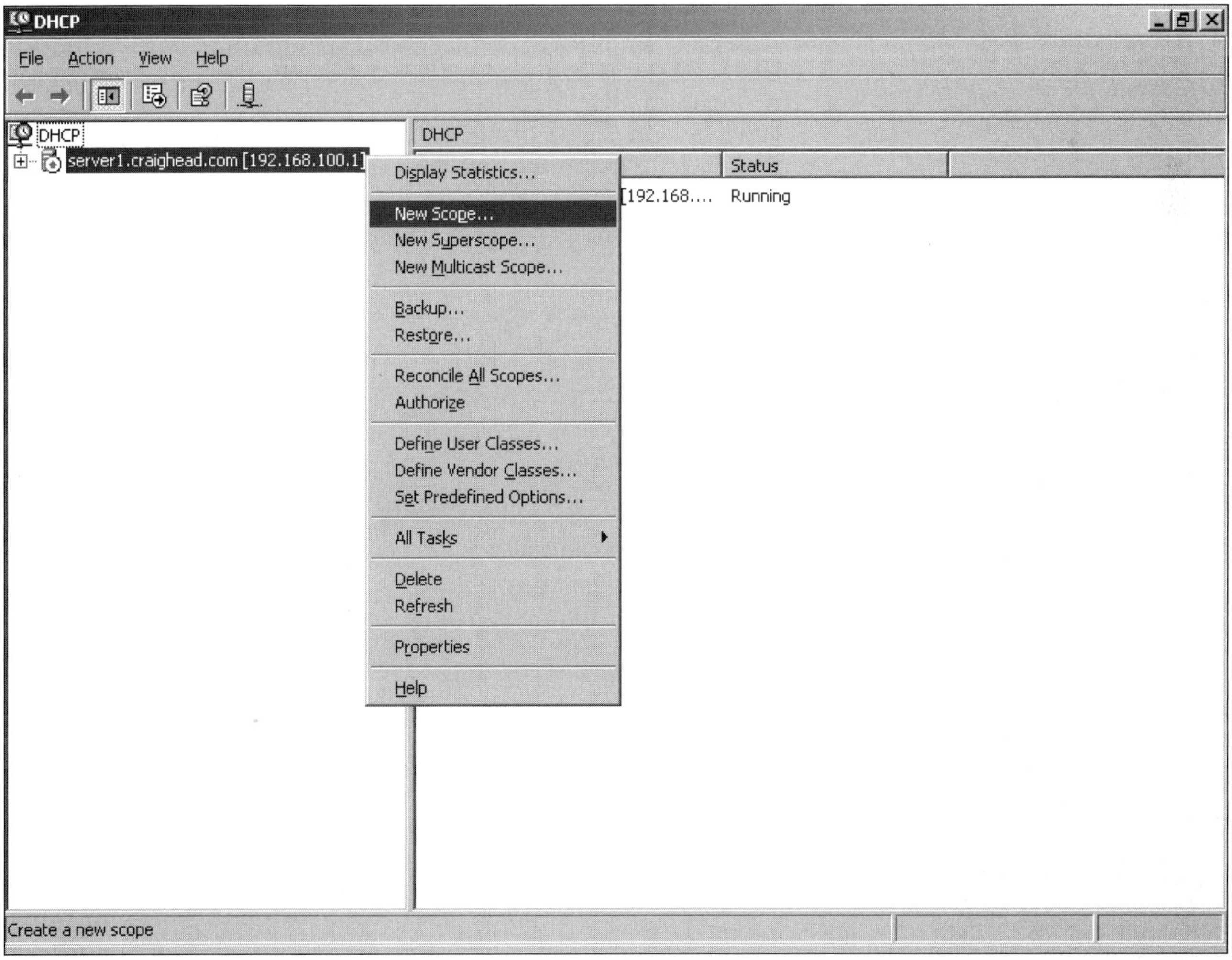

project 10.4

Installing and Configuring DHCP

(cont'd)

exam objective

Basic knowledge

project steps

7. In the **IP Address Range** screen **(Figure 10-8)**, enter a starting IP address of **192.168.100.1** and an ending IP address of **192.168.100.254**. Notice the Wizard automatically sets the subnet mask value to the default for a class C address. Click **Next**.
8. In the **Add Exclusions** screen, type **192.168.100.1** in the **Start IP address** and click **Add**. This will ensure that the DHCP server does not lease the IP address specified for the domain controller. Enter **192.168.100.250** in the **Start IP Address** text box and enter **192.168.100.254** in the **End IP Address** text box. Click **Add**. This will prevent the DHCP server from leasing the addresses you will use for your gateway and printers. Click **Next**.
9. Accept the default **Lease Duration** of 8 days and click **Next**. When prompted to configure DHCP options at this time, select **Yes, I want to configure these options now** and click **Next**.
10. For the default gateway address, type **192.168.100.250**, click **Add**, and click **Next**.
11. In the **Domain Name and DNS Servers** screen, enter **craighead.com** in the **Parent domain** text box. Enter **192.168.100.1** in the **IP address** text box as the address of the computer that will provide primary DNS name resolution. Click **Add**. Enter **192.168.100.250** in the **IP address** text box as the address of the computer that will serve as the secondary DNS name server. Click **Add** and then **Next**.
12. In the **WINS Servers** screen, enter the domain controller's name in the **Server Name** text box and click **Resolve**. The IP address of the domain controller will appear in the **IP Address** text box. Click **Add** and then click **Next**.
13. Ensure that the **Yes, I want to activate this scope now** option button is selected and click **Next**. Click **Finish**.
14. Instructions for authorizing the DHCP server appear in the details pane. Right-click the server name and select **Authorize** to authorize the DHCP server.
15. Close all open dialog boxes and windows.

Figure 10-8 IP Address Range screen

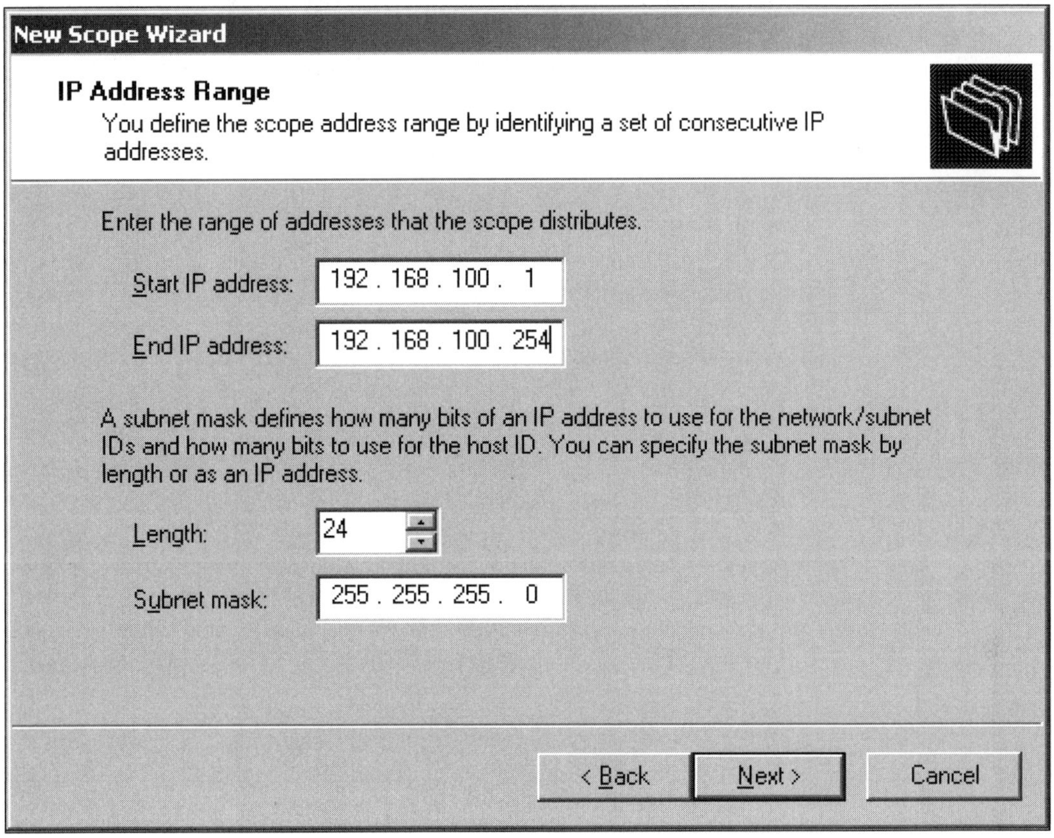

LESSON

11 Introducing WINS, DNS, and RRAS

In the past, network devices were identified on Windows networks through the use of the NetBIOS names. Although NetBIOS names are still supported for backward compatibility, fully qualified domain names (FQDN) are the standard for most TCP/IP networks. When network users want to locate a device on a TCP/IP network using the NetBIOS name, there must be a method for resolving an IP address to the device name. The primary method used in this case is the Windows Internet Name Service (WINS). The WINS database is dynamically updated so that as client computers are assigned different IP addresses by the DHCP server, the database stays current. Setting up some method of NetBIOS name resolution, such as a WINS server, is specifically required for backward compatibility with all Windows 9x and Windows NT computers.

With Windows 2000 and Windows Server 2003, Domain Name System (DNS) is the primary name resolution service utilized. It resolves FQDNs to IP addresses. A FQDN consists of a host name and a domain name including a top-level domain. Name resolution is required so that a user can enter the name of the target computer, and the connection to the other computer can be established. DNS also allows the names of servers providing a service to be located. You cannot have an Active Directory domain-based network without a functioning DNS infrastructure.

To allow clients to access resources on your organization's local area network from a remote location, you can use Windows Server 2003's Routing and Remote Access Service (RRAS). RRAS is installed but disabled by default during the installation of Windows Server 2003. You can configure RRAS to perform the functions of a network router, to provide remote access services, to provide a virtual private network (VPN), or to provide shared Internet access.

This lesson contains projects that will enable you to become more familiar with the different connection methods and authentication protocols used by remote access servers, and the various types of connection equipment available. You will also be able to practice installing and configuring WINS, configuring RAS server options, creating remote access policies, and installing and configuring NAT services.

Scenario

At Craighead College, you will primarily use Domain Name System (DNS) for name resolution on your local area network. However, some legacy systems will require you to install Windows Internet Naming Service (WINS) for backward compatibility. DNS has already been installed on the craighead.com domain controller.

Additionally, several of the faculty and staff of Craighead College want the ability to work from home. Since some of the information transmitted 'off site' will be confidential (i.e. grades, financial aid information, etc.), protection of this data is very important. It will also be important to protect the internal local area network from outside hacking.

Lesson 11 Introducing WINS, DNS, and RRAS

Project	Exam 70-290 Objective
11.1 Installing Windows Internet Name Service (WINS)	Basic knowledge
11.2 Introducing Routing and Remote Access Service (RRAS)	Basic knowledge
11.3 Understanding Remote Access Connections	Basic knowledge
11.4 Configuring Remote Access Services	Basic knowledge
11.5 Creating a Remote Access Policy	Basic knowledge
11.6 Introducing Network Address Translation (NAT)	Basic knowledge

General Requirements

To complete the projects in this lesson, you will need administrative rights on the domain controller for the craighead.com domain and the Windows Server 2003 installation CD-ROM. You may also find it helpful to refer to Lesson 11 in your Prentice Hall Certification Series Exam 70-290 textbook for further information about the topics covered by the projects in this lesson.

project 11.1

Installing Windows Internet Name Service (WINS)

exam objective

Basic knowledge

overview

To enable TCP/IP hosts to communicate on a TCP/IP network using NetBIOS names, a NetBIOS Name Server (NBNS) must be used to resolve the NetBIOS name to an IP address. Microsoft's implementation of NBNS is Windows Internet Name Service (WINS). The computer running WINS is referred to as the WINS server.

Since several of the older computers at Craighead College are not capable of supporting DNS, you want to install and configure WINS for these legacy systems.

learning objective

After completing this project, you will know how to install and configure WINS.

specific requirements

Administrative rights on the domain controller for the craighead.com domain and the Windows Server 2003 installation CD-ROM.

estimated completion time

15 minutes

project steps

1. Click **Start**, point to **Control Panel**, and click **Add or Remove Programs**. Click the **Add/Remove Windows Components** button to start the **Windows Components Wizard**.
2. Highlight **Networking Services** in the **Windows Components** list and click **Details**. Place a checkmark in the box next to **Windows Internet Name Service (WINS)** on the **Subcomponents of Networking Services** list **(Figure 11-1)**. All other selected boxes should not be changed. Click **OK** to close the **Networking Services** dialog box.
3. Click **Next** to open the **Configuring Components** screen while the configuration changes are made. If the domain controller did not already have a static IP address, you would be prompted at this time to assign one. You may be asked to insert the Windows Server 2003 installation CD-ROM. If so, insert the CD and click **OK**.
4. After the components are configured, the **Completing the Windows Components Wizard** screen will open. Click **Finish** to complete the configuration. Close all open windows.
5. Click **Start**, point to **Administrative Tools**, and click **WINS** to open the **WINS** console **(Figure 11-2)**. Expand the domain controller, right-click the domain controller name, and click **Properties**.
6. The **Properties** dialog box for the domain controller opens. On the **General** tab, ensure that a check mark is present to **Automatically update statistics** and change the number of minutes to **30**. Type **C:\backup** in the **Default backup path (Figure 11-3)**, and place a check mark in the **Back up database during server shutdown** check box.
7. On the **Database Verification** tab, place a check mark in the **Verify database consistency** check box. The default of 24 hours will be selected. The default maximum number of records verified in a period will be 30000.
8. On the **Advanced** tab, ensure that burst handling is enabled. Since you are employing a very high-speed multiprocessor server, choose the **High** option button. Click **OK**. Close the WINS server console.

Figure 11-1 Networking Services dialog box

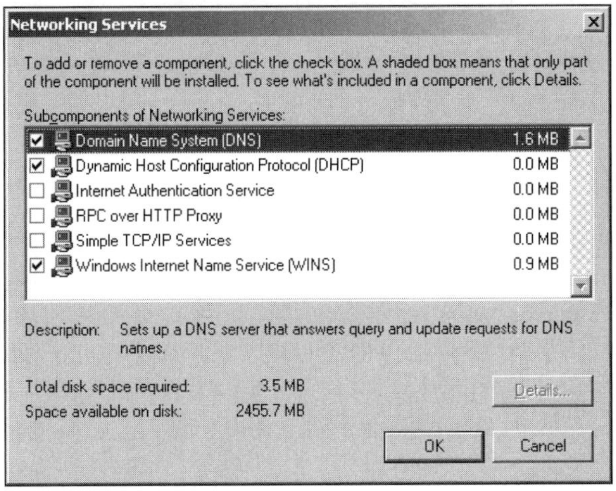

Figure 11-2 WINS console

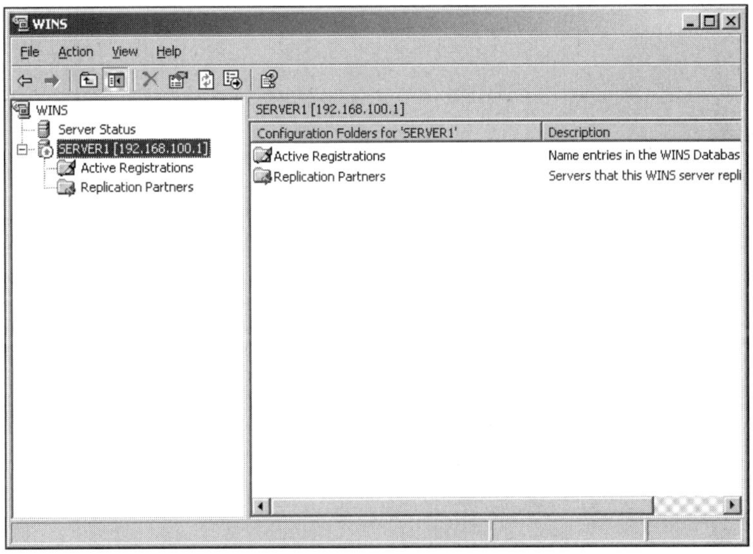

Figure 11-3 WINS Server Properties dialog box

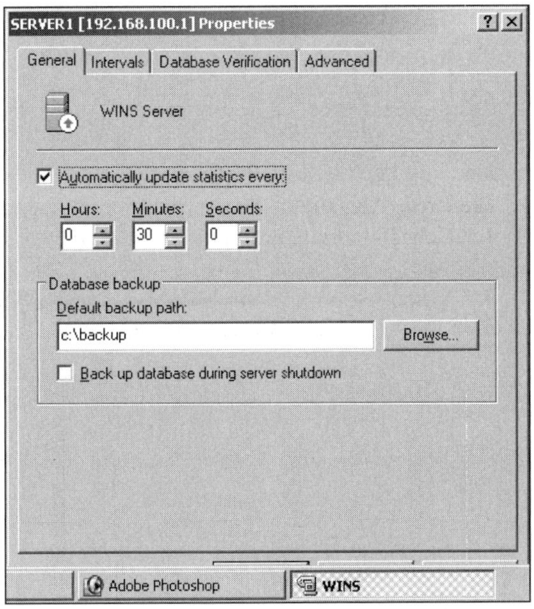

project 11.2

Introducing Routing and Remote Access Service (RRAS)

exam objective

Basic knowledge

overview

When you configure Routing and Remote Access Service (RRAS) to function as a remote access server **(Figure 11-4)**, employees can connect to their office networks and access resources from home, client sites, or from the road. The remote access server (RAS) supports two connection methods: dial-up or virtual private network (VPN).

As network administrator for Craighead College, you need to determine whether you will utilize dial-up connections, VPN connections, or both. Also, you need to decide on the authentication protocol that will be used. Before making the decision, it will be necessary for you to develop a better understanding of the various options. You will prepare a report defining the two connection methods and comparing the various authentication protocols.

learning objective

After completing this project, you will have a better understanding of the connection methods used by remote access servers and the different authentication protocols.

specific requirements

None

estimated completion time

30 minutes

project steps

1. Define dial-up connection and virtual private network connection. Explain the differences and similarities between the two.
2. Write a one paragraph description of each of the follow authentication protocols:
   - Password Authentication Protocol (PAP)
   - Shiva Password Authentication Protocol (SPAP)
   - Challenge Handshake Authentication Protocol (CHAP)
   - Microsoft CHAP (MS-CHAP)
   - Extensible Authentication Protocol (EAP)
   - Point-to-Point Tunneling Protocol (PPTP)
   - Layer Two Tunneling Protocol (L2TP)
3. To establish dial-up connections, Windows Server 2003 uses either the **Point-to-Point Protocol (PPP)** or the **Serial Line Internet Protocol (SLIP)** **(Figure 11-5)**. Windows Server 2003 supports PPP as both a client and a server. However, Windows Server 2003 supports SLIP only as a client. Describe the major advantages of the PPP protocol when compared to SLIP.

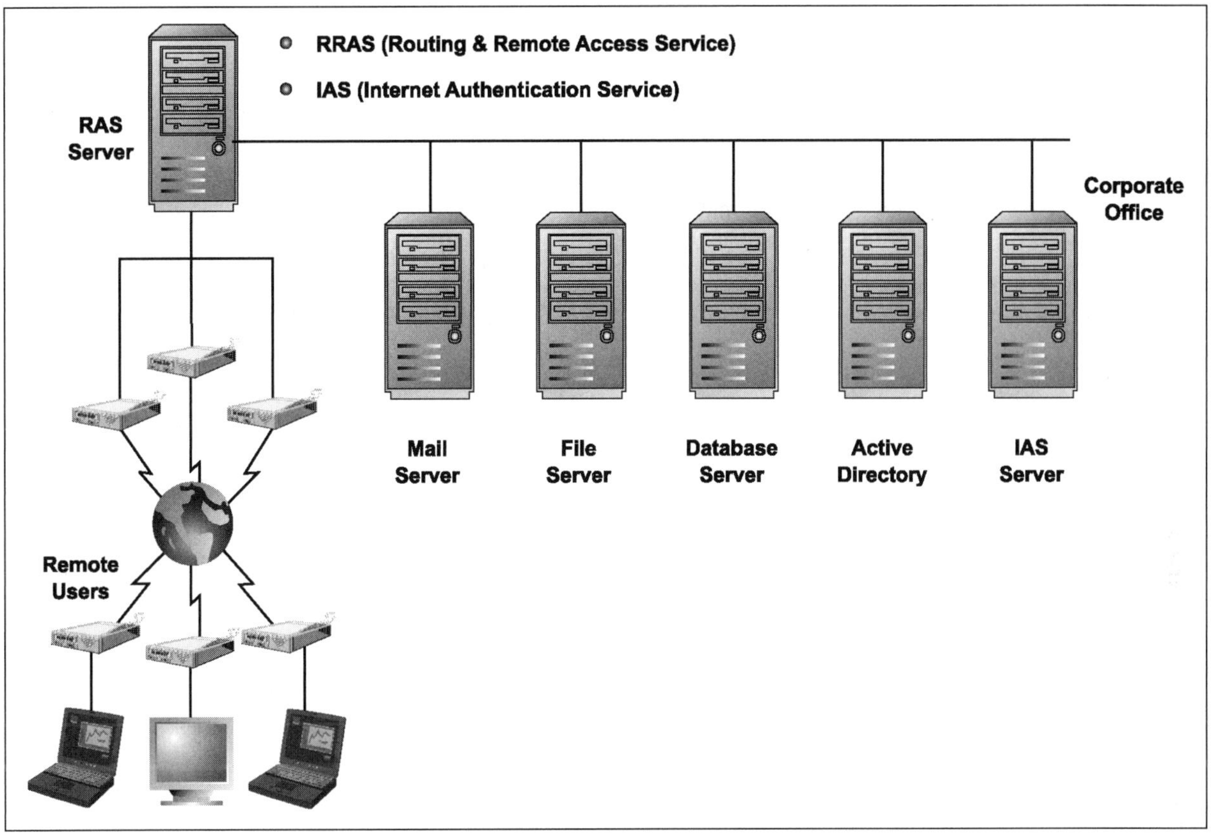

Figure 11-4 Remote Access Servers (RAS)

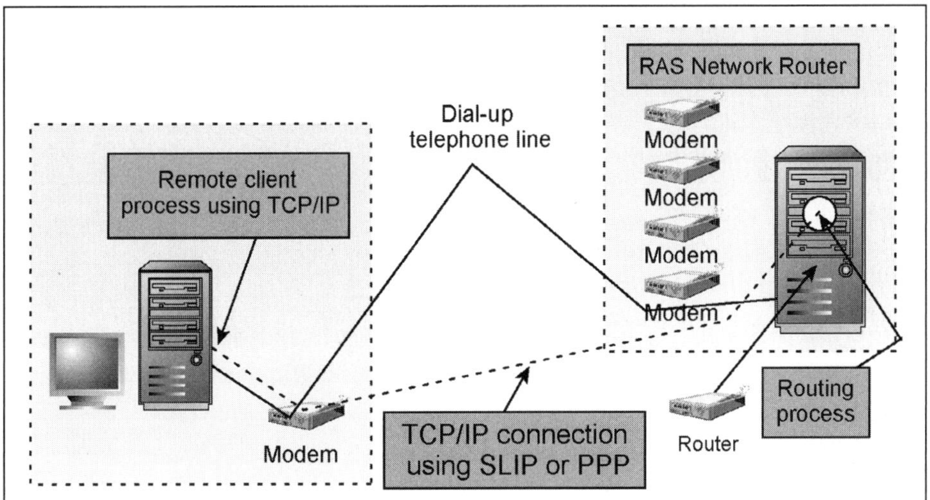

Figure 11-5 SLIP and PPP

- SLIP: No error detection, can only be used on TCP/IP networks, no authentication, does not support dynamically assigned IP addresses
- PPP: Supports multiple networking protocols (IPX, NetBEUI), error-checking, and a variety of authentication protocols

project 11.3

Understanding Remote Access Connections

exam objective

Basic knowledge

overview

To establish a connection between a remote network and a remote access client, you can use several different types of dial-up equipment **(Table 11-1)**. The CIO of Craighead College, Chris Williamson, has requested that you make a presentation of the different types of dial-up equipment available and to make a recommendation on which type to use at Craighead College to handle remote access.

learning objective

After completing this project, you will have a better understanding of the various types of connection equipment available.

specific requirements

None

estimated completion time

15 minutes

project steps

1. Write a one paragraph description of the following equipment:
   - Plain Old Telephone Service (POTS)
   - Integrated Services Digital Network (ISDN)
   - Digital Subscriber Line (DSL)
   - Cable Modem Line
   - Frame Relay
   - X.25 Lines
   - T-Carrier Lines
2. Select the option described in question #1 that best fits the needs of Craighead College and explain your choice.

Table 11-1 Communications Equipment Supported by Windows 2003 RAS

Device	Description
Asynchronous modem	The most common modem type, it uses a special signal or data bit to transmit each unit of data. This data bit displays the start and end of each unit during transmission.
Synchronous modem	This type of modem, which is not in wide use, uses a clocking technique to denote the start and end point of each unit of data during transmission.
Null modem communications	Null modem communications use a specially designed cable to directly connect two computers via their (serial) communications ports (RS-232 ports). Null modem cables are most often used with portable computers so that they can exchange data with each other.
Regular dial-up telephone	The Plain Old Telephone System (POTS) establishes an end-to-end analog connection lines between your computer and a remote network using modems and phone lines.
ISDN lines	The international data transfer formats for sending voice, video, and data over digital telephone lines or normal telephone wires. There are several styles of ISDN (EURO, US). ISDN uses 64 Kbps channels in conjunction with different types of services. The ISDN basic rate interface has three channels: two 64 Kbps channels used to send data, voice, and graphics, and one 16 Kbps channel used to transmit communications signaling.
X.25 lines	Not widely used in the U.S. and Canada, but still used in Europe and other parts of the world, X.25 is an older WAN communication method that originally could only transmit data at speeds up to 64 Kbps, but was upgraded in 1992 so that it can now provide data transfer rates up to 2.048 Mbps.
DSL (Digital Subscriber Line) lines	DSL runs digital signals over Plain Old Telephone System (POTS) lines. DSL uses modulation technology to encode digital or analog signals into a carrier signal. The carrier signal adapts the digital or analog signal to a frequency range that is different from that of the original. Upon reaching the destination, the original signal is separated from the carrier signal using an inverse process called demodulation.
Frame relay	Frame relay is a WAN technique. It is used on packet-switching networks, depends on virtual connection techniques, and can transmit data at speeds between 56 Kbps and 45 Mbps.
Leased telecommunication lines	This term most commonly refers to T-carrier lines, which are digital lines that use multiplexing to send multiple signals over a single communications line. T-1 lines, which are the most commonly used in the U.S., can carry 24 separate signals at a transmission rate of 64 Kbps each, making the total transmission rate 1.544 Mbps. A T-3 line can send 672 separate signals at 64 Kbps each, creating a total transmission speed of 43 Mbps. It can match the transmission speed of 28 T-1 lines. The Internet backbone uses T-3 lines, as well as optical carrier circuits (OC1, OC3, OC12, OC24, and OC48). However, these types of lines are cost-prohibitive and only large enterprises can afford the initial investment. Multiplexing refers to using a device called a multiplexer to combine two or more input signals from various devices into a single data stream that is transmitted over a single transmission medium.

project 11.4 Configuring Remote Access Services

exam objective

Basic knowledge

overview

Routing and Remote Access Service (RRAS) is installed but disabled by default during the installation of Windows Server 2003. Therefore, you must manually enable and configure RRAS to either set up a RAS server, a VPN, NAT, a secure connection between two servers, or a network router.

Since security is an important consideration for remote access at Craighead College, you must secure RAS connections so that only authorized users can access network resources. When a user dials-in to as RAS server, the connection is accepted only after it is authenticated and authorized. In this project, you will configure and enable RRAS to provide this security.

learning objective

After completing this lesson, you will know how to configure RAS server options.

specific requirements

Administrative rights on the domain controller for the craighead.com domain.

estimated completion time

30 minutes

project steps

1. Click **Start**, point to **Administrative Tools**, and click **Routing and Remote Access** to open the RRAS console.
2. Right-click <***Server_name***> **(Local)** and select **Configure and Enable Routing and Remote Access**. In the **Routing and Remote Access Server Setup Wizard Welcome** screen, click **Next**.
3. In the **Configuration** screen **(Figure 11-6)**, select the **Remote access (dial-up or VPN)** option and click **Next**. Select the **Dial-up** check box in the **Remote Access** screen and click **Next**.
4. Since you have a DHCP server on this computer, select the **Automatically** option button in the **IP Address Assignment** screen. The DHCP server will assign IP addresses to the remote access clients. Click **Next**.
5. Select **No, use Routing and Remote Access to authenticate connection requests** when asked to set up this server to work with RADIUS in the **Managing Multiple Remote Access Servers** screen. Click **Next** and then click **Finish**. A message box will appear indicating that you need to configure DHCP Relay Agents. Click **OK**.
6. In the **Routing and Remote Access** console, expand **IP Routing** and right-click **DHCP Relay Agent (Figure 11-7)**. Select **Properties**. In the **Server address** text box, enter **192.168.100.1** and click **Add**. Click **OK**.
7. Right-click the domain controller and choose **Properties**. On the **Logging** tab, select **Log errors only**. On the **Security** tab, click **Authentication Methods** and ensure that **Extensible authentication protocol (EAP), Microsoft encrypted authentication version 2 (MS-CHAP v2),** and **Microsoft encrypted authentication (MS-CHAP)** are the only protocols selected. Click **OK** twice to close the **Properties** dialog box. Close all open windows.

Figure 11-6 Configuration Screen

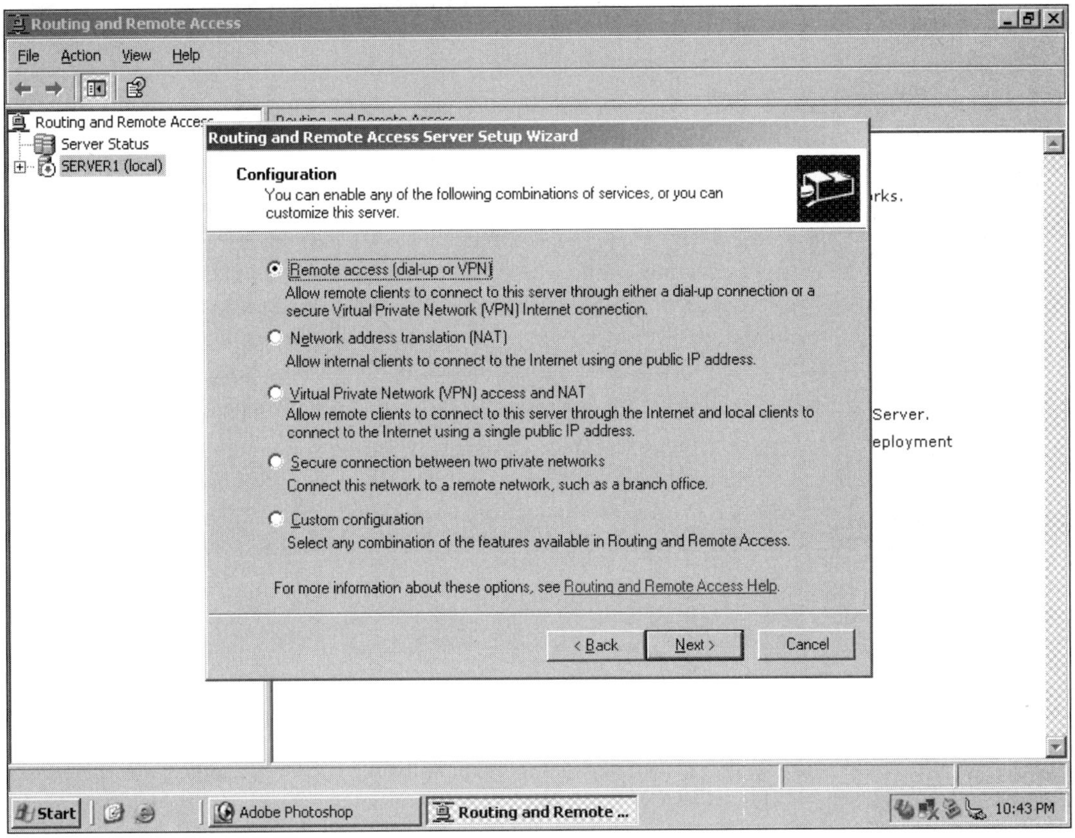

Figure 11-7 Opening the DHCP Relay Agent Properties dialog box

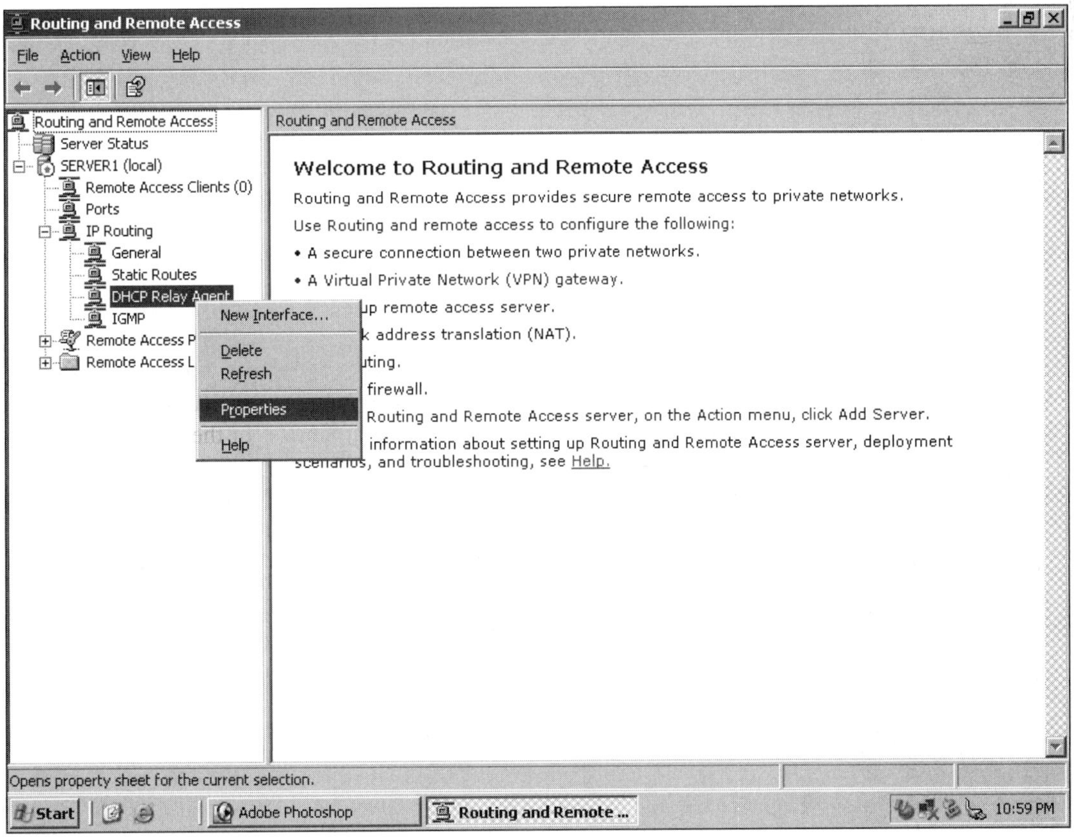

project 11.5 Creating a Remote Access Policy

exam objective

Basic knowledge

overview

A remote access policy consists of a set of rules and conditions that must be met by a connection before a user can gain access. The components of a remote access policy are conditions, permissions, and a profile. Conditions include specifications such as time of day, day of the week, and number dialed. Remote access permissions can be configured to allow or deny user dial-ins. The last thing to apply is the profile. The profile is a list of settings that are offered to the client, and if the client cannot support the offered settings, they are disconnected.

As network administrator of Craighead College, you are to create a remote access policy that will afford the necessary security for the local network. You will include components that will prevent certain dial-up clients from accessing the network during its busiest time periods and maintaining an open idle connection for long periods of time, and address other efficiency issues.

learning objective

After completing this project, you will know how to create remote access policies.

specific requirements

Administrative rights on the domain controller for the craighead.com domain.

estimated completion time

15 minutes

project steps

1. Click **Start**, point to **Administrative Tools**, and click **Routing and Remote Access**. Double-click the RRAS server name to expand the node, if necessary. Select the **Remote Access Policies** node.
2. Right-click the **Remote Access Policies** node and click **New Remote Access Policy** to start the **New Remote Access Policy Wizard**. Click **Next**.
3. Select the **Set up a custom policy** option button in the **Policy Configuration Method** screen and type **Student RAS Policy** as the **Policy name**. Click **Next**.
4. In the **Policy Conditions** screen, click **Add** to open the **Select Attribute** dialog box **(Figure 11-8)**. Double-click **Day-and-Time Restrictions** in the **Name** column. By default, all time slots are denied. Highlight all time periods on Saturday and Sunday and click **Permitted**. Select all times after 6:00 p.m. on Monday—Friday and click **Permitted**. Select all times before 8:00 a.m. on Monday— Friday and click **Permitted**. Dial-ups will not be permitted during the regular working hours on Monday—Friday. Click **OK**.
5. Click **Add** and double-click **Windows-Groups**. Click **Add** and in the **Enter the object names to selec**t text box, type **Staff** and click **OK**. Click **OK** to close the **Groups** dialog box.
6. Click **Next** to open the **Permissions** screen. Select **Grant remote access permission** and click **Next**. Click **Edit Profile** to open the **Edit Dial-in Profile** dialog box.
7. Click the **Dial-in Constraints** tab **(Figure 11-9)**. Place a check in the **Minutes server can remain idle before it is disconnected (Idle-Timeout)** check box and type a value of **10**. Place a check in the **Minutes client can be connected (Session-Timeout)** check box and place a **30** in the value box associated with this option.
8. Click the **Encryption** tab. Clear the check mark from the **No Encryption** check box. Click **OK** to save the changes. Click **Next** and then **Finish**.
9. Close all open dialog boxes and windows.

Figure 11-8 Select Attribute dialog box

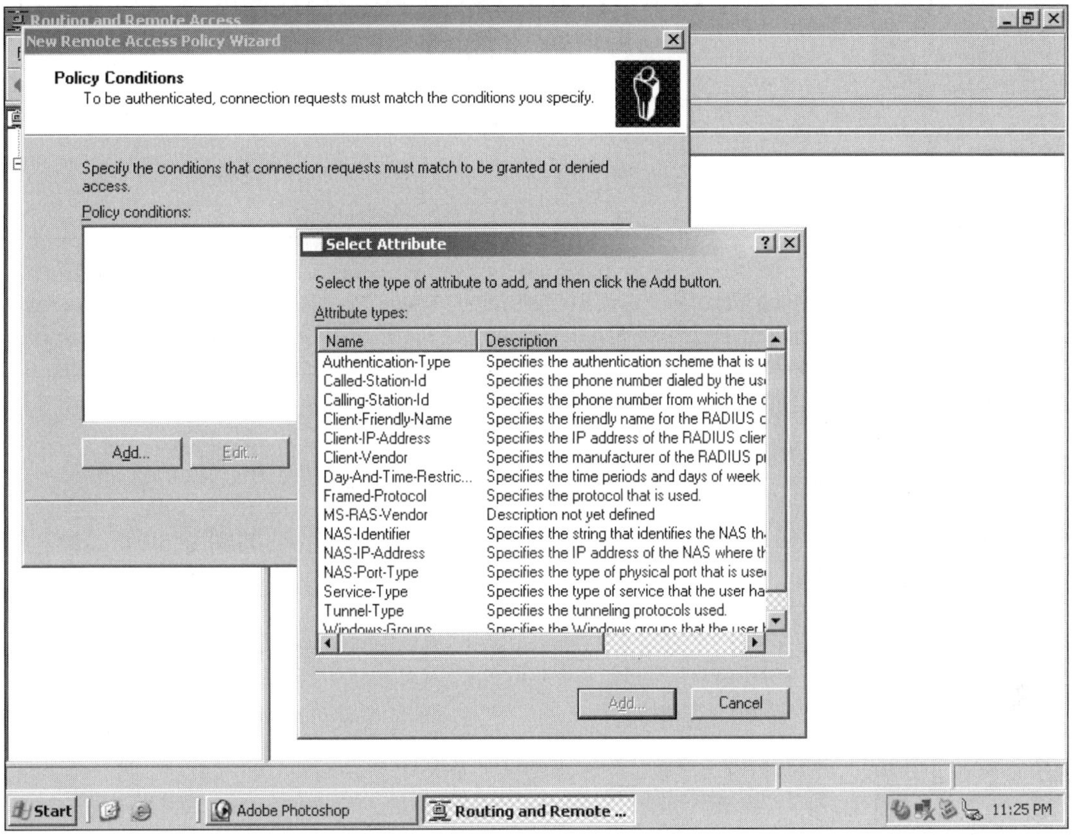

Figure 11-9 Dial-in Constraints tab

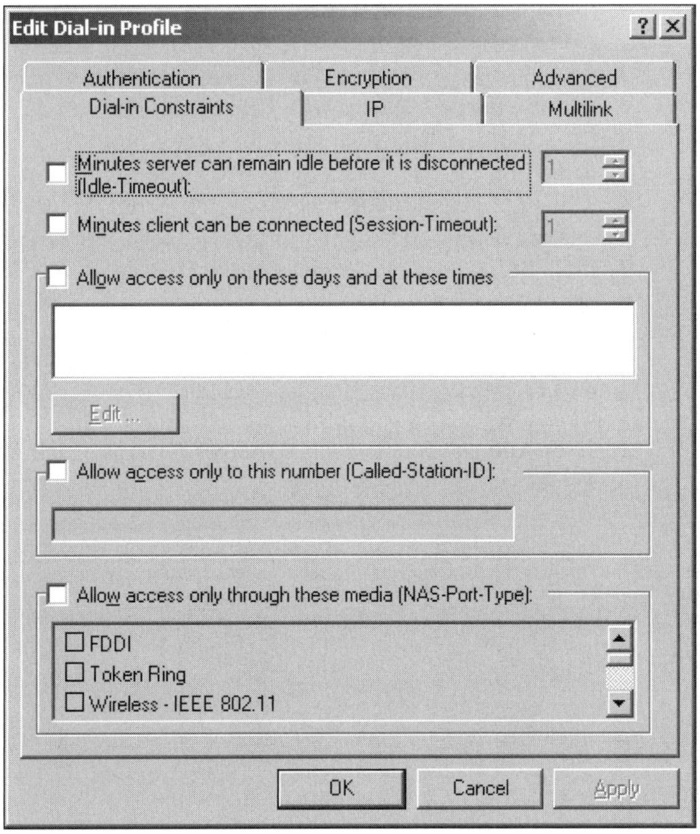

project 11.6

Introducing Network Address Translation (NAT)

exam objective

Basic knowledge

overview

Network Address Translation (NAT) allows computers on a network to share a single Internet connection. NAT can translate private IP addresses to public IP addresses as they are routed to and from the Internet **(Figure 11-10)**. When you enable the basic firewall, you can configure filters to designate the kinds of traffic you will allow to both enter and leave the internal network.

Chris Williamson, CIO of Craighead College, has directed you to install and configure NAT services for all lab computers. The lab computers will utilize private IP addresses and will not be allowed any FTP services, and the Ping utility (ICMP protocol) will be disabled.

learning objective

After completing this project, you will know how to install and configure NAT services.

specific requirements

Administrative rights on the domain controller for the craighead.com domain.

estimated completion time

30 minutes

project steps

1. Click **Start**, point to **Control Panel**, and then click **Add Hardware**. Click **Next**.
2. In the **Is the hardware connected?** screen, click **Yes, I have already connected the hardware**. Click **Next**.
3. Scroll to the bottom of the **Installed hardware** list and select **Add a new hardware device** and click **Next**.
4. When prompted for **What do you want the wizard to do?**, select **Install the hardware that I manually select from a list (Advanced)**.
5. Click **Modems** in the **Common hardware types** list and click **Next**. Place a check mark in the **Don't detect my modem; I will select from a list** check box and click **Next**.
6. Select **Standard 56000 bps Modem** from the **Models** list and click **Next**. Accept the selected port by clicking the port name and clicking **Next**. Click **Finish**.
7. Click **Start**, point to **Administrative Tools**, and click **Routing and Remote Access** to open the console.
8. Right-click the domain controller and click **Disable Routing and Remote Access**. Click **Yes** to confirm. The RAS server will then be disabled.
9. Right-click the domain controller and click **Enable and Configure Routing and Remote Access**. When the wizard starts, click **Next**.

Figure 11-10 NAT

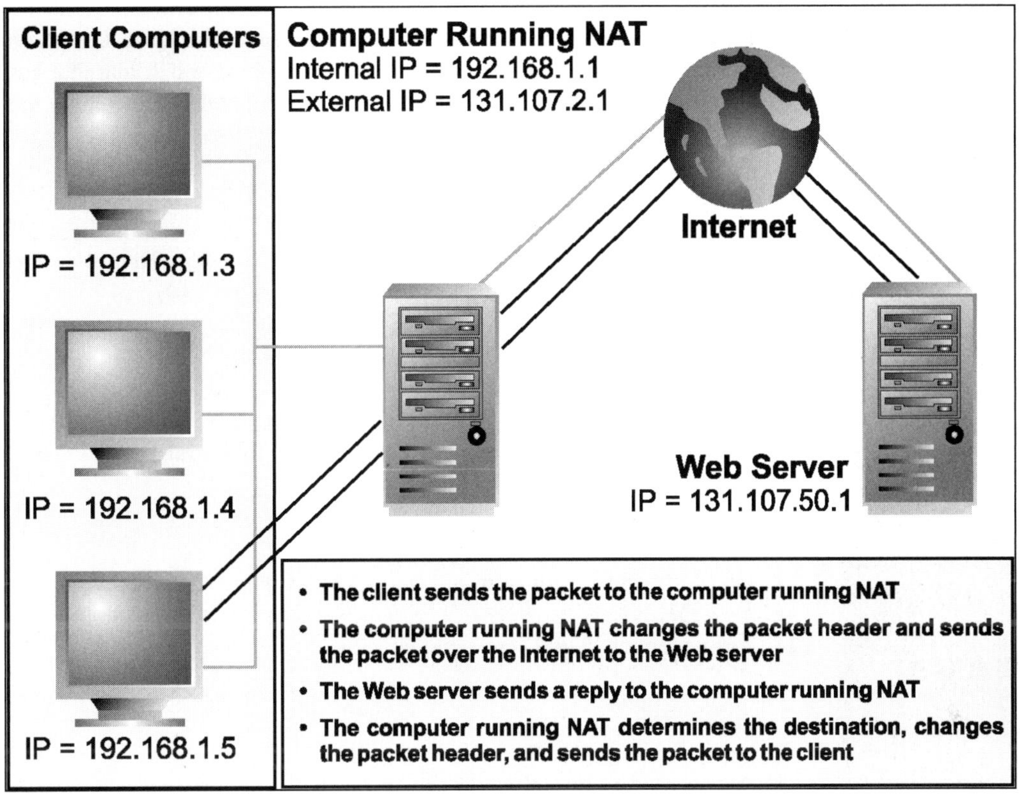

project 11.6 Introducing Network Address Translation (NAT) *(cont'd)*

exam objective

Basic knowledge

project steps

10. In the **Configuration** screen, select **Network Address Translation (NAT)** and click **Next**.

11. In the **NAT Internet Connection** screen **(Figure 11-11)**, make sure that **Create a new demand-dial interface to the Internet** is selected and notice that **Enable security on the selected interface by setting up Basic Firewal**l is selected by default. Click **Next**. Click **Next** again to start the **Demand-Dial Interface Wizard**.

12. In the **Demand-Dial Interface Wizard Welcome** screen, click **Next**. Type **Remote Access Router** in the **Interface name** text box. Click **Next**.

13. Select **Connect using a modem, ISDN adapter**, **or other physical device** and click **Next**. Accept the modem interface displayed by clicking **Next**. For the phone number of the dial-up server, type **8705551234** and click **Next**.

14. In the **Protocols and Security** screen, ensure that only **Route IP packets on this interface** is selected and click **Next**.

15. In the **Dial Out Credentials** screen, type **Administrator** as the **User name**, **CRAIGHEAD.COM** as the **Domain**, and the appropriate password in the **Password** and **Confirm password** text boxes. Click **Next** and then **Finish**. Click **Finish** to complete the RRAS setup wizard.

16. Right-click the **NAT/Basic Firewall** icon (located under **IP Routing**) in the left pane of the RAS console and click **Properties**.

17. On the **Name Resolution** tab, select **Client using Domain Name System (DNS)** and click **OK**.

18. Close all open dialog boxes and windows.

Figure 11-11 NAT Internet Connection screen

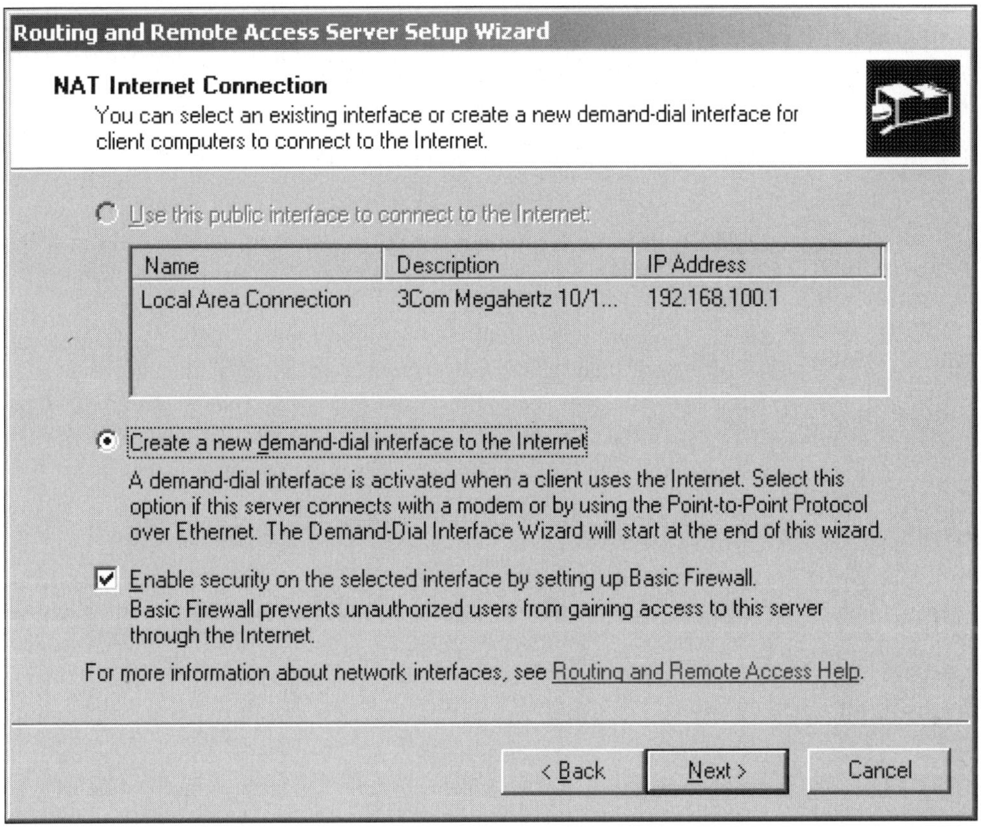

LESSON

12 Implementing Security in Windows 2003 Server

One of the most important concerns within any networking environment is security. When an unauthorized user accesses your network, they can change data, delete important files, become privy to proprietary information, or add malicious content. Windows Server 2003 provides support for Public Key Infrastructure (PKI) and a set of security tools that can be used to combat threats from unauthorized users. PKI supports and augments the basic security functions of network authentication and encryption. Microsoft Certificate Services enables an organization to use digital certificates by providing a local Certification Authority (CA) that issues and revokes certificates.

In addition to PKI support and Certificate Services, Windows Server 2003 also provides other security. As with Windows 2000 Server, the Kerberos protocol is used to enable a server to carry out user authentication for access to network resources. Account lockout policies can be employed to help prevent password guessing. Also, you can utilize security templates, installed on your hard drive at installation, to apply a group of security settings all at once. A security template can include account policies, group membership information, and access controls.

This lesson includes projects that will help you become more familiar with the security concepts underlying PKI. You will also be able to practice creating and assigning IPSec policies, customizing account policies, modifying default security options, customizing user rights assignments, using administrative templates, and working with security tools and templates.

Scenario

Information stored on network servers contains data that is covered by the Family Educational Rights and Privacy Act (FERPA). The CIO of Craighead College has instructed you to make the network more secure to prevent unauthorized access to classified information. Also, security should be in place to prevent unauthorized users from placing malicious content on the network.

You are familiar with the availability of the following Windows 2003 Server security tools:

- Certificate Services
- Kerberos Authentication
- Account Policies
- Security Options
- User Rights Assignments
- Administrative Templates

You will investigate each of these tools and employ them to increase the security level of your network.

Lesson 12 Implementing Security in Windows 2003 Server

Project	Exam 70-290 Objective
12.1 Introducing Public Key Infrastructure	Basic knowledge
12.2 Working with IPSec	Basic knowledge
12.3 Implementing Account Policy	Basic knowledge
12.4 Implementing Security Options	Basic knowledge
12.5 Configuring User Rights Assignments	Basic knowledge
12.6 Configuring Client Security	Basic knowledge
12.7 Working with Security Tools and Templates	Basic knowledge

General Requirements

To complete the projects in this lesson, you will need administrative rights on the craighead.com domain controller and a Windows Server 2003 installation CD-ROM. You also need to have completed the projects in Lessons 6 and 7. You may also find it helpful to refer to Lesson 12 in your Prentice Hall Certification Series Exam 70-290 textbook for further information about the topics covered by the projects in this lesson.

project 12.1

Introducing Public Key Infrastructure

exam objective

Basic knowledge

overview

Public Key Infrastructure (PKI) enables users of unsecured networks to securely exchange data by facilitating the issuance of certificates. The certificates support and enhance authentication and encryption. Before you successfully employ PKI at Craighead College, it is necessary that both you and your staff have a fundamental understanding of the security concepts that are the basis for PKI. You are going to research the topic and prepare a training session for your senior staff.

learning objective

After completing this project, you will be more familiar with security concepts underlying PKI.

specific requirements

None

estimated completion time

30 minutes

project steps

1. Prepare a one-page report explaining the differences between private key (also known as single key or symmetric key) encryption and public key (or asymmetric) cryptography **(Figure 12-1)**. Include the major advantages and disadvantages of each.
2. Certificates can be used for a number of reasons. Explain and give examples of three different reasons to use certificates.
3. Windows 2000 Server and Windows Server 2003 use Encrypting File System (EFS) to encrypt files on NTFS volumes and partitions. Explain the steps used to encrypt with EFS. Include the role of the recovery agent and the Data Recovery Field (DRF).
4. In networking, the terms authentication, integrity, confidentiality, and anti-replay are often used to describe different functions within security management **(Table 12-1)**. Define and give an example of each of these.

Figure 12-1 Public Key Cryptography

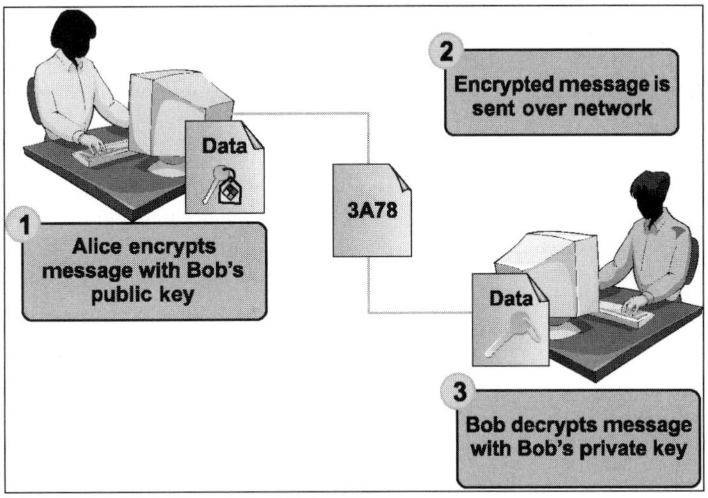

Table 12-1 Security Concepts

Property	Description
Authentication	Process of reliably determining the genuine identity of the communicating host or user. It is based on cryptography and aims to ensure that an attacker eavesdropping on the network cannot gain the information needed to impersonate a valid user.
Integrity	The correctness of the data as it was originally sent. Integrity services protect data from unauthorized medication in transit.
Confidentiality	Ensures that the data is disclosed only to its intended recipients.
Anti-replay	Ensures that datagrams are not retransmitted and that each one sent is unique. This uniqueness prevents attacks in which a message is intercepted and stored, then re-used later to attempt illegal access to information.

project 12.2 Working with IPSec

exam objective

Basic knowledge

overview

IP Security (IPSec) policies can be used both on your intranet and to secure Internet communications. It performs the functions of authentication, packet filtering, and tunneling. IPSec is put into operation using IPSec policies (applied to the local computer) or you can create a GPO to implement them at the domain or OU level. The three preconfigured policies are Server (Request Security), Client (Respond Only), and Secure Server (Require Security).

Since sensitive data will be transmitted across the Craighead College network, you have decided to implement IPSec policies throughout the domain and you have chosen to use the Secure Server (Require Security) template. This template ensures that all communication is encrypted. When this policy is set, unsecured communications with an un-trusted computer are blocked.

learning objective

After completing this project, you will know how to create and assign IPSec policies.

specific requirements

Administrative rights on the craighead.com domain controller.

estimated completion time

30 minutes

project steps

1. Click **Start**, click **Run**, type **mmc** in the **Open** text box, and click **OK**.
2. Click **File** and then click **Add/Remove Snap-in**. In the **Add/Remove Snap-in** dialog box, click **Add** to display the list of available snap-ins.
3. Scroll down and highlight **IP Security Policy Management**. Click **Add**. In the **Select Computer or Domain** dialog box, select the option button for **The Active Directory domain of which this computer is a member** and click **Finish**. Click **Close,** and then click **OK** to return to the MMC console window.
4. Save the current console for future use by clicking **File** and then **Save As**. Enter **IPSec Manager** in the **File name** text box and click **Save**.
5. Double-click **IP Security Policies on Active Directory** and then right-click **IP Security Policies on Active Directory**. Click **Create IP Security Policy (Figure 12-2)** to start the **IP Security Policy Wizard**.
6. Click **Next** and type **Craighead College IPSec Policy** in the **Name** text box. Type **Default IP Security Policy for the Craighead.com domain** in the **Description** text box and click **Next**.
7. Ensure that the **Activate the default response rule** option button is selected, and click **Next**. You will be given the option to select between various authentication methods. Select **Active Directory default (Kerberos V5 protocol)** and click **Next**.
8. In the **Completing the IP Security Policy Wizard** screen, ensure that **Edit properties** is checked and click **Finish**. In the **Craighead College IPSec Policy Properties** dialog box **(Figure 12-3)**, click **Add** to start the **Security Rule Wizard**. Click **Next**.
9. In the **Tunnel Endpoint** screen, select **This rule does not specify a tunnel** and click **Next**. Select **All network connections** in the **Network Type** screen, and click **Next**.
10. In the **IP Filter List** screen, click the **All IP Traffic** option button, and then click **Edit**. Read the information associated with the filter item and click **OK** and then **Next**.
11. In the **Filter Action** screen **(Figure 12-4)**, select **Require Security** and click **Next**. Accept **Active Directory default (Kerberos V5 protocol)** as the authentication method, click **Next**, and then click **Finish**. Close all open dialog boxes and windows.
12. Click **Start**, point to **Administrative Tools**, and click **Domain Security Policy**.
13. Click **IP Security Policies on Active Directory** at the bottom of the left pane. In the right pane, right-click **Craighead College IPSec Policy**. No IPSec policies are assigned to a computer by default. You could assign this policy simply by selecting **Assign** from the menu. Leave the policy unassigned and close all open windows. Save changes to the MMC console when prompted.

Figure 12-2 The Create IP Security Policy command

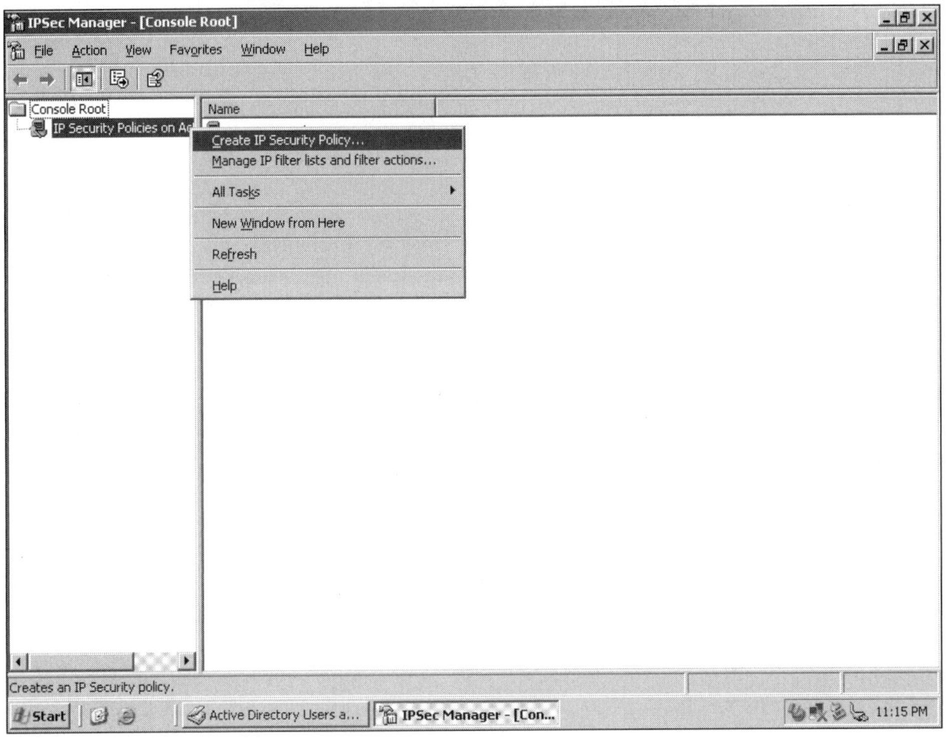

Figure 12-3 Craighead College IPSec Policy Properties dialog box

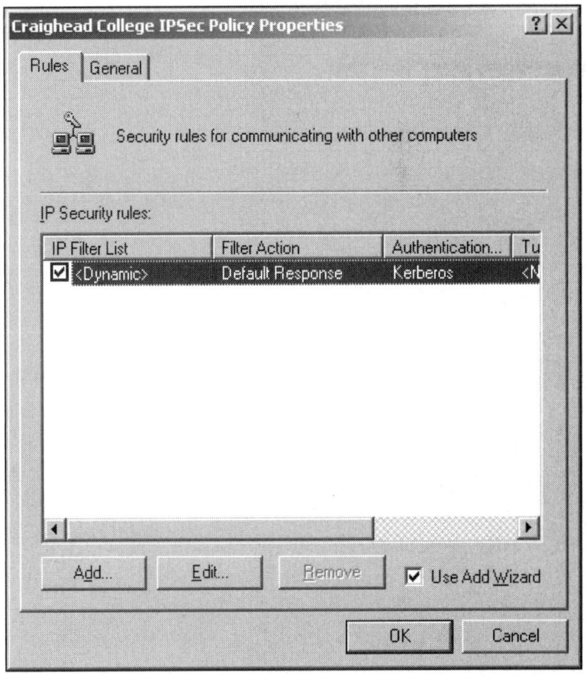

Figure 12-4 Filter Action screen

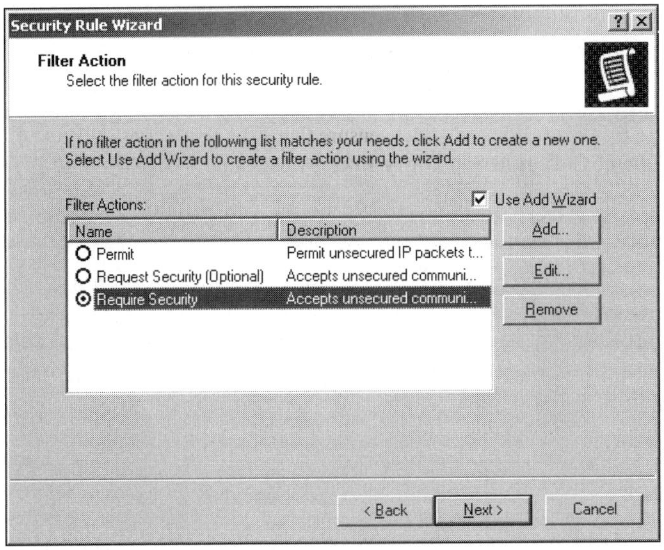

project 12.3 Implementing Account Policy

exam objective

Basic knowledge

overview

There are three types of account policies: Account Lockout, Password, and Kerberos. Account Lockout policies are used to limit the amount of invalid login attempts allowed before the account is locked out from further use. This helps to reduce 'password guessing' intruders. Password policies dictate how users must manage their passwords by specifying options, such as length, complexity, frequency of change, etc. This helps to keep passwords harder to compromise. Default Kerberos policies are normally suitable for most networks and rarely need to be changed. However, in some situations, you may want to decrease the lifetime of the tickets issued by Kerberos servers to reduce the possibility of a hacker stealing passwords.

To increase the level of security on the network at Craighead College, you have decided to edit the default policies for your domain. You will make the necessary changes to all three types of account policies.

learning objective

After completing this project, you will know how to customize account policies to enhance the security of your network.

specific requirements

Administrative rights on the craighead.com domain controller.

estimated completion time

15 minutes

project steps

1. Click **Start**, point to **Administrative Tools**, and select **Domain Security Policy**.
2. Expand **Account Policies** in the left pane and click **Password Policy**. All of the existing domain password policies will appear in the right pane of the window **(Figure 12-5)**.
3. Double-click **Maximum password age** and change the existing value to **15** and click **OK**. Double-click **Minimum password length** and change the value to **8** and click **OK**. Double-click **Enforce password history** and change the number of passwords remembered to **10** and click **OK**.
4. Click **Account Lockout Policy** in the left pane. All of the existing lockout policies for the domain will appear in the right pane **(Figure 12-6)**.
5. Double-click **Account lockout threshold** and change the value to **3** and click **OK**. Click **OK** to accept the suggested values for the other to lockout fields.
6. Double-click **Reset account lockout counter after** and change the value to **60** minutes and click **OK**. Click **OK** to accept the suggested value for **Account lockout duration**.
7. Double-click **Account lockout duration** and change the value to **1440** minutes and click **OK**. These settings will now lock out an account for 24 hours if three invalid logins are attempted within one hour.
8. Click **Kerberos Policy** in the left pane. All of the existing Kerberos settings for the domain will appear in the right pane **(Figure 12-7)**.
9. Double-click **Maximum lifetime for user ticket** and change the value to **5** hours and click **OK**. Accept the suggested change in value for **Maximum lifetime for service ticket** by clicking **OK**. Close all open windows.

Figure 12-5 Default Domain Password Policies

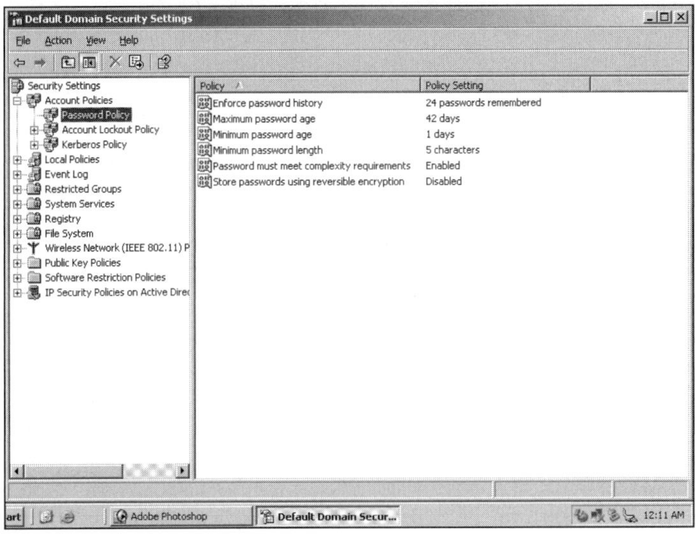

Figure 12-6 Default Domain Account Lockout Policies

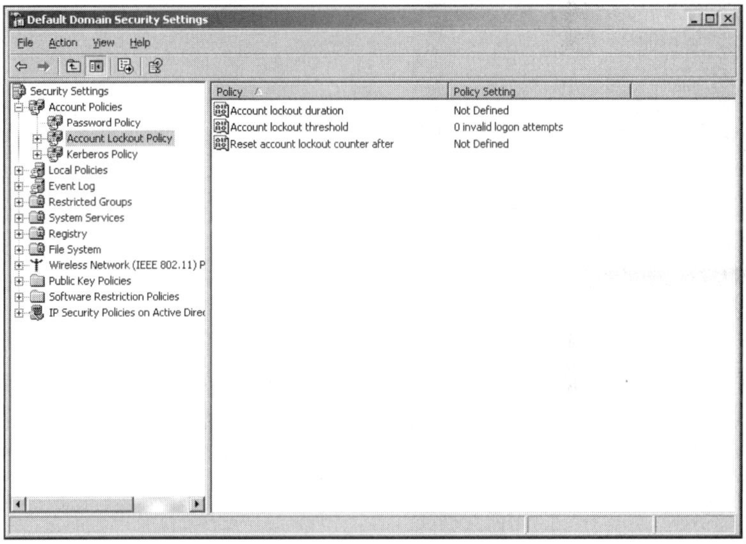

Figure 12-7 Default Domain Kerberos Policies

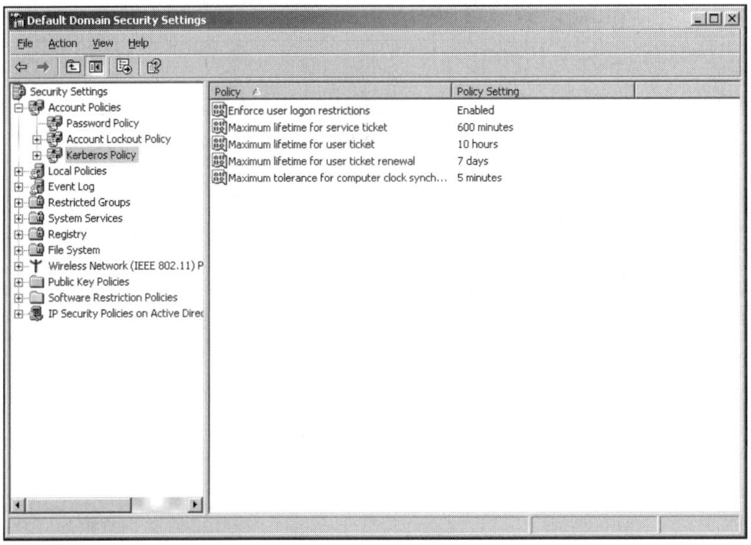

project 12.4 Implementing Security Options

exam objective

Basic knowledge

overview

You can further enhance the security of your network by implementing the security options available with Windows 2003 Server. As the network administrator for Craighead College, there are several security options that you wish to use. Before implementing the changes on a domain-wide basis, you have decided to test them by editing the default local security policy on the domain controller first.

learning objective

After completing this project, you will know how to change the default local security options.

specific requirements

Administrative rights on the craighead.com domain controller.

estimated completion time

15 minutes

project steps

1. Click **Start**, click **Run**, type **mmc** in the **Open** text box, and click **OK**.
2. Click **File** and then **Add/Remove Snap-in**. In the **Add/Remove Snap-in** dialog box, click **Add** to display the list of available snap-ins.
3. Scroll down the list, click **Group Policy Object Editor**, and then click **Add**. Accept **Local Computer** as the **Group Policy Object** and click **Finish**. Close all open dialog boxes.
4. Click **File** on the Menu bar, select **Save As**, and then type **Group Policy Editor** in the **File name** text box. Then click **Save** or press **[Enter]** to save the console.
5. Expand **Local Computer Policy**, **Computer Configuration**, **Windows Settings**, **Security Settings** and then **Local Policies**. Click **Security Options**. A list of the possible security options will appear in the left pane **(Figure 12-8)**. They are divided into 14 general categories.
6. Double-click **Accounts: Rename guest account** and type **Student** in the text box. Click **OK**.
7. Double-click **Devices: Unsigned Driver Installation Behavior** and select **Do not allow installation** from the drop-down list. This will prevent installation of unsigned drivers on the computer. Click **OK**.
8. Double-click **Interactive logon: Do not display last user name** and select **Enabled**. This will prevent a user from seeing the name of the last logged on user. Click **OK**.
9. Double-click **Interactive logon: Message text for users attempting to log on**. Type **The use of this network is for academic purposes only**. **All other uses are strictly prohibited**. Click **OK**.
10. Double-click **Interactive logon: Message title for users attempting to log on**. Type **Read the Following Use Restrictions** in the text box and click **OK**.
11. Double-click **Shutdown: Clear virtual memory pagefile**, select **Enabled**, and click **OK**. Close all open windows and save changes to the MMC when prompted.

Figure 12-8 Security Options

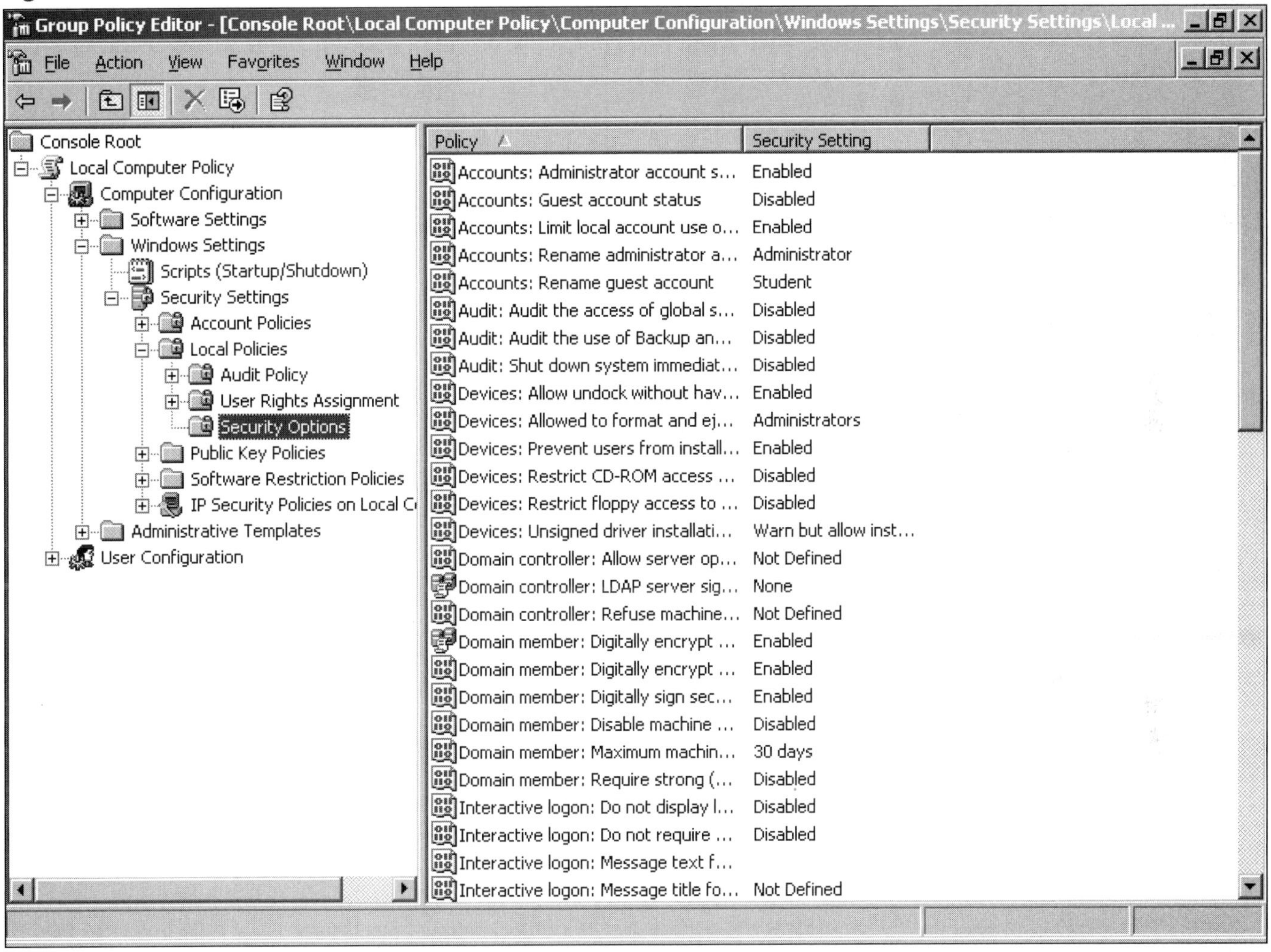

project 12.5

Configuring User Rights Assignments

exam objective

Basic knowledge

overview

User rights assignments define the users and groups that are allowed to perform tasks on an individual computer or throughout the domain. The rights are divided into two categories: logon rights and privileges. Logon rights designate who can log on to a computer and how they log on. Privileges permit users to interact with the operating system and with system-wide resources.

You currently have five network support technicians working in your department. They are all members of the IT Staff group (see Lessons 6 and 7). You want to enable these technicians to perform certain administrator tasks without making them members of the Administrators group.

learning objective

After completing this lesson, you will be able to customize user rights assignments for the domain.

specific requirements

Administrative rights on the craighead.com domain controller. You also must have completed the projects in Lessons 6 and 7.

estimated completion time

10 minutes

project steps

1. Click **Start**, click **Run**, and type **mmc** in the **Open** text box. In the empty console screen, select **File** on the Menu bar, and then double-click **Group Policy Editor** in the Explorer list.
2. If necessary, expand **Local Computer Policy**, and then expand **Computer Configuration**, **Windows Settings**, **Security Settings**, and **Local Policies**.
3. When you click **User Rights Assignments**, a list of the different policies available will appear in the right pane of the window **(Figure 12-9)**.
4. Double-click **Allow log on through Terminal Services** and click **Add User or Group**. Type **IT Staff** in the **Enter the object names to select** text box and click **OK**. The **IT Staff** group now appears in the **Properties** dialog box. Click **OK** to close the Properties dialog box.
5. Double-click **Perform volume maintenance tasks** and click **Add User or Group**. Type **IT Staff**, click **OK**, and then **OK** again. Close all open dialog boxes and windows, and save changes to the MMC when prompted.

Figure 12-9 User Rights Assignment

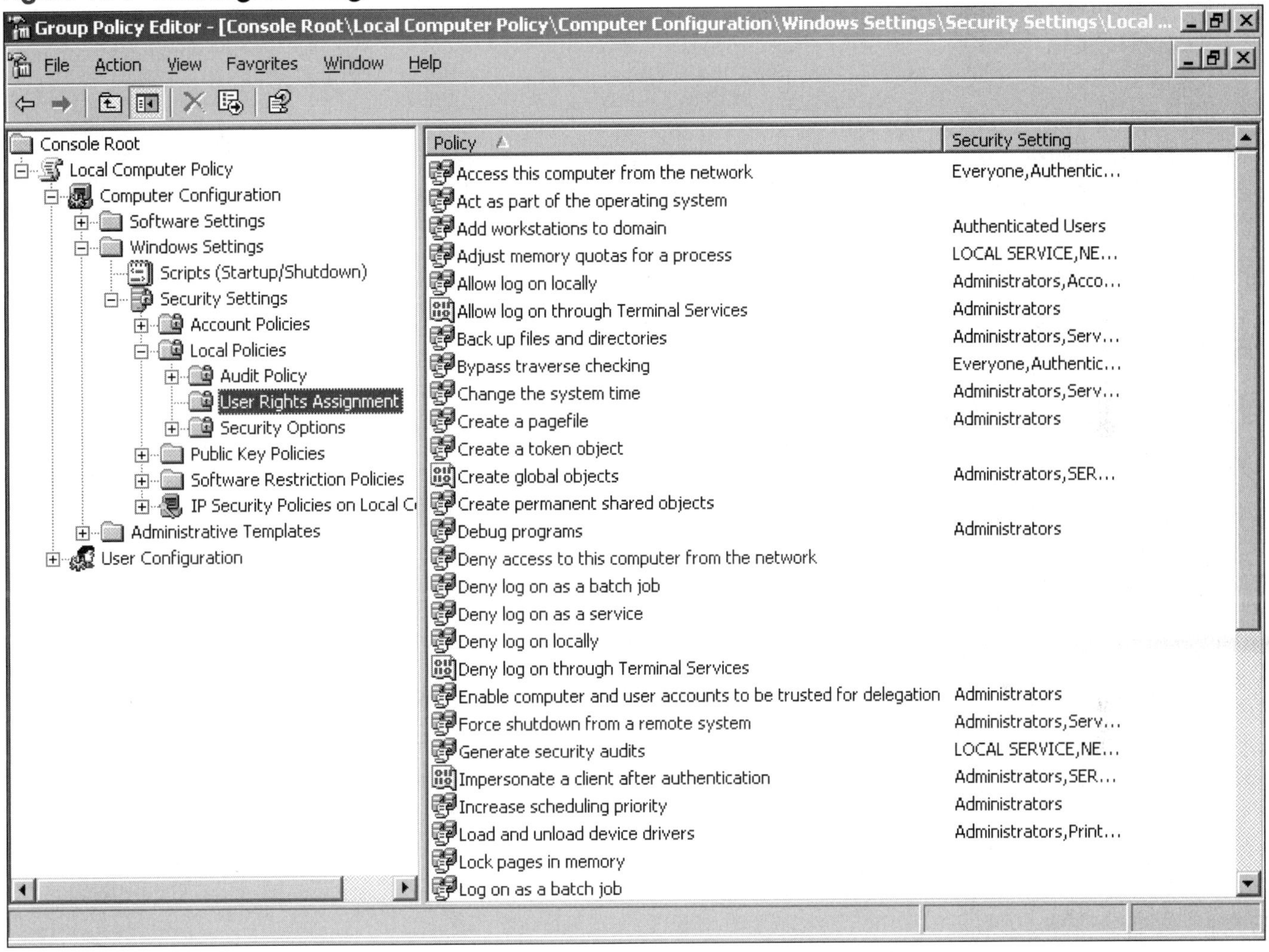

project 12.6 Configuring Client Security

exam objective

Basic knowledge

overview

Administrative template policies can be used to improve security and to provide a consistent desktop environment for all clients. These policies can be applied locally or at the site, domain, or OU level. There are multiple classes of access restrictions located within the User Configuration/Administrative Template node. The types of policies you can set from each of these are shown in **Figure 12-10**.

At Craighead College, all student accounts are located in the Student OU. When these students access computers in the computer labs, certain functions of the desktop should be prohibited. You are going to modify an administrative template to provide this restricted environment.

learning objective

After completing this project, you will know how to use administrative templates to customize the desktop environment for users.

specific requirements

Administrative rights on the craighead.com domain controller. You also must have completed the projects in Lessons 6 and 7.

estimated completion time

30 minutes

project steps

1. Click **Start**, point to **Administrative Tools**, and click **Active Directory Users and Computers**.
2. Right-click the **Students** OU and click **Properties**. On the **Group Policy** tab, click **New** to create a new group policy for this OU. Type **Student Group Policy** in the highlighted text box **(Figure 12-11)**.
3. Click **Edit**. In the **Group Policy Object Editor**, expand **Administrative Templates** under **User Configuration** and then expand **Windows Components**. Click **Internet Explorer**. Click the **Standard** view tab located at the bottom of the left pane in the window **(Figure 12-12)**.
4. Double-click each of the following settings and change the value in each to **Enabled**:
   - Disable changing home page settings
   - Disable changing language settings
   - Disable changing connection settings
   - Disable Internet Connection Wizard

   Then click **OK**.
5. Click **Start Menu and Taskbar** under **Administrative Templates**. In the left pane, double-click each of the following and change the value to **Enabled**:
   - Remove Search menu from Start Menu
   - Prevent changes to Taskbar and
   - Remove Favorites from Start Menu
   - Remove My Network Places icon

   Then click **OK**.
6. Click **Control Panel** under **Administrative Templates**, and then double-click **Prohibit access to the Control Panel** in the right pane of the window. Change the value to **Enabled** and click **OK**.
7. Expand **System** under **Administrative Templates**, and click **[Ctrl]+[Alt]+[Del] Options**. In the left pane, double-click **Remove Lock Computer**. Change the value to **Enabled** and click **OK**. Close all open windows.
8. To test the changes you just made, log off as **Administrator** and log on as **NathanS** with a password of **p@$$w0rd**. You created **NathanS** in a previous project and placed his user object in the **Students OU**.

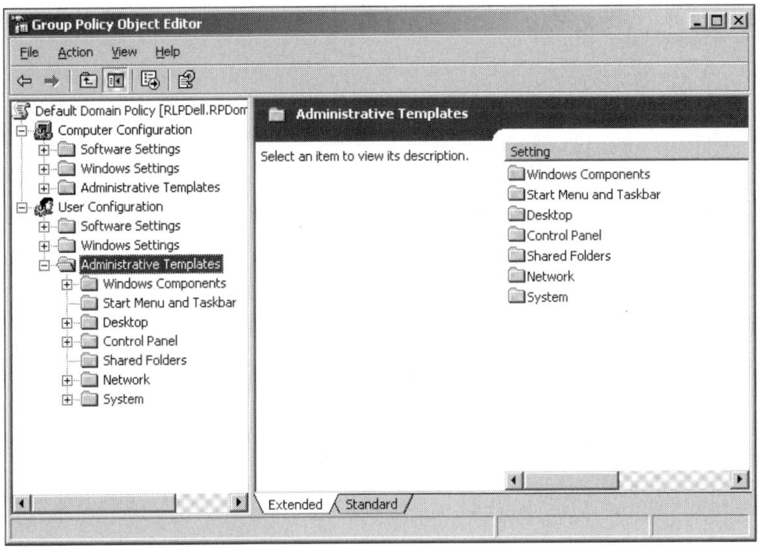

Figure 12-10 The Administrative Templates node in the Group Policy Object Editor

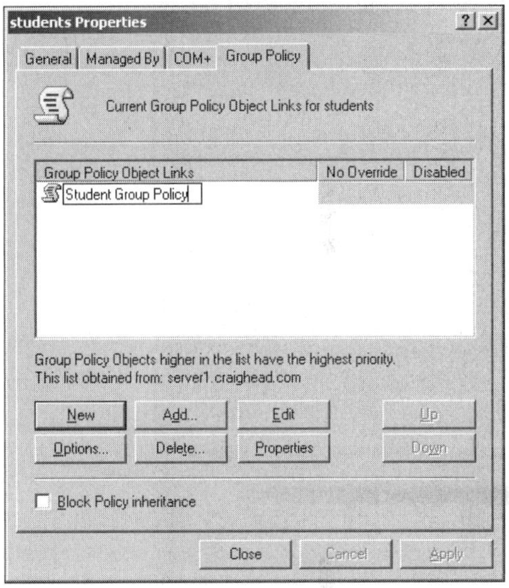

Figure 12-11 The Group Policy tab

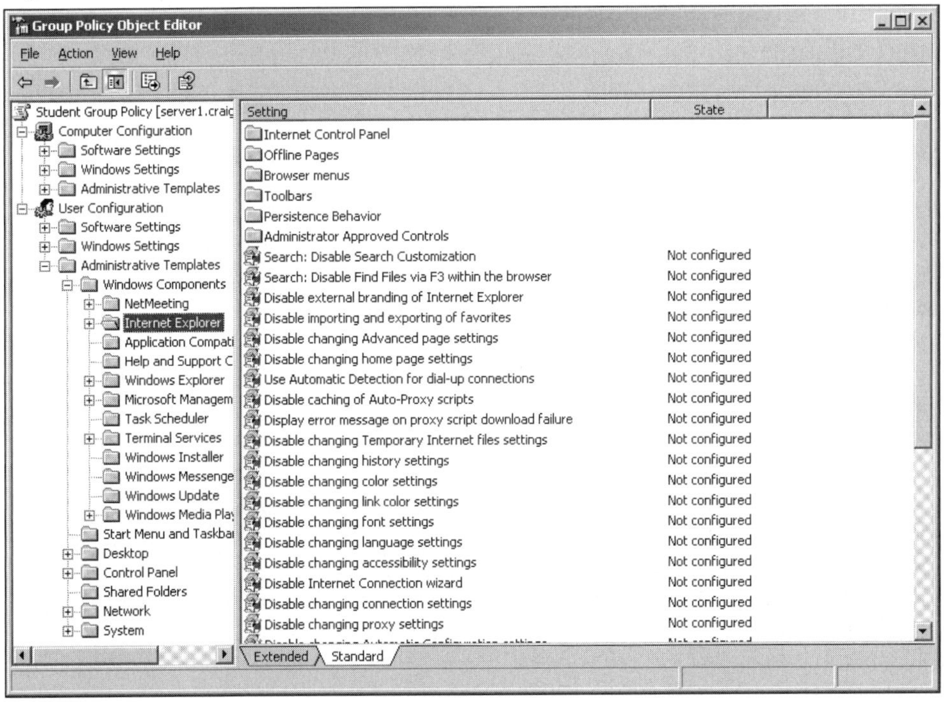

Figure 12-12 Internet Explorer settings

project 12.7

Working with Security Tools and Templates

exam objective

Basic knowledge

overview

The Security and Configuration Analysis snap-in can be used for several different tasks. It can be used to compare the current security configuration of the computer to one of the security templates, to create custom templates, and to apply a selected template to either the local computer or to a Group Policy object.

Because the craighead.com domain controller is functioning as a domain controller, file server, and print server, it is important to have a high degree of security set on this computer. You want to compare the high security domain controller template, provided with Windows Server 2003, to the domain controller and determine if current settings are at a high enough level of security.

learning objective

After completing this project, you will know how to work with security tools and templates to evaluate security levels of computers within the domain.

specific requirements

Administrative rights on the craighead.com domain controller.

estimated completion time

30 minutes

project steps

1. Click **Start**, click **Run**, and type **mmc** in the **Open** text box Then click **OK** or press **[Enter]**.
2. Click **File**, and then click **Add/Remove Snap-in** to open the **Add/Remove Snap-in** dialog box. Click **Add** to display the list of available snap-ins.
3. Scroll down and highlight **Security Configuration and Analysis**, and click **Add**. Highlight **Security Templates** and click **Add**.
4. Click **Close** and then click **OK** to return to the MMC console window.
5. Save the new MMC console by clicking **File**, then clicking **Save As**, and then typing **Security** in the **File name** text box. Click **Save**.
6. Expand **Security Templates**, **C:\WINDOWS\security\templates**, and then **hisecdc** to display the template settings available **(Figure 12-13)**.
7. After viewing the various settings within the **hisecdc** template (browse through the various Account Policies and Local Policies), you wish to increase the security to a higher level.
8. Click **Account Lockout Policy** located under **Account Policies**. Double-click **Account lockout threshold** in the right pane. Change the existing value for invalid logon attempts to **3** and click **OK**. Double-click **Account lockout duration** and change the existing value to **60** minutes and click **OK**.
9. Right-click **hisecdc** in the right pane and select **Save As (Figure 12-14)**. Type **CustomDC** in the **File name** text box and click **Save**.
10. In the left pane, right-click **Security Configuration and Analysis** and select **Open Database**. In the **File name** text box, type **SecurityDB** and click **Open**. You will be prompted to select **Import Template**. Click **CustomDC.inf** and click **Open**.
12. Right-click **Security Configuration and Analysis** and click **Analyze Computer Now**. Click **OK** to accept the default location for the error log.

Figure 12-13 Security Templates List

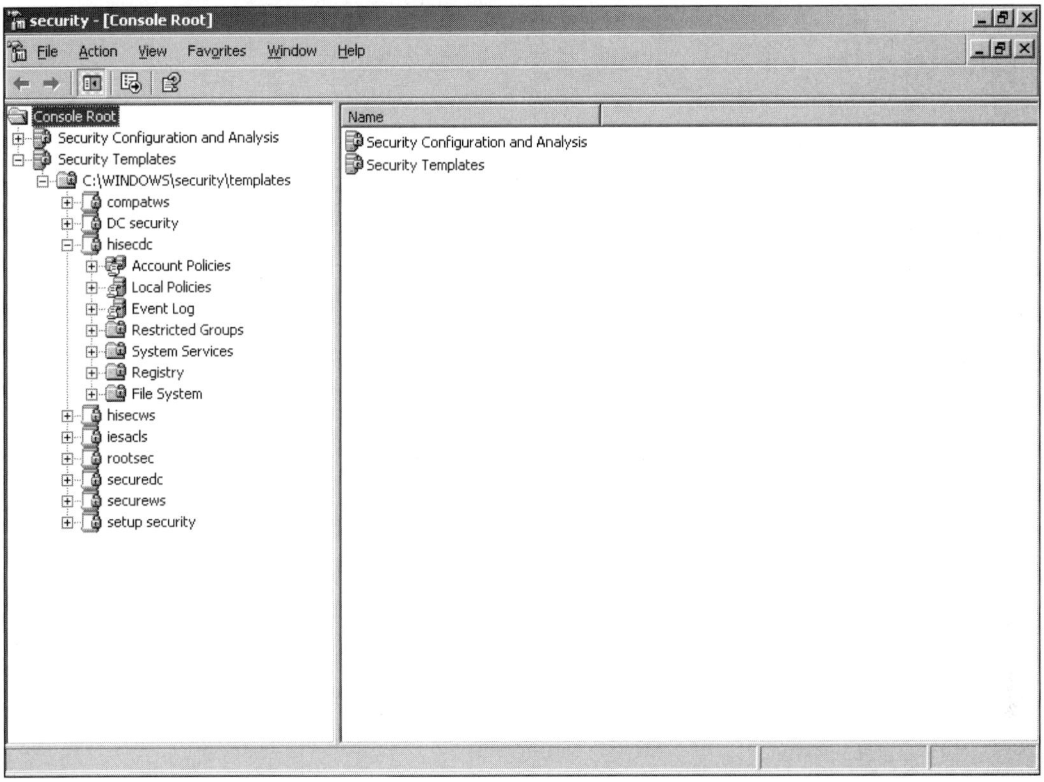

Figure 12-14 Saving the new Security Template

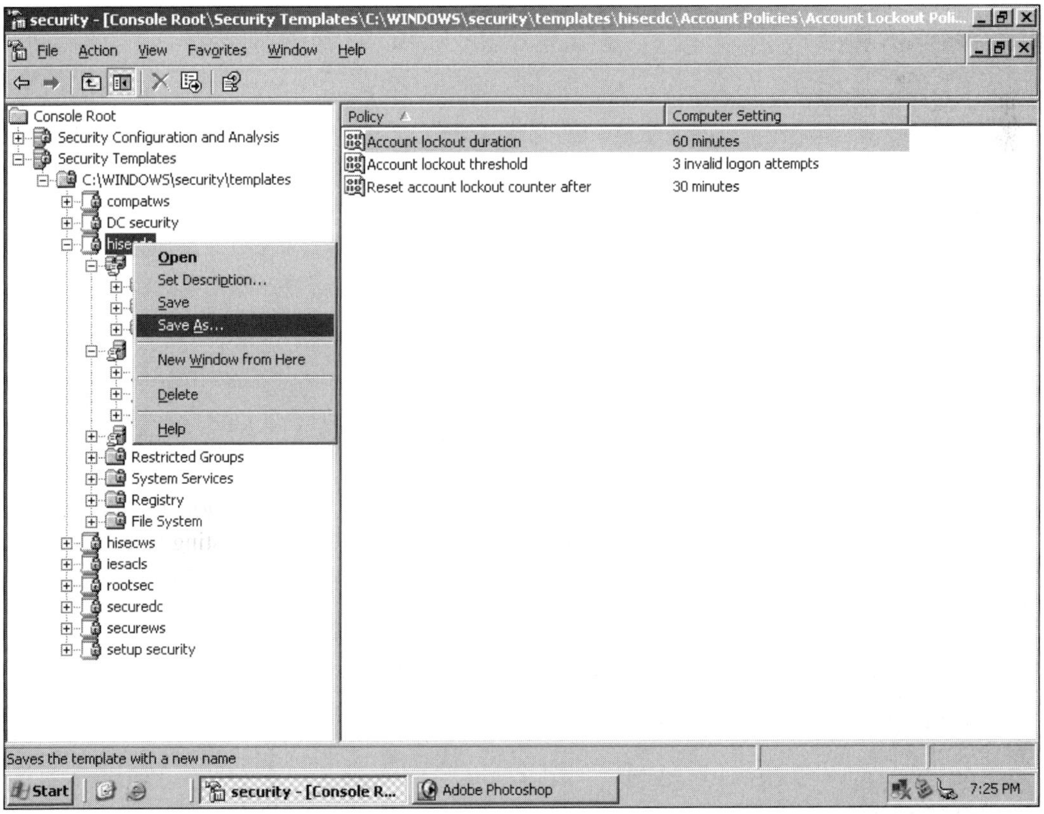

project 12.7

Working with Security Tools and Templates *(cont'd)*

exam objective

Basic knowledge

project steps

13. Expand **Security Configuration and Analysis** and then expand **Account Policies**. When you click **Password Policy**, a list of all the password policies appears in the right pane of the window **(Figure 12-15)**. If a red **X** appears, then the current settings of the domain controller do not meet the minimum security settings of the **CustomDC** template. If a green check mark appears, then the domain controller meets or exceeds the template guidelines.
14. To bring the current settings of the domain controller to the security minimums set forth in the template, right-click **Security Configuration and Analysis** and click **Configure Computer Now**. Accept the default location for the error log file by clicking **OK**.
15. To check the configuration, right-click **Security Configuration and Analysis** and click **Analyze Computer Now**. Accept the default location for the error log file by clicking **OK**.
16. Expand **Security Configuration and Analysis** and then **Account Policies**. Click **Password Policy** and notice that all policies in the right pane appear with a green checkmark **(Figure 12-16)**. Close all windows and save settings to the MMC when prompted.

Figure 12-15 Pre-configuration Analysis Results

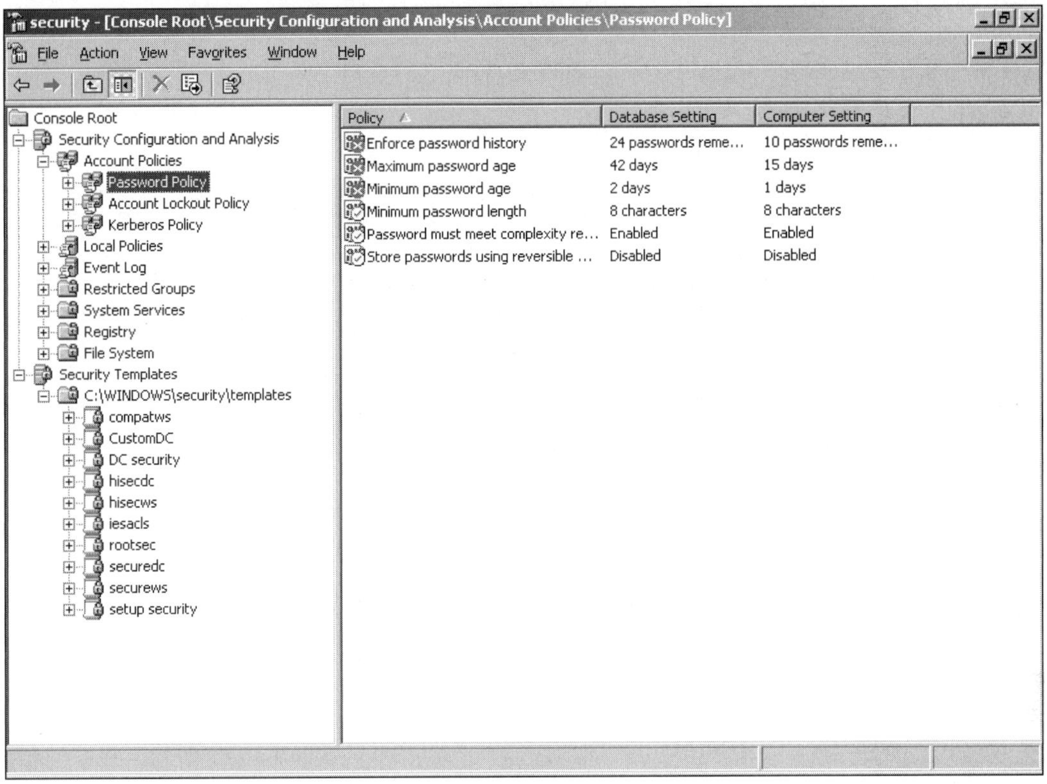

Figure 12-16 Post-configuration Analysis Results

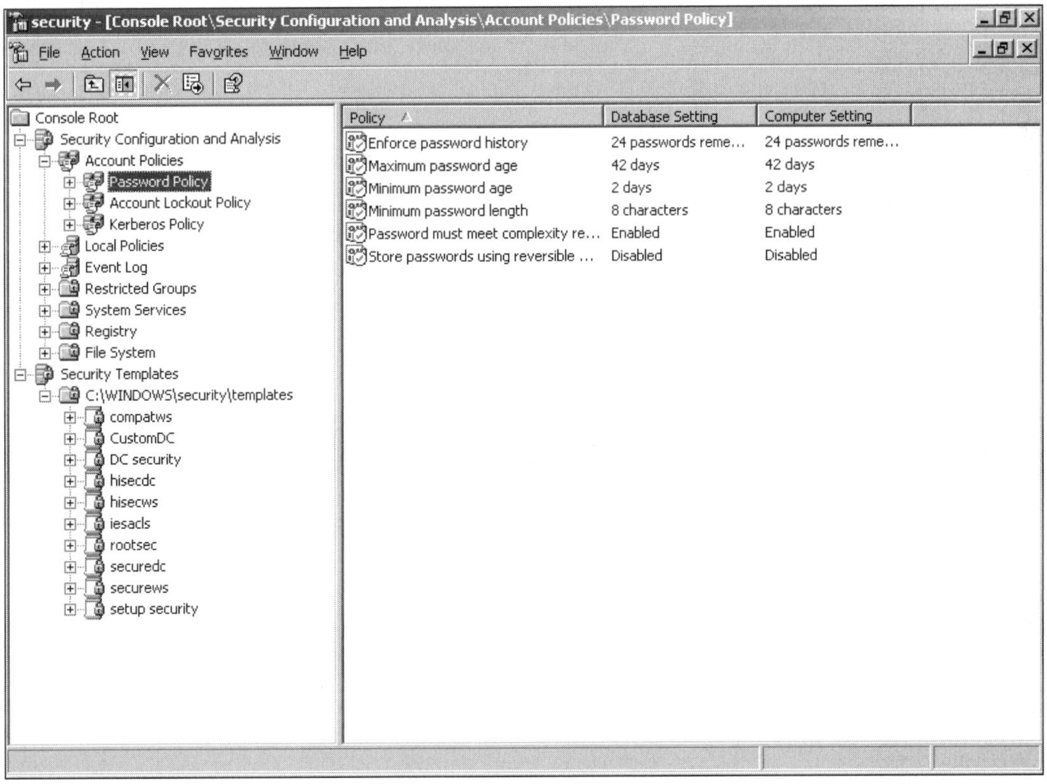

LESSON 13

Implementing Data and System Recovery

Windows Server 2003 has several wizards within the Backup utility that are used to protect your data and system in the event of a catastrophe such as a disk drive crash, a virus, or a power outage. These utilities include the Backup Wizard, the Restore Wizard, and the Automated System Recovery Wizard.

When you are booting a server and a problem occurs that prevents the operating system from starting, Windows Server 2003 allows the user to boot in Safe Mode. You can use Safe Mode to remove corrupt drivers, fix driver conflicts, or uninstall and reinstall applications to resolve possible difficulties. The Last Known Good Configuration can be useful if you have installed a driver that is not compatible with your hardware or is defective.

The Volume Shadow Copy Service (VSS) can be configured so that previous versions of saved files that are stored on a share can be recovered if they are accidentally deleted or overwritten. One of the major advantages of VSS is that it can be used to back up locked files that are in use by other services or applications, without the need for special software.

This lesson includes projects that will let you practice backing up and restoring data files and System State data on a domain controller, using the Last Known Good Configuration, installing and using the Recovery Console, and configuring Volume Shadow Copy Services.

Scenario

Since Craighead College is storing its financial data and student transcripts on the domain controller, data will be backed up on a daily basis. In addition, System State data will be backed up on a regular basis. In the event of domain controller hardware failure, all of the IT staff should be acquainted with the use of Last Known Good Configuration and the Recovery Console. Also, in case files are accidentally deleted, VSS will be employed to allow recovery of those files.

Lesson 13 Implementing Data and System Recovery

Project	*Exam 70-290 Objective*
13.1 Using the Windows Backup Utility to Back Up and Restore Files	Manage backup procedures. Verify the successful completion of backup jobs. Recover from server hardware failure. Restore backup data.
13.2 Using the Windows Backup Utility to Back Up and Restore System State Data	Manage backup procedures. Back up files and system state data to media. Verify the successful completion of backup jobs. Recover from server hardware failure. Restore backup data.
13.3 Using the Last Known Good Configuration	Perform system recovery for a server.
13.4 Working with the Recovery Console	Perform system recovery for a server. Recover from server hardware failure.
13.5 Configuring the Volume Shadow Copy Service	Restore data from shadow copy volumes.

General Requirements

To complete the projects in this lesson, you will need administrative rights on the craighead.com domain controller created in Lesson 3 and a blank floppy diskette. You may also find it helpful to refer to Lesson 13 in your Prentice Hall Certification Series Exam 70-290 textbook for further information on the topics covered by the projects in this lesson.

project 13.1 Using the Windows Backup Utility to Back Up and Restore Files

exam objective

Manage backup procedures. Verify the successful completion of backup jobs. Recover from server hardware failure. Restore backup data.

overview

When you back up user data, you can either back up all the files and folders on a computer or only specific files and folders. If you have configured the user's home directory and mail account to be stored on a central server, all user data can be backed up by selecting those folders on that particular server.

In order to back up data, you must have the necessary user rights or permissions to access the data being backed up. Users can back up files as long as they have at least the Read permission. By default, local Administrators and Backup Operators can back up and restore any file or folder on the local machine. Domain Administrators and members of the Backup Operators group on a domain controller can back up any file or folder in the domain. To restore data, users must have at least the Write permission. Domain Administrators and members of the Backup Operators group have the Restore files and directories user right by default and can restore any backup file or folder on the domain.

At Craighead College, all users will store their My Documents folder and all incoming mail on the domain controller for the craighead.com domain. You will schedule a backup of all user data on a daily basis. The backup will take place in the evening when no users are present.

learning objective

After completing this project, you will know how to perform a backup and restore data files on a Windows Server 2003 computer.

specific requirements

Administrative rights on the craighead.com domain controller and a blank floppy diskette.

estimated completion time

15 minutes

project steps

Back up selected folders.

1. Click **Start**, click **Run**, type **ntbackup** in the **Open** text box, and click **OK** to start the **Backup or Restore Wizard**.
2. Click **Next**. Ensure that **Back up files and settings** is selected and click **Next**. When asked **What to Back Up**, select **Let me choose what to back up**. Click **Next**.
3. In the **Items to Back Up** windows, expand **My Computer**, expand **Local Disk (C:)**, and then place a check mark in the box next to the **deploy** folder **(Figure 13-1)**. Note that this folder is selected for demonstration only. Normally, you would select the folder(s) that contain the users' documents and mail files. Click **Next**.
4. When prompted for the backup destination, click **Browse** and select **Local Disk (C:)** from the drop down box and click **Save**. Click **Save** again, click **Next**, and then click **Finish**. Note that you would not normally back up files to the same disk. This is done for demonstration purposes only.
5. After you click the **Finish** button, the **Backup Progress** dialog box **(Figure 13-2)** will appear and track the number of files completed. To view the backup details, click **Report**. Close all open windows.
6. Simulate data loss by deleting the **deploy** folder under **C:**. You can accomplish this by using Windows Explorer, right-clicking the **deploy** folder and selecting **Delete**. Click **OK** to confirm the deletion.

Figure 13-1 Items to Back Up screen

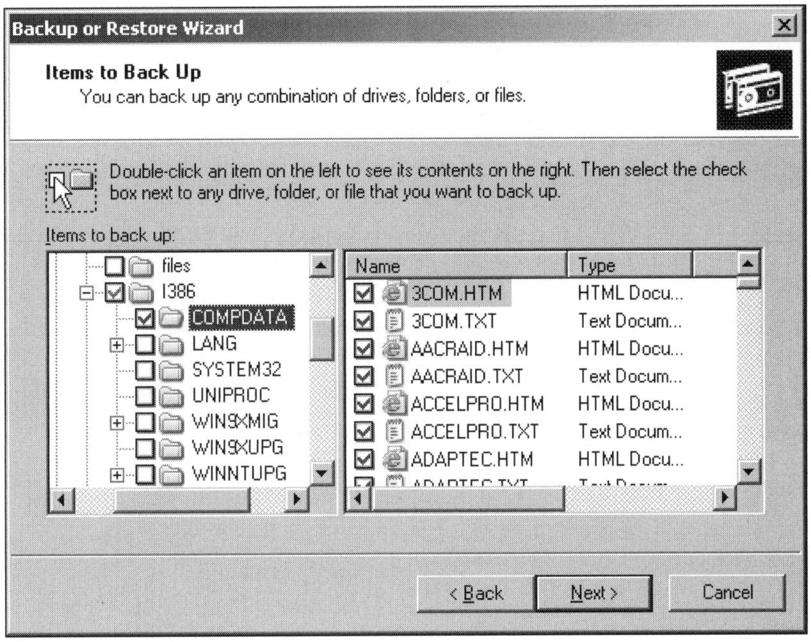

Figure 13-2 Backup Progress dialog box

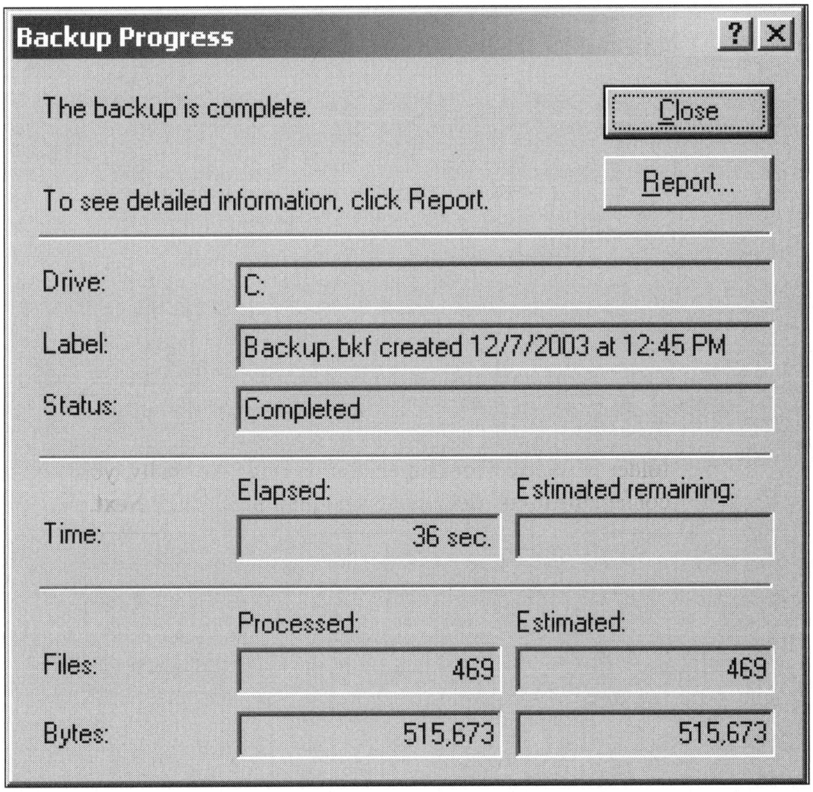

project 13.1

Using the Windows Backup Utility to Back Up and Restore Files *(cont'd)*

exam objective

Manage backup procedures. Verify the successful completion of backup jobs. Recover from server hardware failure. Restore backup data.

project steps

Restore files from a backup.

7. Click **Start**, click **Run**, type **ntbackup** in the **Open** text box, and click **OK** to start the **Backup or Restore Wizard**.
8. Click the **Advanced Mode** link to open the **Backup Utility Advanced Mode** window.
9. Click the icon associated with **Restore Wizard (Advanced)**. Click **Next**. A list of all the backups will appear in the **What to Restore** screen **(Figure 13-3)**.
10. Expand **File** in the left pane, then expand **Backup.bkf**, and place a check mark in the box beside the C: folder. Click **Next**.
11. Click **Finish** to begin the restore. Insert the floppy disk used for the backup, if necessary. Close all open windows.

Figure 13-3 Selecting items to restore

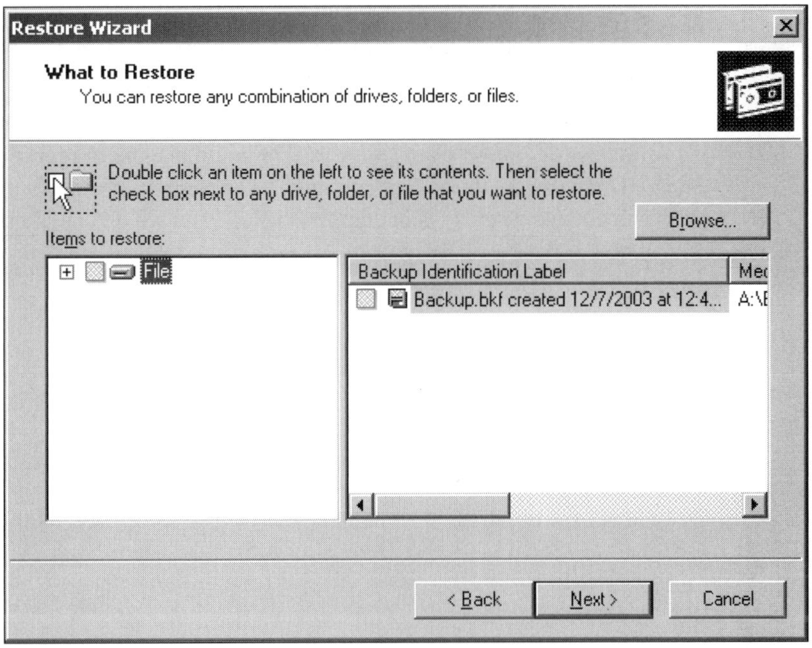

project 13.2 Using the Windows Backup Utility to Back Up and Restore System State Data

exam objective

Manage backup procedures. Back up files and system state data to media. Verify the successful completion of backup jobs. Recover from server hardware failure. Restore backup data.

overview

The System State data on a domain controller includes the SYSVOL folder and the Active Directory database. In addition, on all servers, the System State data contains the Registry, the COM+ Class Registration database, system boot files, Certificate Services database (if installed), and the DNS zones (if DNS is installed).

A System State restore is performed on a clean installation of the operating system to recover all of the configuration changes. A restore could also be triggered by the need to restore the Active Directory database. System State backups should be performed frequently because the data will change when system components change, which can happen quite often.

Due to the ever-changing configuration of your domain controller, you have determined to back up the System State data on a weekly basis. This backup procedure will be performed separately from the data backup.

learning objective

After completing this project, you will know how to back up and restore the System State data on a domain controller.

specific requirements

Administrative rights on the craighead.com domain controller and a blank floppy diskette.

estimated completion time

15 minutes

project steps

Back up the System State data.

1. Click **Start**, click **Run**, type **ntbackup** in the **Open** text box, and click **OK** to start the **Backup or Restore Wizard**.
2. Click the **Advanced Mode** link to open the **Backup Utility Advanced Mode** window **(Figure 13-4)**. Click the icon associated with **Backup Wizard (Advanced)**.
3. Click **Next** on the **Welcome** screen. Select **Only back up the System State data** and click **Next**.
4. When prompted for the backup destination, click **Browse** and select **3 ½ Floppy** from the drop-down list. Click **Save** and then **Next**. To begin the backup, click **Finish**.
5. The **Backup Progress** dialog box will open and the System State backup will begin. In approximately 2-5 minutes, you will receive a message that **The Disk is full**. This is because a normal System State backup requires approximately 500 MB of storage space. After reviewing the current progress (**Figure 13-5**), click **Cancel** to end the backup procedure. Close all open dialog boxes and windows.

Restore the System State data on a domain controller.

6. Restart the domain controller. In the text portion of booting, press **[F8]** when prompted to open the **Advanced Options Menu**. Highlight **Directory Services Restore Mode** and press **[Enter]**.
7. Windows Server 2003 will now boot in **Safe mode – Directory Services Restore**. Log on as an **Administrator** with the Directory Services Restore Mode password, **Restore**. This password was set in Project 3.3 when the server was promoted to a domain controller. Click **OK** to acknowledge that the computer is running in safe mode.
8. To restore the System State data, you would now run **Ntbackup** and follow Steps 7-11 used in **Project 13.1**. Since you did not complete the full System State Backup in Step 5 above, you will be unable to complete the restore. Reboot the domain controller normally.

Figure 13-4 Backup Utility Advanced Mode window

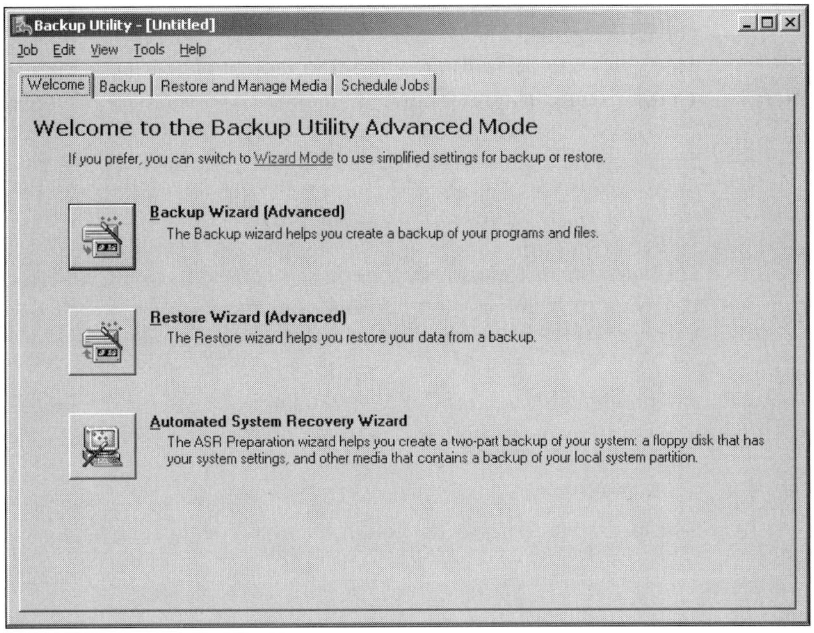

Figure 13-5 Backup Progress screen

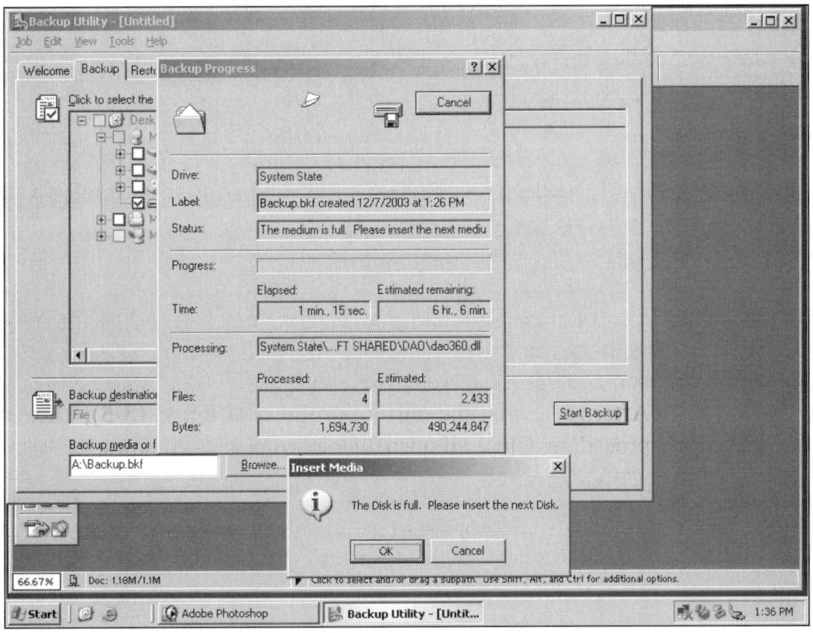

project 13.3

Using the Last Known Good Configuration

exam objective

Perform system recovery for a server.

overview

The Last Known Good Configuration (LKGC) contains settings saved in the Registry the last time a user successfully logged on to the computer. After every successful logon, the data used for configuring the computer is copied to the Last Known Good Configuration entry. The LKGC is useful if you incorrectly edited the Registry, added an incompatible driver, or disabled a critical driver. However, if a hardware device problem is occurring and you forget to choose LKGC, and you successfully log on, the LKGC will be updated and you will no longer be able to revert to the pre-change state.

The hardware on the domain controller is constantly being updated. As network administrator, you want to become more familiar with the use of the Last Known Good Configuration. You have developed the following scenario for practice.

learning objective

After completing this project, you will know how to use the Last Known Good Configuration to assist in recovery from several types of hardware problems.

specific requirements

Administrative rights on the craighead.com domain controller.

estimated completion time

15 minutes

project steps

Create a configuration problem.

1. Click **Start**, right-click **My Computer**, and select **Properties**. On the **Hardware** tab, select **Device Manager** to display the list of currently installed devices **(Figure 13-6)**.
2. Double-click **DVD/CD-ROM Drives** and right-click your existing CD-ROM driver **(Figure 13-7)**. Select **Disable** and click **Yes** to accept your selection.
3. In the text portion of the boot process, press **[F8]** when prompted to display the **Advanced Options Menu**. Select **Last Known Good Configuration** and press **[Enter]**. When prompted to **Please select the operating system to start**, select **Windows Server 2003, Enterprise [or Standard]**.
4. When the server completes the reboot process, logon as an **Administrator**. Check the status of the CD-ROM by clicking **Start**, right-clicking **My Computer**, and selecting **Properties**. On the **Hardware** tab, select **Device Manager** and expand **DVD/CD-ROM Drives**. Notice that the CD-ROM does not have a red “X” on the icon. A red “X” would indicate a disabled driver.

Figure 13-6 Device Manager

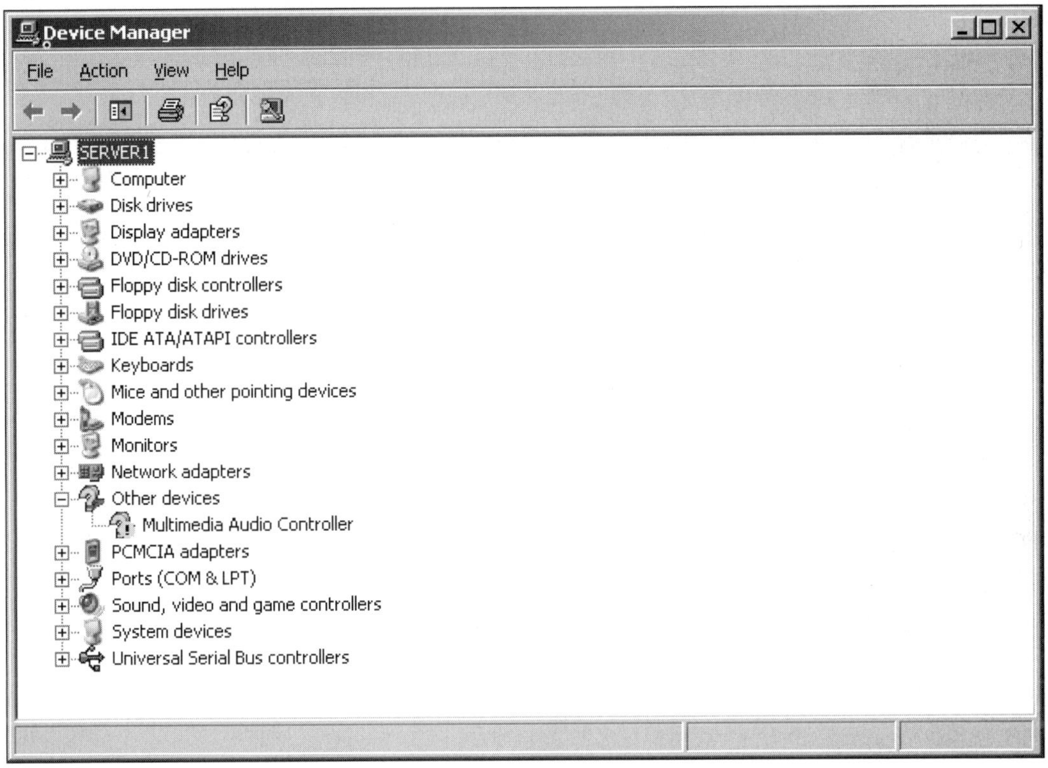

Figure 13-7 DVD/CD-ROM drives node expanded

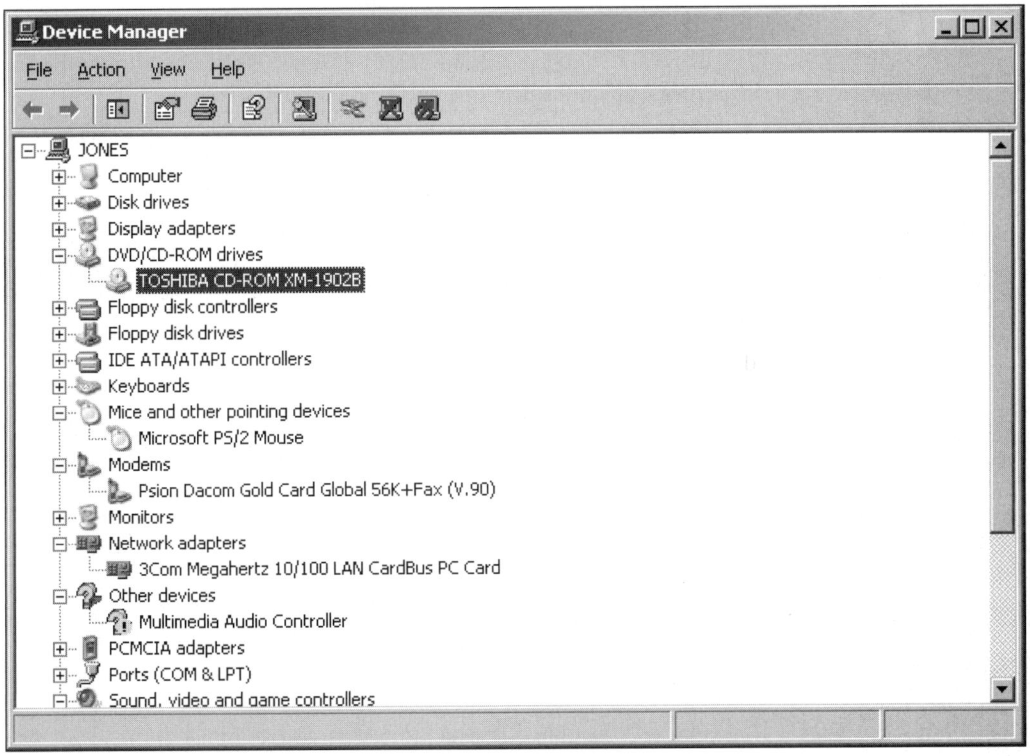

project 13.4 Working with the Recovery Console

exam objective

Perform system recovery for a server. Recover from server hardware failure.

overview

The Recovery Console enables booting the computer to allow the user to stop specific software or drivers from loading that are causing a problem. Since the Recovery Console open the Registry, you can use it to restore the Registry from a backup, if necessary. It is a command-line interface that allows limited access to the hard drive to view and repair certain files and folders.

As a preventive measure, you want to install the Recovery Console on every server, so that it will be included as a boot option. This will eliminate the necessity of having an installation CD available. After installation, you want to experiment with several of the Recovery Console commands you have learned.

learning objective

After completing this project, you will know how to install and use Recovery Console.

specific requirements

Administrative rights on the craighead.com domain controller, a blank floppy diskette, and a Windows 2003 Server installation CD-ROM.

estimated completion time

15 minutes

project steps

1. Insert the Windows Server 2003 installation CD in the CD-ROM drive.
2. Click **Start**, click **Run**, type ***x:*\i386\winnt32.exe /cmdcons** (where *x:* represents the letter of your CD-ROM drive) in the **Open** text box and click **OK**.
3. A **Windows Setup** screen will appear and ask if you wish to install the Recovery Console as a startup option. Click **Yes** to install.
4. Windows will attempt to obtain updated setup files from the Windows Update Web site. If you are not connected to the Internet, select **Skip this step and continue installing Windows** when prompted **(Figure 13-8)** and click **Next**.
5. Windows will now copy the necessary files to your hard drive. After completion, you will receive a message that the Recovery Console has been successfully installed. Click **OK**.
6. Click **Start** and then click **Shut Down**. Select **Restart** in the **What do you want the computer to do** drop-down box and select **Operating System: Reconfiguration** in the **Shutdown Event Tracker** drop-down box **(Figure 13-9)**. Click **OK**.
7. During the text portion of the boot process, select **Microsoft Windows Recovery Console** on the list of operating systems by using the down arrow key and then pressing **[Enter]**.
8. You will be prompted to select which installation you would like to log on to. If your system has only one operating system installed, type **1** and press **[Enter]**.
9. Enter the Directory Services Restore Mode password, **Restore**. Type **help**, then press **[Enter]** to get a list of available commands.
10. Type **chkdsk** and then press **[Enter]** to check the hard drive and display a status report.
11. To display a list of current environment variables, type **set** and then press **[Enter]**. This command also allows you to change current variable settings.
12. Type **listsvc** at the command prompt and then press **[Enter]** to see a partial listing of the services and drivers currently on the computer. To view additional services and drivers, press **[Enter]**. To stop the listing, press **[Esc]**. If a service or driver is causing a problem, you could use the **disable** command.
13. Type **exit** and then press **[Enter]** to restart your computer.

Figure 13-8 Getting Updated Setup Files screen

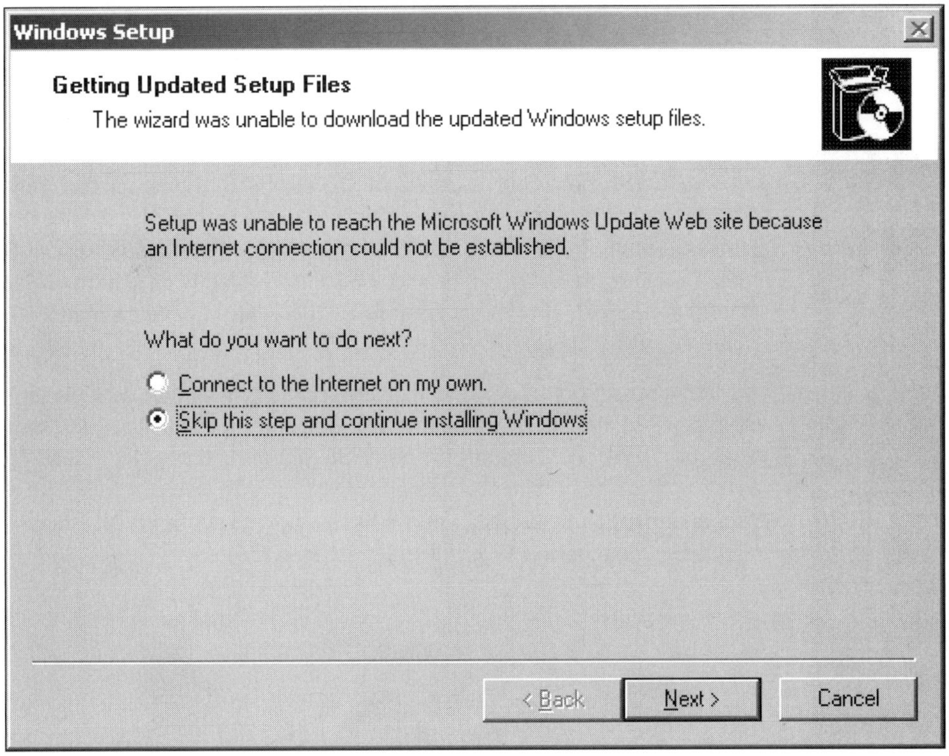

Figure 13-9 Shut Down Windows dialog box

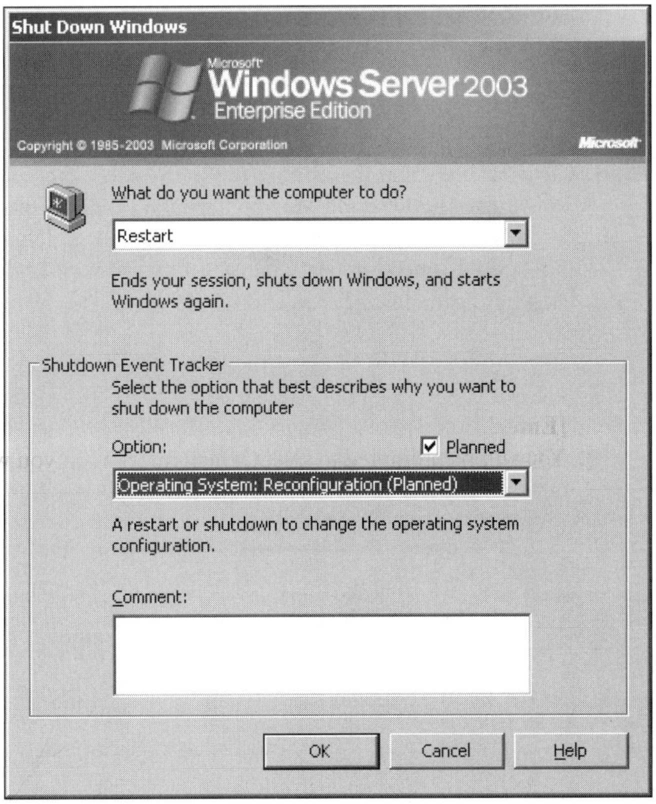

project 13.5 Configuring the Volume Shadow Copy Service

exam objective

Restore data from shadow copy volumes.

overview

The Volume Shadow Copy Service (VSS) provides two major features in Windows Server 2003. First, it can be used by applications to access locked files or files that are in use by other services. Secondly, you can configure VSS so that previous versions of saved files that are stored on a network share can be accessed and restored from shadow copies that are created at scheduled intervals. Previous versions of files that have been inadvertently deleted can be recovered on the file server.

Due to the possibility of accidental deletion of files at Craighead College, you have decided to implement Volume Shadow Copy Service on your domain controller. This is important because the domain controller contains the home directories and My Documents folder for all users.

learning objective

After completing this project, you will know how to configure Volume Shadow Copy Service to facilitate the recovery of accidentally deleted files.

specific requirements

Administrative rights on the craighead.com domain controller.

estimated completion time

15 minutes

project steps

1. Click **Start**, right-click **My Computer**, and click **Manage** to open the **Computer Management** console.
2. Click the **Disk Management** option in the left pane of the console. Right-click the volume in the right pane and then click **Properties**.
3. On the **Shadow Copies** tab, click **C:** in the **Select a volume** text box. Click **Enable** and click **Yes** to confirm in the **Enable Shadow Copies** dialog box.
4. Click **Settings** and then **Schedule** to change the configuration. The default schedule is 7:00 am and 12:00 noon Monday through Friday **(Figure 13-10)**.
5. Click **New** to create a new schedule and in the **Schedule Task** list box, select **Daily**. In the **Start time** spin box, enter **4:00 AM (Figure 13-11)**.
6. Close all open dialog boxes and windows.

Figure 13-10 Default schedule for Volume Shadow Copy Service

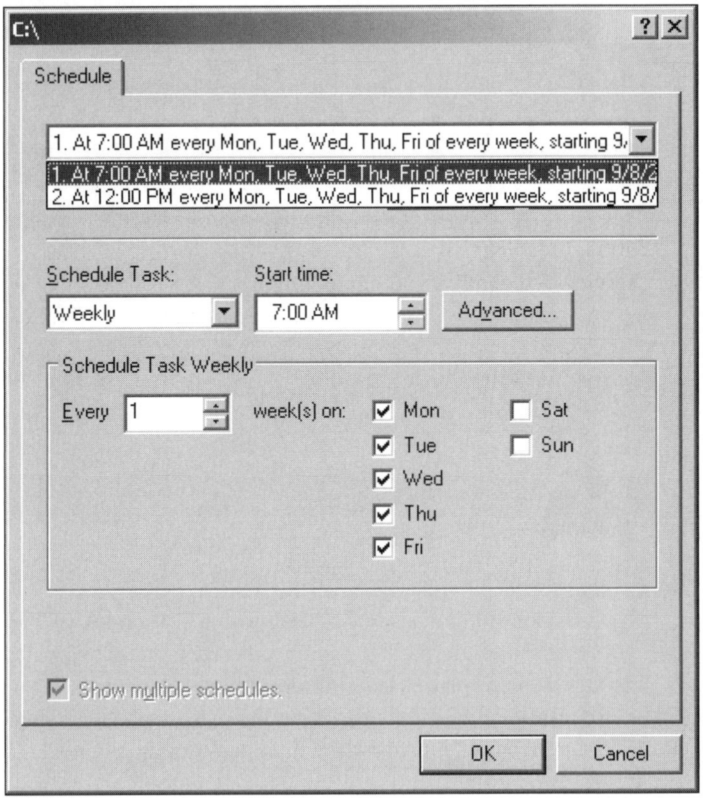

Figure 13-11 Revised Volume Shadow Copy Service schedule

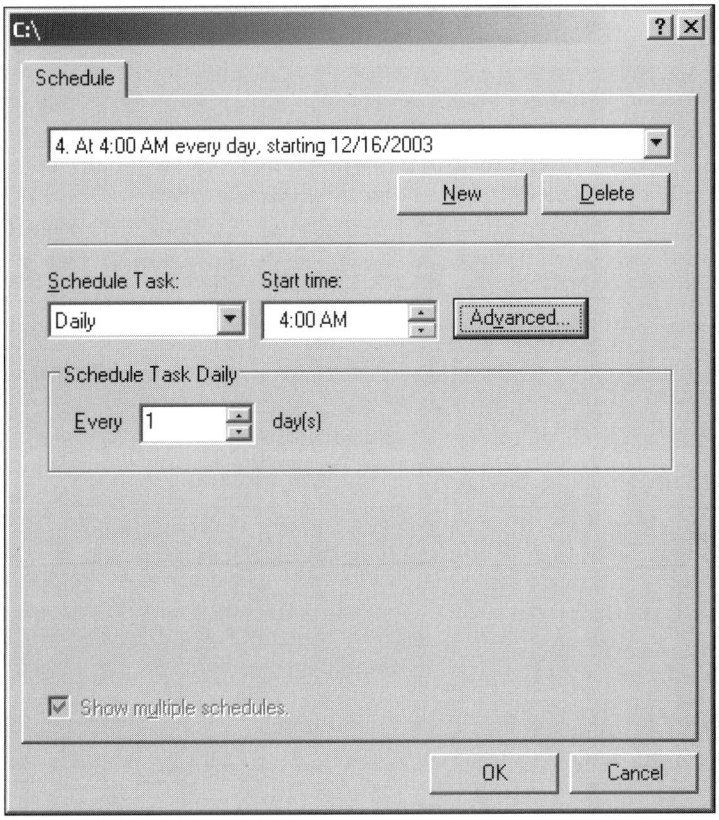

LESSON

14 Monitoring Windows Server 2003 Performance

As a network administrator, an important part of your job is to ensure that the servers on the network are functioning optimally. This includes optimizing the storage on the network and monitoring systems to anticipate and resolve resource problems. Windows Server 2003 provides useful tools to monitor the server's performance.

System Monitor can be used to diagnose a bottleneck on the network. A bottleneck refers to an overtaxed resource that causes other resources to be delayed. Task Manager is used to manage system processes and monitor performances. You can use Task Manager to stop malfunctioning applications or stalled processes. The Check Disk and Disk Defragmenter tools are used to improve hard disk performance. Check Disk inspects your hard disk for errors and bad sectors, while Disk Defragmenter rearranges disk space to decrease the access time needed to read from the disk. Compression can be used to conserve disk space, while disk quotas can be used to limit the amount of space for each user. Auditing can observe and record the events that occur on the network. These events are recorded in the Security event log.

Scenario

To ensure that the network at Craighead College operates at optimum efficiency, you have decided to become more familiar with the various performance monitoring tools provided by Windows Server 2003. It is your plan to use these tools on a regularly scheduled basis.

Lesson 14 Monitoring Windows Server 2003 Performance

Project	Exam 70-290 Objective
14.1 Optimizing Hard Disk Performance	Optimize server disk performance. Defragment volumes and partitions.
14.2 Optimizing Disk Storage Performance	Optimize server disk performance. Monitor disk quotas.
14.3 Working with Task Manager	Monitor file and print servers. Monitor server hardware for bottlenecks. Monitor and optimize a server environment for application performance.
14.4 Working with Performance Logs and Alerts	Monitor file and print servers. Monitor server hardware for bottlenecks. Monitor system performance. Monitor memory performance objects. Monitor and optimize a server environment for application performance.
14.5 Tracking Windows Server 2003 Activities with Audit Policy	Basic knowledge
14.6 Viewing the Security Log	Basic knowledge

General Requirements

To complete the projects in this lesson, you need administrative rights on the domain controller for Craighead College. In addition, you also may find it helpful to refer to Lesson 14 in your Prentice Hall Certification Series textbook for further information about the topics covered by the projects in this lesson.

project 14.1 Optimizing Hard Disk Performance

exam objective

Optimize server disk performance. Defragment volumes and partitions.

overview

Windows Server 2003 includes three major utilities to optimize hard disk performance. These are Check Disk, Disk Cleanup, and Disk Defragmenter.

Check Disk is a tool designed to check the hard disk for file system errors and bad sectors on volumes formatted with FAT, FAT32, or NTFS. Check Disk identifies errors and fixes them automatically.

Disk Cleanup is designed to clean out old files on the hard disk in order to create more free storage space. It locates files you are likely to want to delete, such as temporary Internet files, temporary files, and downloaded program files.

Disk Defragmenter reorganizes files on a partition or volume that has become fragmented. Fragmentation occurs because files are saved in the first available space on the hard drive by the controller. This causes pieces, or fragments, of large files to be scattered over different parts of the hard disk. As the files become increasingly fragmented, the computer takes longer to access the files.

As network administrator for Craighead College, you decide to call a meeting of the members of your IT Staff to demonstrate the use of the various utilities that optimize hard disk performance. The domain controller for Craighead College will be used to demonstrate the utilities.

learning objective

After completing this project, you will know how to optimize hard disk performance using the utilities included with Windows Server 2003.

specific requirements

See general requirements.

estimated completion time

30–45 minutes (depending upon size of hard disk)

project steps

Run Check Disk.

1. Click **Start**, click **My Computer**, and click **Properties**.
2. Right-click **Local Disk (C:)** and click **Properties**. On the **Tools** tab, click the **Check Now** button associated with **Error-checking** to open the **Check Disk Local Disk (C:)** dialog box **(Figure 14-1)**.
3. Place a check mark in the **Scan for and attempt recovery of bad sectors** check box, and click **Start**. This process will take several minutes to complete. Click **OK** when finished.

Run Disk Cleanup.

4. On the **General** tab, click **Disk Cleanup**. **Disk Cleanup** will scan your hard disk to calculate how much space you will be able to recover. This process will take several minutes. After completion, the results will be displayed.
5. On the **Disk Cleanup** tab **(Figure 14-2)**, place a check mark in the appropriate box for each of the following, and then click **OK** and **Yes** to confirm:
   - Downloaded Program Files
   - Temporary Internet Files
   - Temporary Files

Figure 14-1 Check Disk options

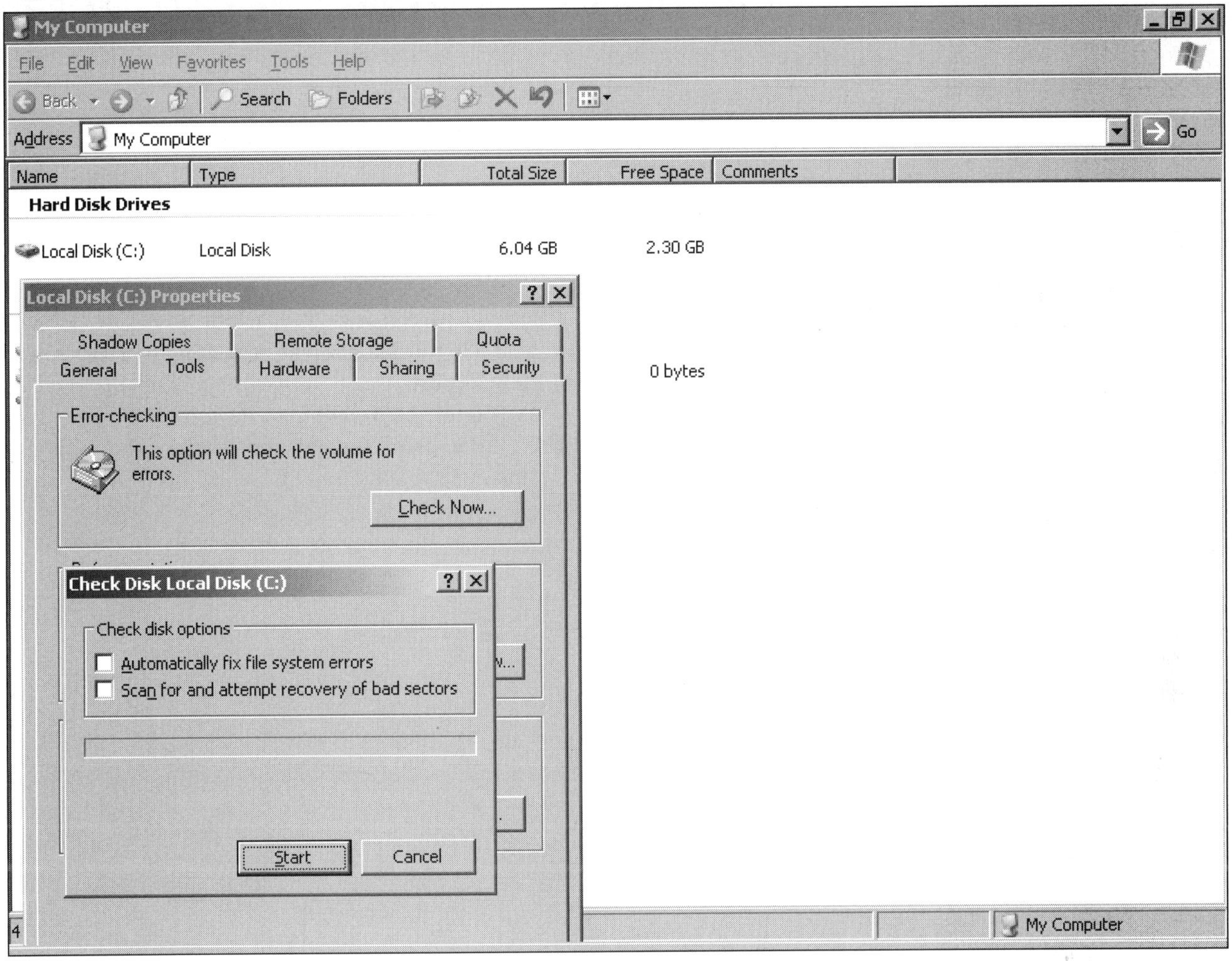

Figure 14-2 Disk Cleanup results

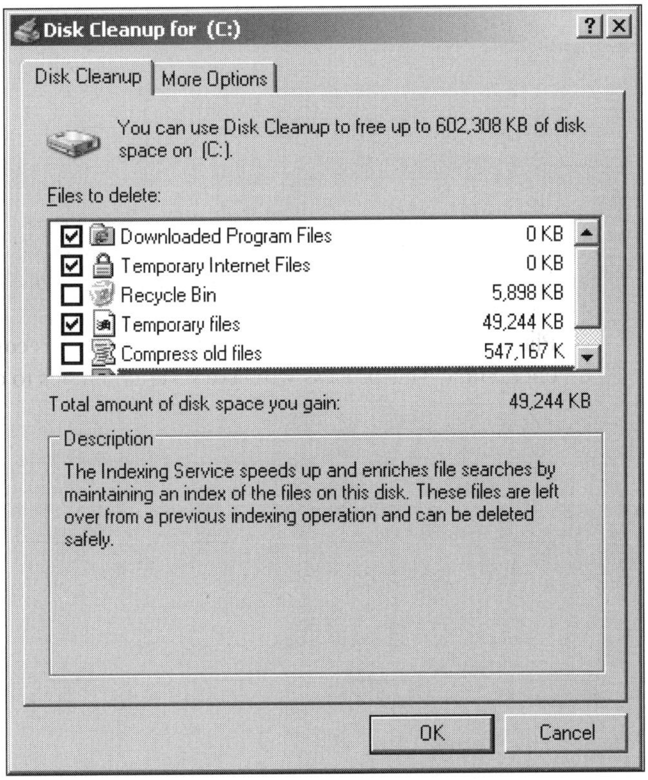

project 14.1

Optimizing Hard Disk Performance

(cont'd)

exam objective

Optimize server disk performance. Defragment volumes and partitions.

project steps

Run Disk Defragmenter.

6. On the **Tools** tab, click **Defragment Now**. With the **C:** volume highlighted, click **Analyze**.
7. After the analysis is complete, you will receive a screen indicating whether you should defragment the volume. Click **View Report**.
8. The **Analysis Report** dialog box **(Figure 14-3)** will provide volume information and a list of the most fragmented files. Because defragmentation can take several hours, you will not perform the process at this time. Click **Close**. Close all open dialog boxes and windows.

Figure 14-3 Analysis Report dialog box

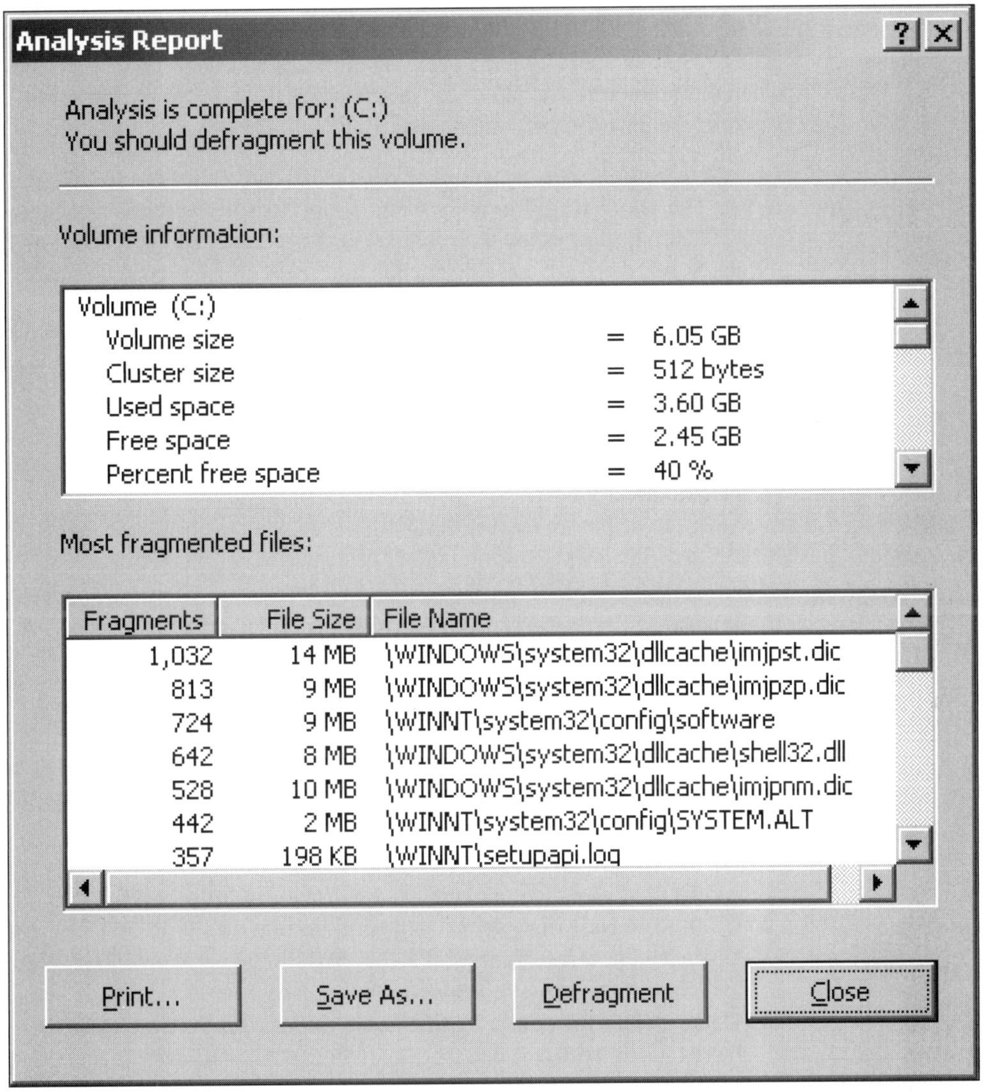

project 14.2

Optimizing Disk Storage Performance

exam objective

Optimize server disk performance. Monitor disk quotas.

overview

To help in optimizing disk storage, there are two primary tools: data compression and disk quotas. On NTFS volumes, you can store files and folders in a compressed state to conserve storage space. You can use disk quotas to optimize disk storage by allocating a specific amount of disk space to each user. Disk quotas can deny further storage space to the user when this amount is reached. You can also use disk quotas to track disk usage without denying space to users who exceed their quota limit.

As network administrator, you have decided to limit all users to 500 MB of storage on the server. The only exception, other than members of the administrator group, will be AmyB. Because AmyB teaches the architectural design course, you will be allowing 2 GB of storage for her. In addition, you have decided to compress all files located in the deploy folder on the server.

learning objective

After completing this project, you will know how to optimize disk storage performance by enabling disk quotas.

specific requirements

See general requirements.

estimated completion time

15 minutes

project steps

Set up disk quotas.

1. Click **Start** and then click **My Computer**. In the left pane of the window, right-click **Local Disk (C:)** and click **Properties**.
2. On the **Quota** tab **(Figure 14-4)**, place check marks in the **Enable quota management** and **Deny disk space to users exceeding quota limit** check boxes.
3. Click the **Limit disk space to** option button, and type **500** in the text box provided. Change the measurement from **KB** to **MB**. In the **Set warning level to** text box, type **400** and change the measurement from **KB** to **MB**.
4. Under **Select the quota logging options for this volume**, place a check mark in both boxes. Click **Apply**. A message box will appear, warning you that you should only enable disk quotas if you intend to use quotas on the volume **(Figure 14-5)**. Click **OK** to confirm. The operating system will now calculate the current disk usage for every user. Notice that the traffic light changes from red to green to indicate that disk quotas are now enabled.
5. Click **Quota Entries** to specify a different quota for the **AmyB** user account. Click **Quota** on the Menu bar, and then click **New Quota Entry**. Type **AmyB** in the **Enter the object names to select** text box and click **OK**.
6. The **Add New Quota Entry** dialog box opens **(Figure 14-6)**. Click the **Limit disk space to** option button and type **2** in the text box. Change the measurement to **GB**. In the **Set warning level to** text box, type **1.5**, and change the measurement to **GB**. Click **OK**. Close all open dialog boxes and windows.

Figure 14-4 Quota tab

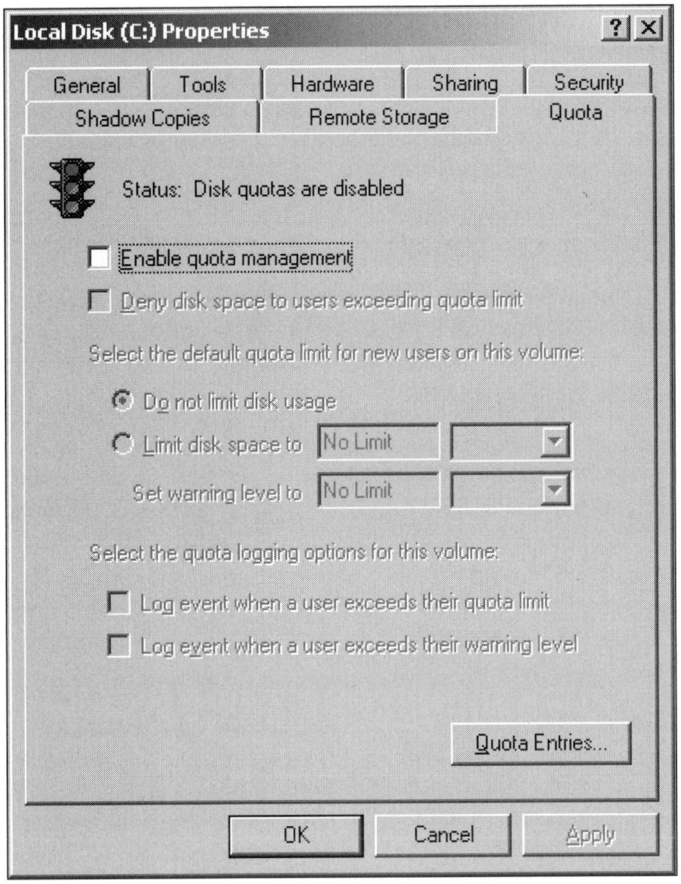

Figure 14-5 Disk Quota warning message

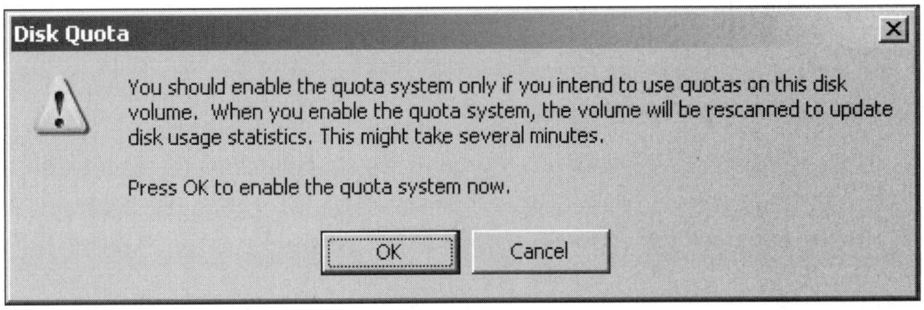

Figure 14-6 Add New Quota Entry dialog box

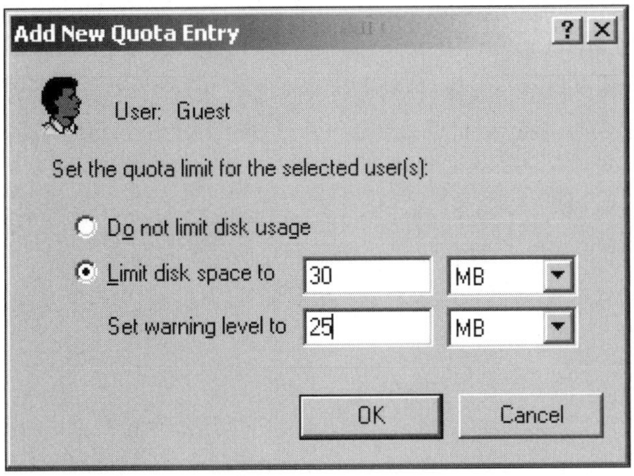

project 14.3 Working with Task Manager

exam objective

Monitor file and print servers. Monitor server hardware for bottlenecks. Monitor and optimize a server environment for application performance.

overview

Task Manager can be used for a variety of purposes. You can use Task Manager to view the status of applications, and stop and start them. You can view information about the processes that are currently running on a computer. Graphs of the CPU and memory usage are also available in Task Manager. Network interface cards (NICs) can be monitored along with total network utilization. Finally, current users can be viewed and, if necessary, disconnected.

You want to better acquaint your IT Staff with the various functions of Task Manager. You will hold a short briefing to demonstrate how it can be used.

learning objective

After completing this project, you will know how to use Task Manager to monitor your computer.

specific requirements

See general requirements.

estimated completion time

20 minutes

project steps

1. Right-click in an empty space on the Taskbar and click **Task Manager**.
2. Click **Start**, point to **All Programs**, point to **Accessories**, and then click **Calculator**. The **Calculator** task will appear on the **Applications** tab of the **Windows Task Manager** dialog box.
3. On the **Processes** tab, you will see a listing of all of the currently running processes **(Figure 14-7)**. This tab also indicates the amount of memory used by the individual processes.
4. To determine which process(es) are associated with currently running applications, right-click **Calculator** on the **Applications** tab and click **Go to Process**. The processes associated with the selected application will be highlighted on the **Processes** tab **(Figure 14-8)**.
5. To terminate the Calculator application, click **Calculator** on the **Applications** tab. Click **End Task**.
6. On the **Performance** tab, a graph of the current CPU and page file usage is displayed **(Figure 14-9)**. In addition, memory usage information is displayed.
7. On the **User** tab, a list of currently connected user accounts is displayed. If you want to close any files a user has open and log the user off, you would click the **Logoff** button.
8. On the **Networking** tab, you can monitor the NICs installed on the server.
9. After you have finished reviewing the contents of each tab, close all open dialog boxes and windows.

Figure 14-7 Task Manager Processes tab

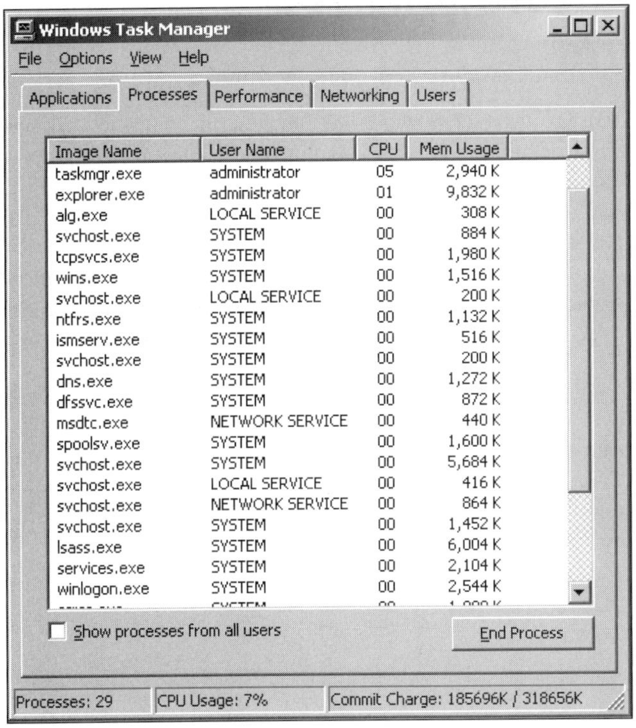

Figure 14-8 Processes associated with various applications

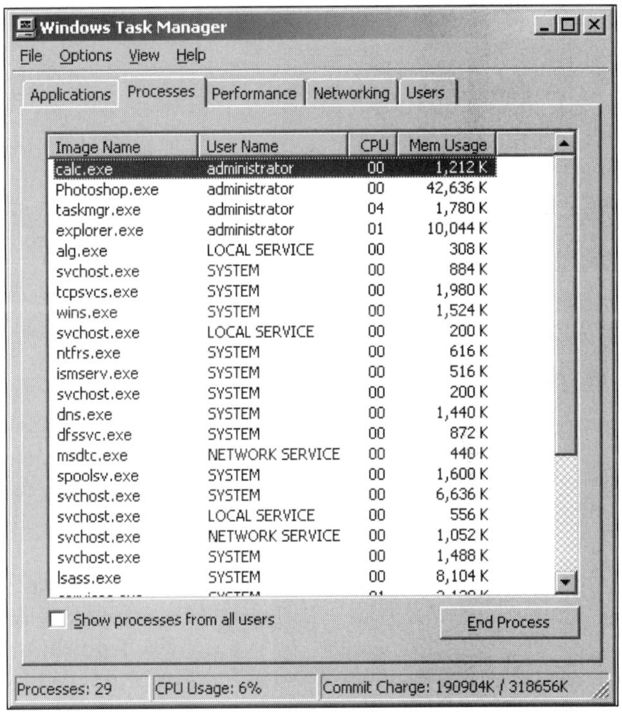

Figure 14-9 Task Manager Performance tab

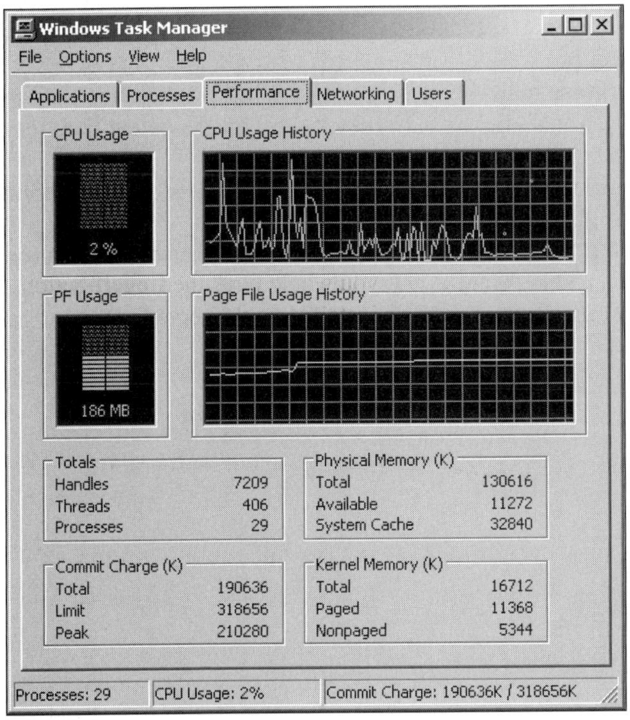

project 14.4 Working with Performance Logs and Alerts

exam objective

Monitor file and print servers. Monitor server hardware for bottlenecks. Monitor system performance. Monitor memory performance objects. Monitor and optimize a server environment for application performance.

overview

While System Monitor displays real-time representations of the performance measures for various objects, Performance Logs and Alerts are used to store the data for future reference. In addition, you can create an alert for situations in which the operating system will monitor user-defined critical factors and notify you when a critical threshold has been reached.

One of the security problems at Craighead College involves guessing passwords to crack security on the server. You want to set up an automatic alert that informs you when a password-guessing program has been used.

learning objective

After completing this project, you will know how to create alerts.

specific requirements

See general requirements.

estimated completion time

15 minutes

project steps

1. Click **Start**, click **Run**, type **mmc** in the **Open** text box, and click **OK**.
2. Click **File**, click **Add/Remove Snap-in**, and then click **Add** to display a list of available snap-ins.
3. Click **Performance Logs and Alerts**, click **Add**, click **Close**, and then click **OK**. In the **Console1** window, click **File** on the Menu bar, click **Save**, and then type **Performance Monitor** in the text box. Click **Save**.
4. Expand **Performance Logs and Alerts** in the left pane of the window. Right-click **Alerts** and click **New Alert Settings**. Type **Hacker Alert** in the text box and click **OK**.
5. On the **General** tab of the **Hacker Alert** dialog box **(Figure 14-10)**, type **Password Cracker Alert** in the **Comment** box.
6. Click **Add**. In the **Add Counters** dialog box **(Figure 14-11)**, select **Server** on the **Performance object** drop-down list. Highlight **Errors Logon** on the **Select counters from list** drop-down list, and click **Add**. Click **Close**.
7. Make sure that the **Alert when the value is** text box contains **Over** and type **3** in the **Limit** text box. The default sample interval is 5 seconds.
8. On the **Action** tab **(Figure 14-12)**, place a check mark in the **Send a network message to** check box, and type the domain controller's name in the text box. Click **OK**. Close all open dialog boxes and windows, and save changes to **Performance Monitor** when prompted.

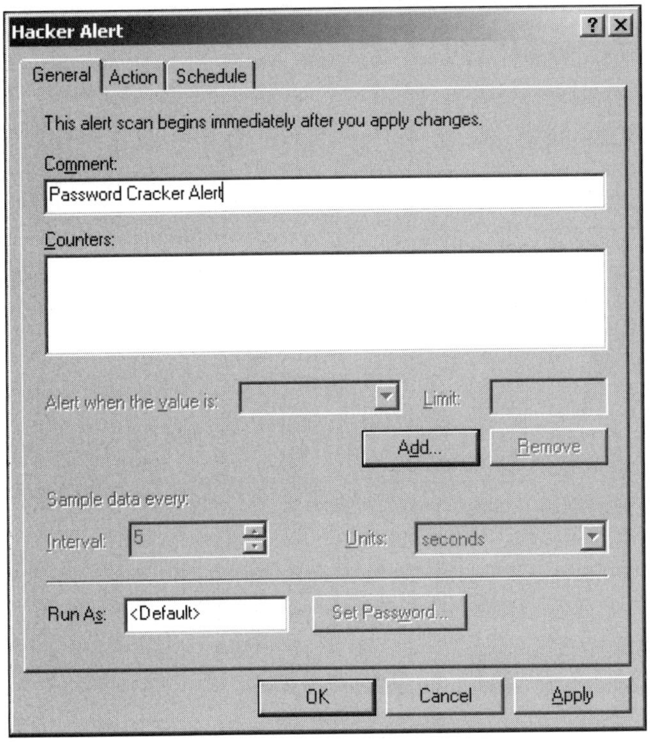

Figure 14-10 Hacker Alert dialog box

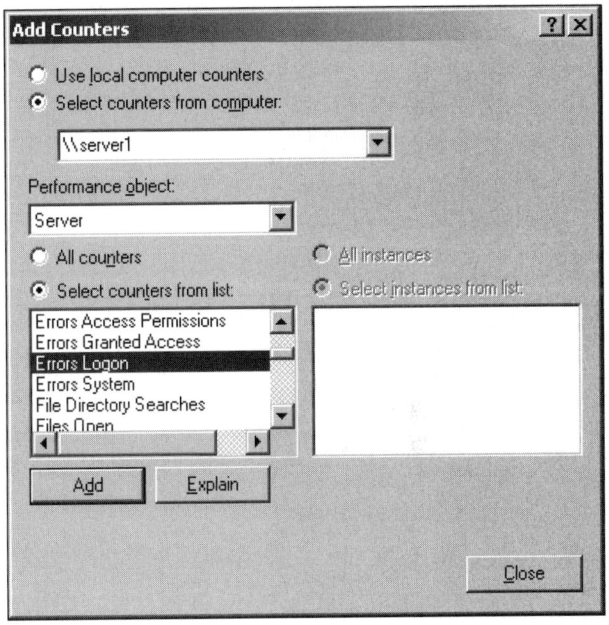

Figure 14-11 Add Counters dialog box

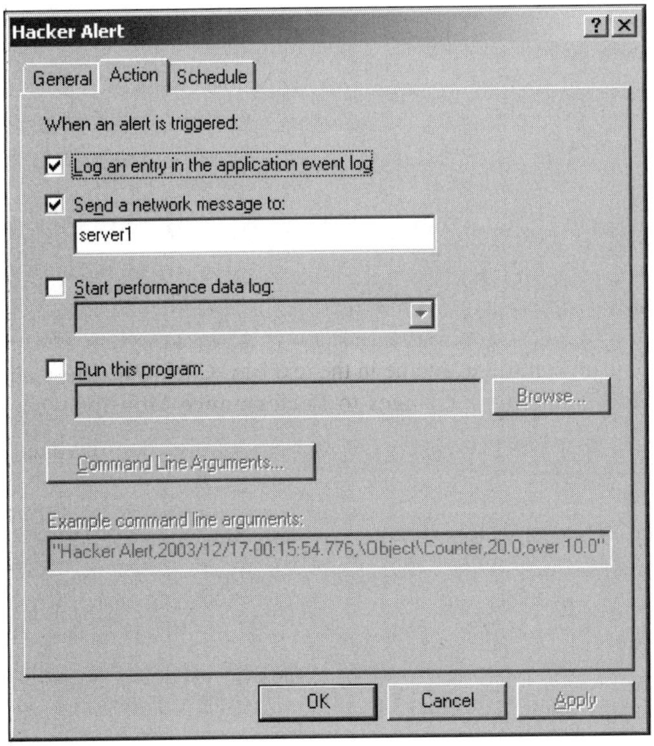

Figure 14-12 Action tab in the Hacker Alert dialog box

project 14.5

Tracking Windows Server 2003 Activities with Audit Policy

exam objective

Basic knowledge

overview

Users perform a number of different activities, including logging on to the domain, accessing files, using printers, or accessing Active Directory. These events can be monitored at the network administrator's discretion. As network administrator, you may want to track and monitor certain events on a regular basis to ensure the security and seamless functioning of the computers on the network. Auditing is used to track these activities or events.

When creating your audit policy, you must determine what events you wish to monitor. In addition, you must determine what group of users, if not everyone, you wish to monitor. Also, you can monitor the success or failure of an event. The most common reason to monitor the failure of an event is security related. For example, someone may be attempting to access a file for which they do not have the proper rights. A common reason to monitor the success of an event is to conduct resource planning. For example, you may monitor successful access to a file or folder to determine what group of users, if any, is utilizing that file or folder.

Protection against unauthorized logon attempts is important. As an added security precaution, you have decided to audit failed logon attempts to the domain controller.

learning objective

After completing this project, you will know how to implement an audit policy.

specific requirements

See general requirements.

estimated completion time

15 minutes

project steps

1. Click **Start**, point to **Administrative Tools**, and then click **Active Directory Users and Computers**.
2. Right-click the **Domain Controllers** organizational unit and click **Properties**. On the **Group Policy** tab, click **Edit**.
3. Expand the **Computer Configuration**, **Windows Settings**, **Security Settings**, and **Local Policies** nodes. Click **Audit Policy (Figure 14-13)**.
4. In the right pane of the **Group Policy Object Editor** window, double-click **Audit account logon events** and place a check mark in the **Failure** check box. Click **OK**. Close the **Group Policy Object Editor** and click **OK** in the **Domain Controllers Properties** dialog box. Close all open dialog boxes and windows.
5. Log off as an **Administrator** and attempt to log on as **BadUser** with no password. When the error message box appears, click **OK**. Attempt to log on as an **Administrator** with no password. When the error message box appears, click **OK**.
6. Log on as an **Administrator** successfully. Click **Start**, point to **Administrative Tools**, and then click **Event Viewer**. Click **Security** in the left pane. Scan the list of events in the right pane of the window. Double-click the first one entitled **Failure Audit** to open the **Event Properties** dialog box. This event was caused by attempting to log on as an **Administrator** with no password.
7. Click the down arrow button to view the next **Failure Audit**. This **Event Properties** entry was created when you attempted to log on as **BadUser**. Close all open dialog boxes and windows.

Figure 14-13 Audit Policy

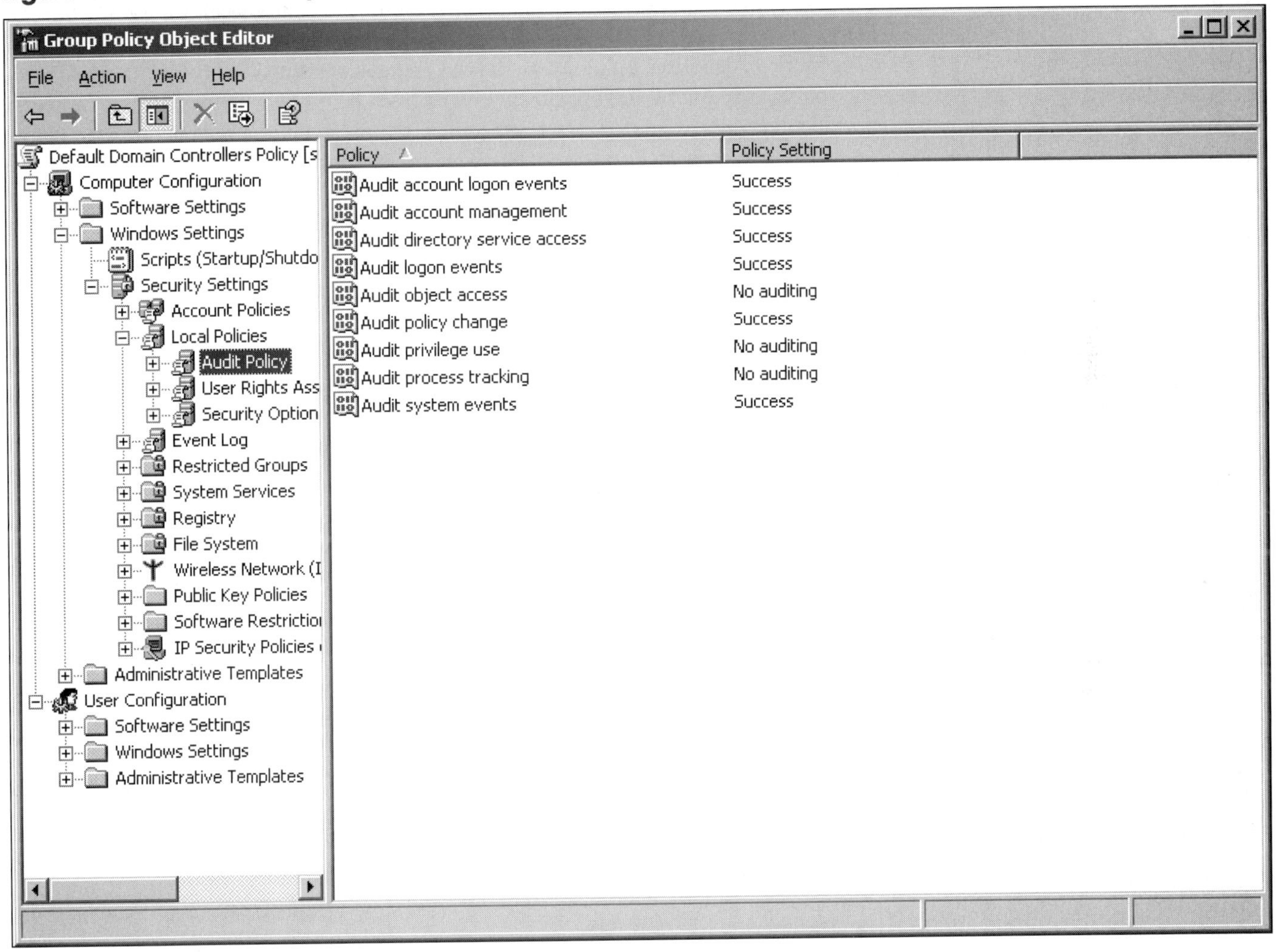

project 14.6 Viewing the Security Log

exam objective

Basic knowledge

overview

When auditing is enabled, the overhead on the CPU will be greatly increased. This emphasizes the fact that you should only audit those events that are most important. Once you have selected the events you wish to audit, you must set a schedule to check the Security log regularly. You can specify a maximum file size for the log. When the maximum size is reached, you can choose to either overwrite old records as needed, set a specific age for the events you want to overwrite, or prevent events from being overwritten. If you choose to overwrite old records as needed or set a specific age, you could lose data before you archive it. If you choose to prevent events from being recorded, you must make sure that you monitor the Security log often enough to archive and clear the log before it becomes full. If not, when the log is full, the operating system will stop recording events.

At Craighead College, you have decided to archive and clear the Security log every Friday afternoon. You have also decided to dedicate 250 MB of storage for the Security log.

learning objective

After completing this project, you will know how to change the properties of the Security log. In addition, you will know how to archive and clear the entries in the log.

specific requirements

See general requirements.

estimated completion time

15 minutes

project steps

1. Click **Start**, point to **Administrative Tools**, and then click **Event Viewer**.
2. Right-click **Security** in the left pane of the window and click **Properties**.
3. In the **Security Properties** dialog box (**Figure 14-14**), change the **Maximum log size** to **250000**. Select the **Do not overwrite events (clear log manually)** option button. Click **OK**. You will receive a message stating that the log size must be in 64K increments and the amount entered will be rounded. Click **OK**.
4. Right-click **Security** and click **Clear all events**. When prompted to **save "Security" before clearing it?**, click **Yes**.
5. In the **Save "Security" As** dialog box, type **C:\SecurityLog** in the **File name** text box and click **Save**. When you click **Security**, the only entry will be a **Success Audit** that states the security audit log was cleared. Close all open windows.

caution

You would not normally archive the Security log to the hard disk of the local computer. This is done for demonstration purposes only.

Figure 14-14 Security log properties

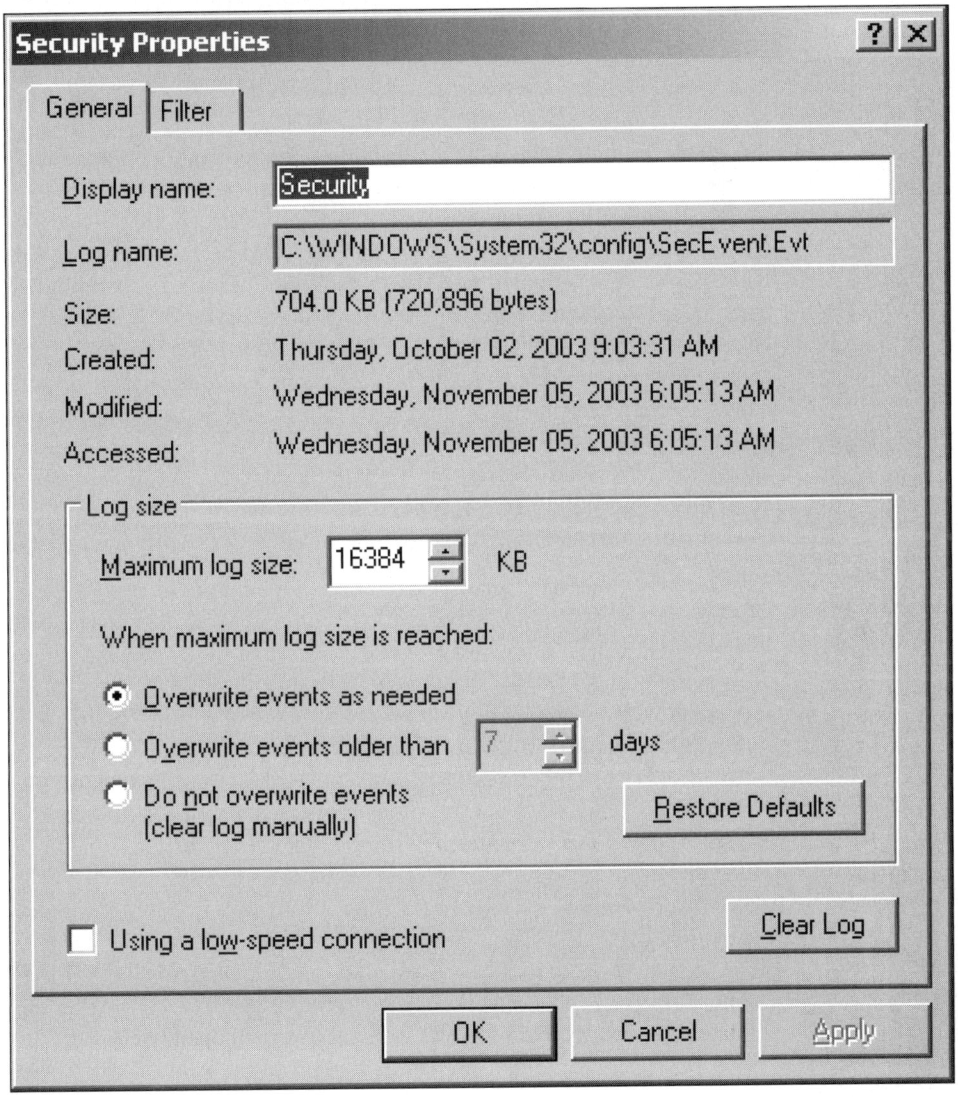

LESSON

15 Configuring a Windows Server 2003 Application Server

Terminal Services is the Windows Server 2003 component that enables users to execute applications on a remote server. Terminal Services supports a full range of clients, including so-called "thin clients" as well as Windows 98, NT, CE, 2000, and XP Professional computers. With the help of third-party software, it will also support Unix, Unix-based, X-terminals, and Macintosh computers. The Terminal Services software is installed on the client, the client receives the Windows GUI from the terminal server, users enter keystrokes and mouse clicks, and the commands are sent to the terminal server for execution. Another benefit is the ability to run applications on older computers and on legacy hardware, thus reducing hardware expense. Terminal Services also provides an easier way to update software. It also includes two important tools: Remote Desktop for Administration and Remote Desktop Assistance. Remote Desktop for Administration is used to manage a computer from nearly any computer on your network and Remote Assistance allows a trusted party to remotely access your system in order to provide assistance.

Another important Windows Server 2003 component is Internet Information Services (IIS) 6.0. IIS allows the Windows Server 2003 computer to function as a Web Server. It includes WWW, FTP, NNTP and SMTP services, and FrontPage 2002 Server Extensions. IIS 6.0 management and security features help ensure the reliability of the content on the Web server, as well as enhancing the security of the Web environment. This allows users to safely publish and share information over an intranet or the Internet.

Scenario

Since the computer labs at Craighead College are located in several different buildings, you have decided to install Terminal Services to allow you to manage all computers from a central location. Also, the current domain controller will serve as the host for Web services for the college. As network administrator, you will install and configure Internet Information Services on the domain controller.

Lesson 15 Configuring a Windows Server 2003 Application Server

Project	Exam 70-290 Objective
15.1 Working with Remote Desktop for Administration	Manage servers remotely. Manage a server by using Terminal Services remote administration mode. Manage a server by using available support tools.
15.2 Configuring Terminal Services	Manage a server by using available support tools.
15.3 Managing IIS	Manage a Web server. Manage IIS. Manage security for IIS.
15.4 Configuring IIS Security	Manage a Web server. Manage IIS. Manage security for IIS.
15.5 Administering the Web Environment	Manage a Web server. Manage IIS. Manage security for IIS.

General Requirements

To complete the projects in this lesson, you will need administrative rights on the domain controller for Craighead College and the Windows Server 2003 installation CD-ROM. IIS 6.0 must be installed on the domain controller. You may also find it helpful to refer to Lesson 15 of your Prentice Hall Certification Series Exam 70-290 textbook for further information about the topics covered by the projects in this lesson.

project 15.1

Working with Remote Desktop for Administration

exam objective

Manage servers remotely. Manage a server by using Terminal Services remote administration mode. Manage a server by using available support tools.

overview

Remote Desktop for Administration allows the user to manage a computer remotely from anywhere on the network. Almost any task can be performed, including the shut down and restart of a server on the network. An administrator can configure, maintain, and troubleshoot a computer from home or while on the road. No additional licensing is required for Remote Desktop for Administration and the service is disabled by default in Windows Server 2003.

You have decided to allow Remote Desktop for Administration on all computers within the craighead.com domain. The first step will be to allow remote administration on the domain controller and to test the installation of the connection client.

learning objective

After completing this project, you will know how to enable Remote Desktop for Administration and install the Remote Desktop Connection client.

specific requirements

See general requirements.

estimated completion time

15 minutes

project steps

Enable Remote Desktop for Administration on the server.

1. Click **Start**, right-click **My Computer**, and click **Properties**.
2. On the **Remote** tab **(Figure 15-1)**, place a check mark in the **Allow users to connect remotely to this computer** check box.
3. The **Remote Sessions** dialog box will inform you that only accounts that have passwords will be allowed to connect. Click **OK**. Click **OK** to close the **System Properties** dialog box.

Install the Remote Desktop connection client.

4. Click **Start** and then click **Windows Explorer**. Expand **My Computer**, **Local Disk (C:)**, **Windows**, **System32**, **clients**, and **ts client**.
5. Click **win32** in the left pane of the Window Explorer window. In the right pane, double-click **setup** to start the **Remote Desktop Connection – InstallShield Wizard**. Click **Next**.
6. After reading the **License Agreement**, click the **I accept the terms in the license agreement** option button **(Figure 15-2)**, and click **Next**.
7. In the **Customer Information** screen, ensure that **Anyone who uses this computer (all users)** is selected, click **Next**, and then click **Install**. After the installation is completed, click **Finish** and close all open dialog boxes and windows.

caution

Normally you would use the administrator's computer, not the domain controller, to administer other computers in the domain. However, for the purposes of this project, you will install the client on the domain controller.

Figure 15-1 Remote tab in the System Properties dialog box

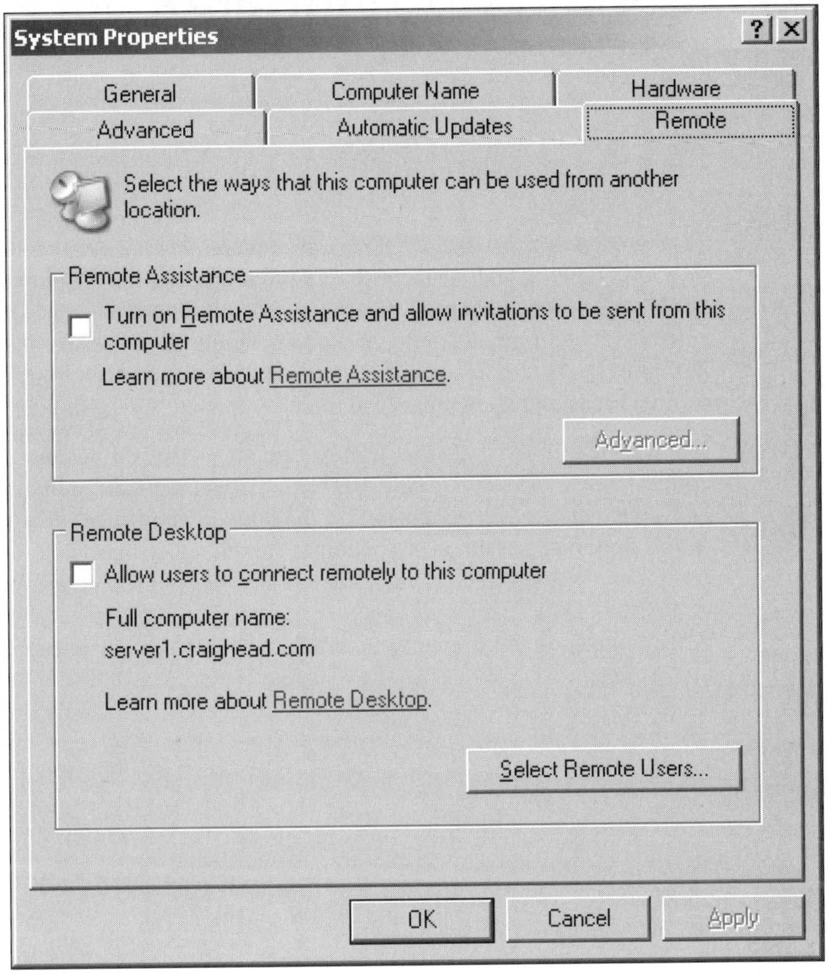

Figure 15-2 Remote Desktop Connection License Agreement

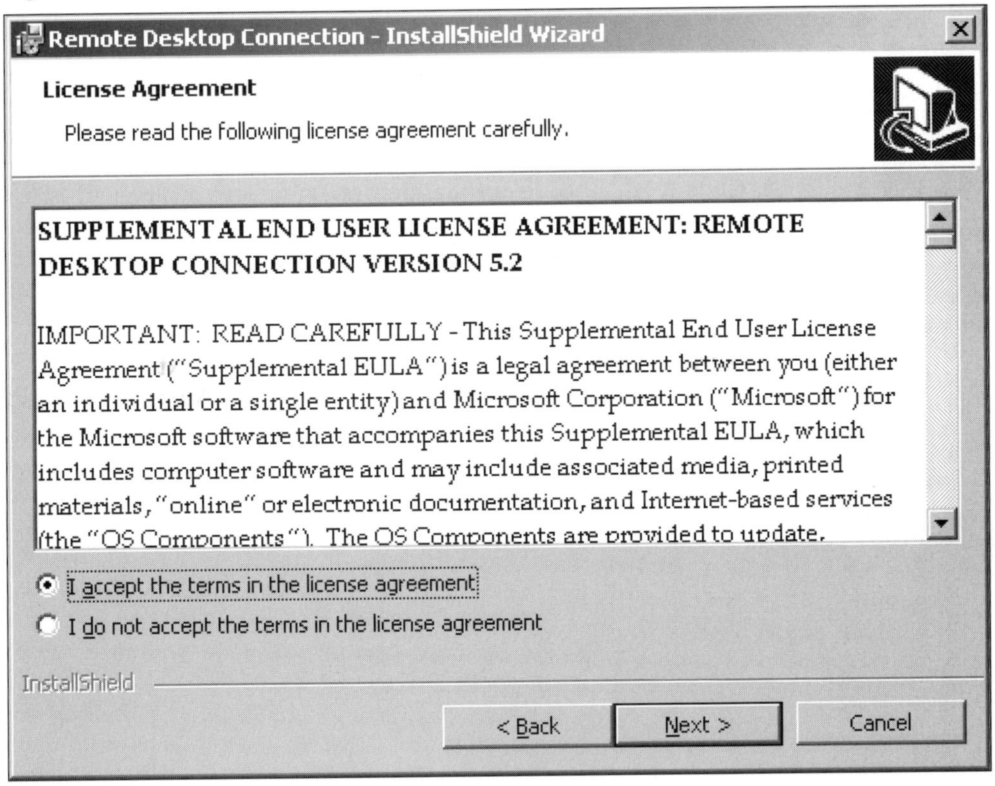

project 15.2 Configuring Terminal Services

exam objective

Manage a server by using available support tools.

overview

Terminal Services is used to deliver and manage Windows-based applications by delivering a Windows desktop and Windows-based programs to various computers. These computers do not have to meet the normal requirements to run these applications, since they will be executed remotely. Terminal Services supports multi-session access to applications, which allows multiple clients to access multiple applications concurrently. Terminal Services comes with its own licensing requirements and these components are detailed in **Table 15.1**.

Since there still exist several legacy computers that do not meet the requirements to run certain critical Windows-based applications, you have decided to install Terminal Services and Terminal Services Licensing on the domain controller. Note that normally you should install Terminal Services on a member server rather than on a domain controller because processing Active Directory requests will slow down the response to terminal sessions.

learning objective

After completing this project, you will know how to install and configure Terminal Services.

specific requirements

See general requirements.

estimated completion time

25 minutes

project steps

1. Click **Start**, point to **Control Panel**, and then click **Add or Remove Programs**.
2. Click **Add/Remove Windows Components** to start the **Windows Components Wizard**.
3. In the **Components** list, locate **Terminal Server** and **Terminal Server Licensing**. Place a check mark in the corresponding boxes. If **Internet Explorer Enhanced Security Configuration** is enabled, a **Configuration Warning** message box will appear, as shown in **Figure 15-3**. Click **Yes** to proceed.
4. Click **Next**. In the **Terminal Server setup** screen, you will be informed that only members of the local Administrators group will be able to connect to this terminal server. Click **Next**.
5. In the **Terminal Server Setup** screen, select **Full Security** to provide the most secure environment for Terminal Services. Click **Next**.
6. In the **Terminal Server Licensing Setup** screen, indicate that the license will serve **Your entire enterprise (Figure 15-4)**. Accept the default location for the license installation and click **Next**.
7. Insert the Windows Server 2003 installation CD-ROM, when prompted. When completed, click **Finish**. Remove the CD-ROM and click **Yes** to restart your computer when prompted.

Table 15-1 Components of Terminal Services Licensing

Component	Description
Microsoft Clearinghouse	A database maintained by Microsoft that stores information about all activated license servers and client license key packs that have been issued. The Microsoft Clearinghouse, which is accessed by running the Licensing Wizard in the Terminal Services Licensing snap-in, activates license servers and distributes client license key packs.
Terminal server	A Windows Server 2003 computer on which Terminal Services is installed and configured. When a user logs on to the Terminal Server, the client license must be validated. If no client license is presented, the Terminal Server contacts the license server to have one issued.
License server	All Terminal Services client licenses that have been installed for a Terminal Server are stored on a license server. The license server also monitors licenses that have been issued to client computers and terminals. The license server, which must be activated through the Microsoft Clearinghouse, must be connected to all Terminal Servers on the network.
Client licenses	Each terminal or client computer that connects to a Terminal Server must have a license. The license is stored on the local computer so that it can be presented to the Terminal Server for validation each time a connection is established.

Figure 15-3 Configuration Warning message box

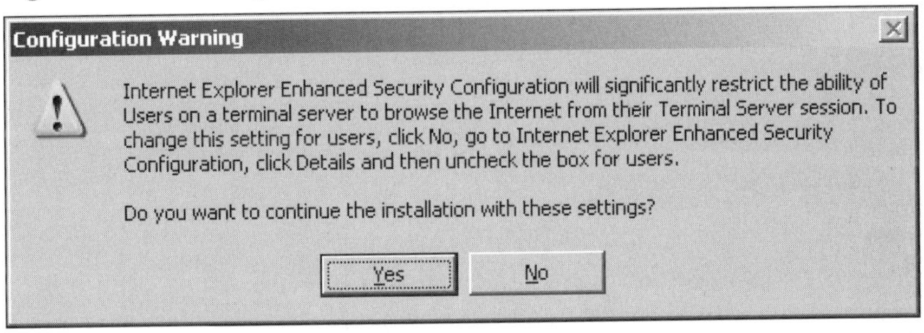

Figure 15-4 Terminal Services Licensing Setup screen

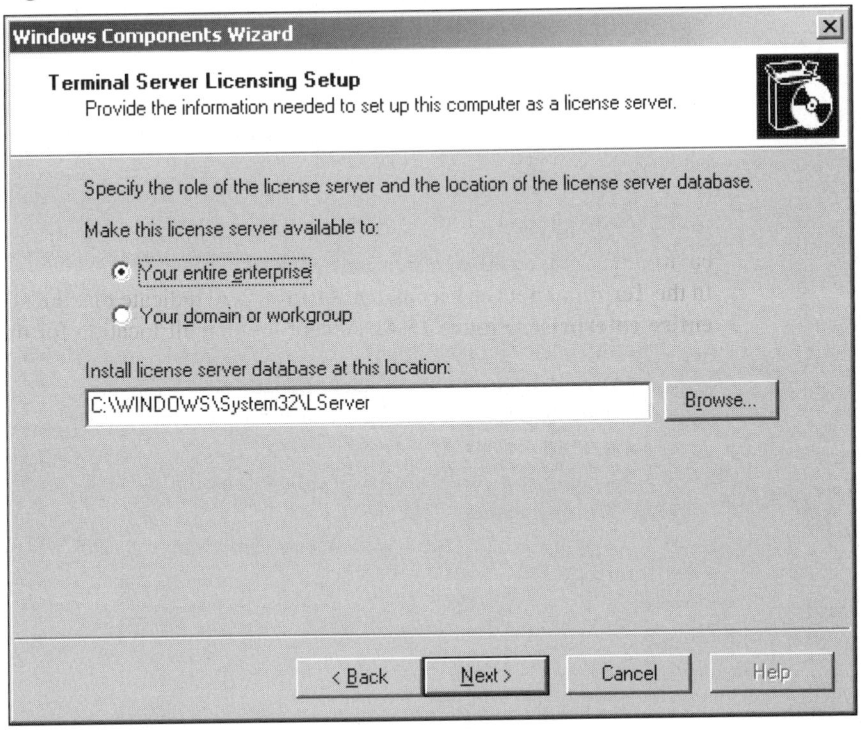

project 15.3

Managing IIS

exam objective

Manage a Web server. Manage IIS. Manage security for IIS.

overview

Once IIS is installed, the administrator can use Internet Information Services Manager to configure the appropriate properties. These could include IP address management, performance settings, authentication methods, site ratings, default document types, and error message customization.

The Web sites hosted by the domain controller are for use only by employees and students of Craighead College. Access will be granted only to those individuals that possess valid domain accounts. As network administrator for Craighead College, you should customize the default settings for all Web sites hosted on the domain controller to facilitate a more enjoyable user experience and to enhance security. You will use the Internet Information Services (IIS) Manager snap-in to manage the Web server.

learning objective

After completing this project, you will know how to configure setting within Internet Information Services (IIS).

specific requirements

See general requirements.

estimated completion time

15 minutes

project steps

1. Click **Start**, point to **Administrative Tools**, and click **Internet Information Services (IIS) Manager**.
2. Expand the local computer node, if necessary. Right-click **Application Pools** and click **Properties**.
3. On the **Performance** tab **(Figure 15-5)**, type **10** in the text box entitled **Shutdown worker processes after being idle for (time in minutes)**.
4. On the **Health** tab, type **3** in the **Failures** text box. Click **OK**.
5. Right-click **Web Sites** in the left pane of the window and click **Properties**.
6. On the **Performance** tab, click the **Connections limited to** option button and type **100** in the associated text box **(Figure 15-6)**.
7. On the **Directory Security** tab, click the **Edit** button associated with **Authentication and access control**.
8. Clear the check mark in the **Enable Anonymous access** check box. Place a check mark in the **Digest authentication for Windows domain servers** check box **(Figure 15-7)**. You will receive a warning message, stating that only Windows Active Directory domain accounts can use Digest authentication. Click **Yes** to proceed. Click **OK**.
9. On the **HTTP Headers** tab, click **Edit Ratings**. Place a check mark in the box entitled **Enable ratings for this content**. Click each of the categories: **Violence**, **Sex**, **Nudity**, and **Language**. Ensure that the rating level is set to **0** for each. Click **OK**.
10. Click **OK** to close the **Web Sites Properties** dialog box. An **Inheritance Overrides** dialog box will appear. Click **Select All** to use the new values for all child nodes. Click **OK** to close. Leave the **Internet Information Services (IIS) Manager** window open for next project.

Figure 15-5 Application Pools Properties dialog box

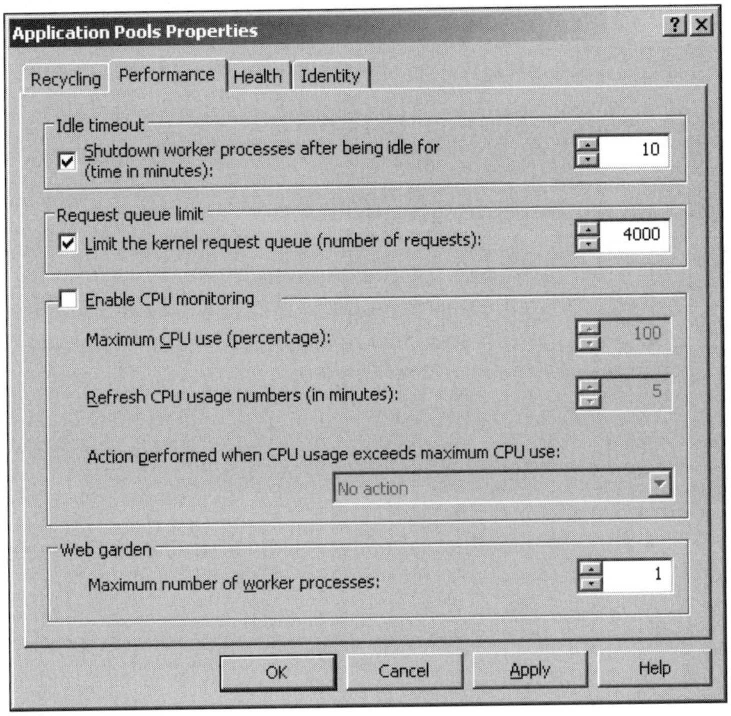

Figure 15-6 Performance tab in the Web Sites Properties dialog box

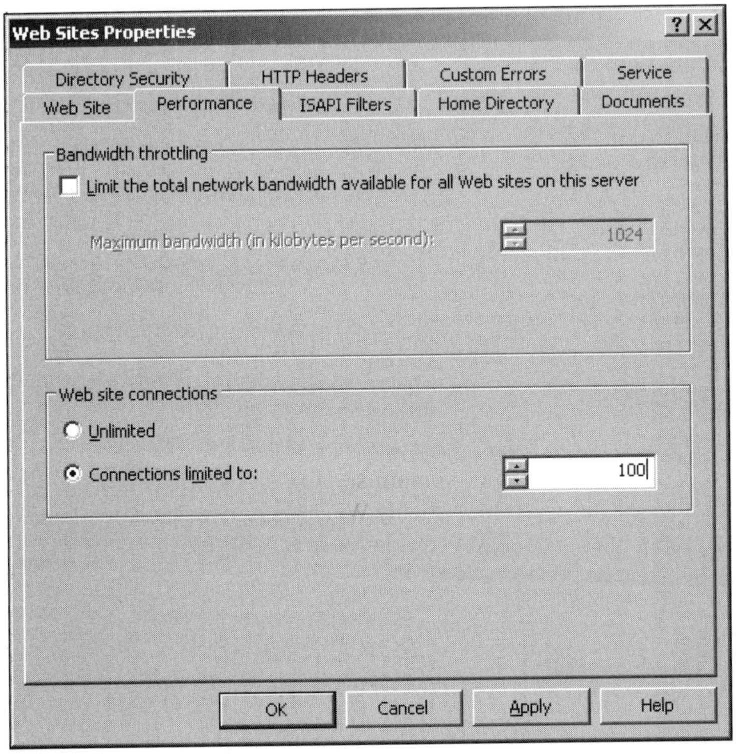

Figure 15-7 Authentication Methods dialog box

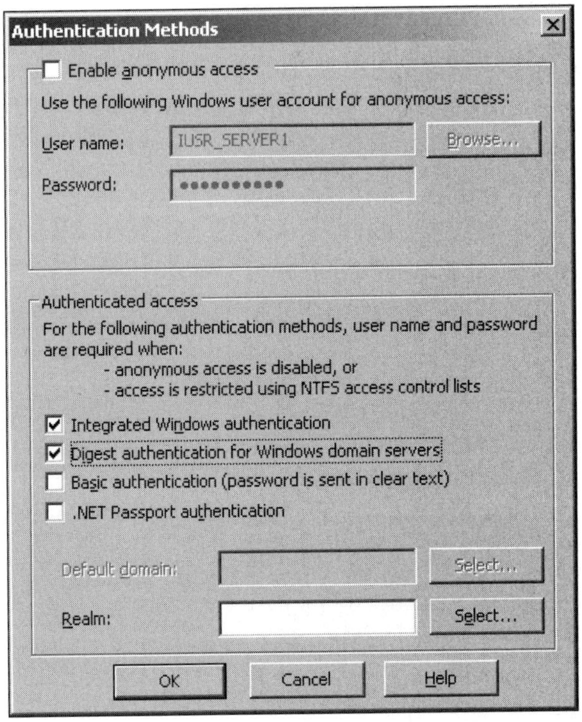

project 15.4 Configuring IIS Security

exam objective

Manage a Web server. Manage IIS. Manage security for IIS.

overview

IIS security includes the ability to validate and certify users, regulate access, encrypt information, and audit usage. Access can be controlled through both NTFS permissions (discussed earlier) and HTTP permissions. The Web permissions are detailed in **Table 15-2**. If there is a conflict between the permissions, the more restrictive permission is applied. If sensitive data is transmitted through the Web site, encryption is essential. IIS security allows the administrator to set a minimum level of encryption to access the Web site.

Since student financial information is stored on the Web site, you have decided to require 128-bit encryption for access to the Web site. Also, you will allow the Read and Directory Browsing Web permission for all users.

learning objective

After completing this project, you will know how to configure IIS security.

specific requirements

See general requirements.

estimated completion time

20 minutes

project steps

1. Expand the **Web Sites** folder in the left pane of the **Internet Information Services (IIS) Manager** window, if necessary.
2. Right-click **Default Web Site** and click **Properties**. On the **Web Site** tab **(Figure 15-8)**, type **Student Information Services** in the **Description** text box.
3. On the **Directory Security** tab, click the **Edit** button associated with **Secure communications**.
4. In the **Secure Communications** dialog box **(Figure 15-9)**, place a check mark in the **Require secure channel (SSL)** check box. Also, place a check mark in the **Require 128-bit encryption** check box. Click **OK**.
5. On the **Home Directory** tab, place a check mark in the **Directory browsing** check box. Close all open dialog boxes and windows.

Table 15-4 Web Permissions

Read	This permission, which is selected by default, allows users to view file content and properties.
Write	Allows users to change file content and properties.
Script Source Access	Allows users to access the source code for files, for example, the scripts in an Active Server Pages (ASP) application. You can only select this permission if you have also assigned either the Read or Write permission. It also allows users to access source files. If you have assigned the Read permission, users can only read the source code. If you have assigned the Write permission, users can also write source code. Assigning the Script Source Access permission in conjunction with the Write permission presents a security risk and should rarely, if ever, be done. You do not want to allow users to both read and write source code.
Directory browsing	Allows users to view file lists and collections.
Log visits	When this permission is selected, a log entry will be created for each visit to the Web site.
Index this resource	When this permission is selected, the Indexing Service is permitted to index this resource.

Figure 15-8 Default Web Site Properties dialog box

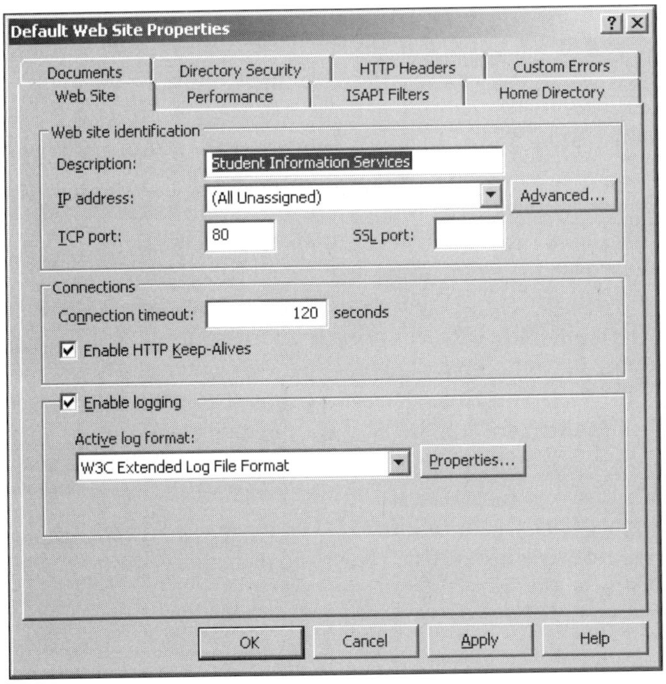

Figure 15-9 Secure Communications dialog box

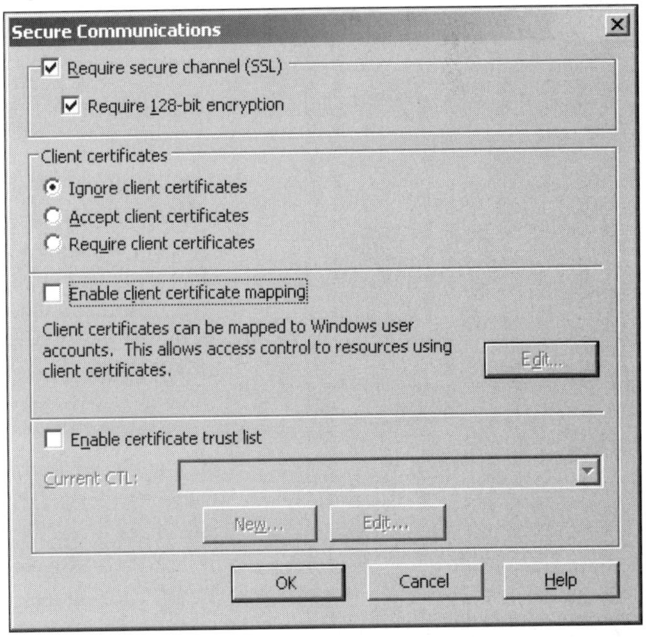

project 15.5

Administering the Web Environment

exam objective

Manage a Web server. Manage IIS. Manage security for IIS.

overview

IIS supports the hosting of multiple Web sites on a single server. Every Web site must have a home directory, which generally contains a home page. The home page will often contain links to other pages on the site and is placed in the home directory.

Virtual directories can be created and used to make a directory appear to be located within the home directory, when in reality is located elsewhere. An alias is used to identify the virtual directory to the Web browser while the full path is hidden from the user. This provides greater security.

Administration wants the ability to access student financial records through the Web browser. However, security is of the utmost concern. The student financial records will be stored in the SFR folder located on the C: drive of the Craighead College domain controller. As network administrator, you need to create the folder and then create the Web site for access. You should use all possible security precautions to protect the data.

learning objective

After completing this project, you will know how to create and secure a Web site using Internet Information Services (IIS) Manager.

specific requirements

See general requirements.

estimated completion time

25 minutes

project steps

1. Use **Windows Explorer** to create a folder named **SFR** under the **C:** drive on the domain controller.
2. Click **Start**, point to **Administrative Tools**, and click **Internet Information Services (IIS) Manager**.
3. Expand the local computer icon, if necessary. Right-click the **Web Sites** folder, click **New**, and then click **Web Site** to start the **Web Site Creation Wizard**. Click **Next**.
4. Type **Student Financial Records** in the **Description** text box and click **Next**.
5. In the **IP Address and Port Settings** screen **(Figure 15-10)**, type **2100** as the **TCP port this Web site should use (Default: 80)**. This will provide added security by requiring users to specify the port number in their browser to access the Web site. Click **Next**.
6. Click the **Browse** button in the **Web Site Home Directory** screen. Expand **Local Disk (C:)** and click **inetpub**. Click **Make New Folder**. Type **sfrroot** as the name of the new folder and click **OK**. Clear the check mark in the **Allow anonymous access to this Web site** check box. Click **Next**.
7. In the **Web Site Access Permissions** screen **(Figure 15-11)**, place check marks in the **Read**, **Run scripts**, and **Execute** check boxes. Click **Next** and then click **Finish**.

Figure 15-10 IP Address and Port Settings screen

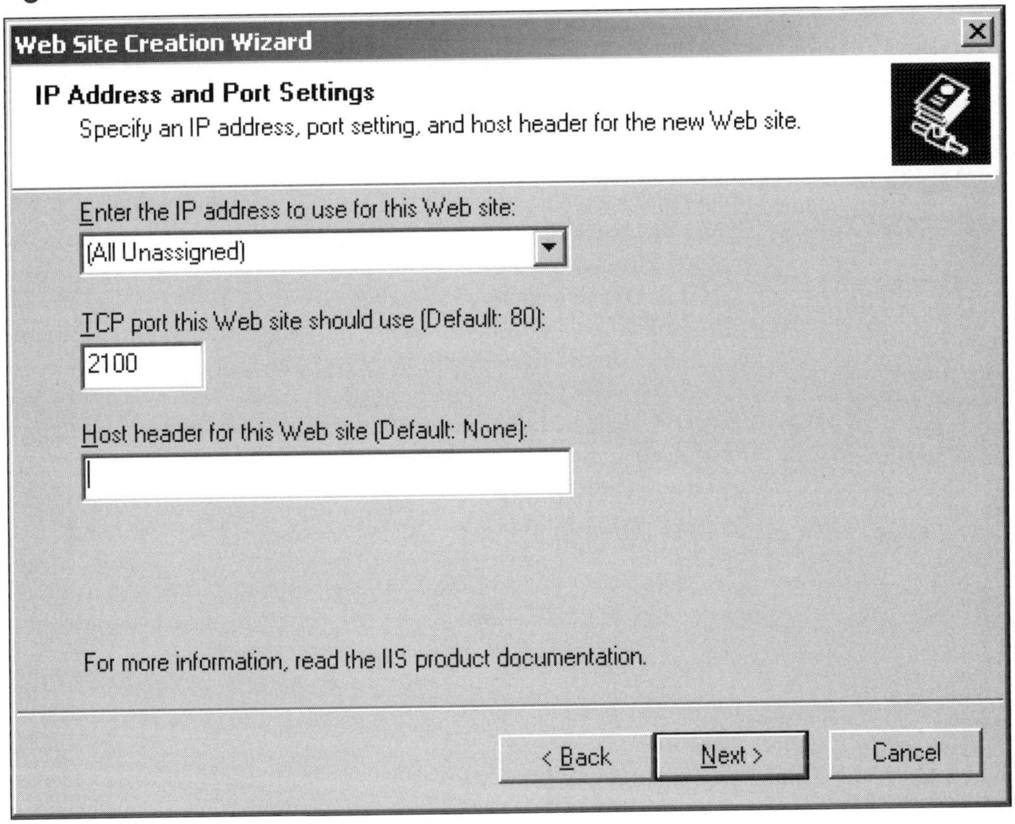

Figure 15-11 Web Site Access Permissions screen

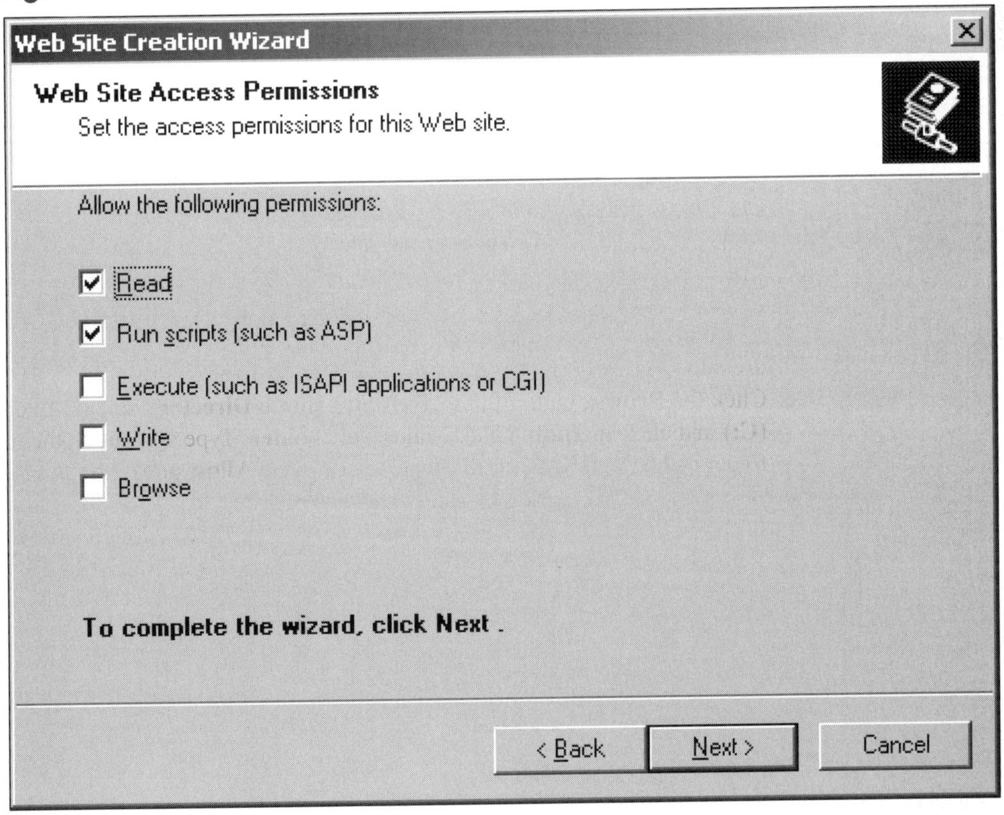

project 15.5

Administering the Web Environment

(cont'd)

exam objective

Manage a Web server. Manage IIS. Manage security for IIS.

project steps

8. Right-click the **Student Financial Records** Web site in the left pane and click **Properties**.
9. On the **Directory Security** tab, click the **Edit** button associated with **Secure communications**. Place check marks in the **Require secure channel (SSL)** and the **Require 128-bit encryption** check boxes. Click **OK**.
10. Click the **Edit** button associated with **Authentication and access control**. Place a check mark in the **Digest authentication for Windows domain servers** check box. Click **Yes** to continue. Click **OK** to close the **Authentication Methods** dialog box.
11. Click **OK** to close the **Student Financial Records Properties** dialog box. Right-click **Student Financial Records** Web site and point to **New**. Click **Virtual Directory** to start the **Virtual Directory Creation Wizard**. Click **Next**.
12. Type **SFR** as the **Alias (Figure 15-12)** and click **Next**.
13. Type **C:\SFR** in the **Path** text box to specify the path to the virtual directory. Click **Next**.
14. Place check marks in the **Read**, **Run scripts**, and **Execute** access permission check boxes. Click **Next** and **Finish**. Close all open dialog boxes and windows.

Figure 15-12 Virtual Directory Creation Wizard

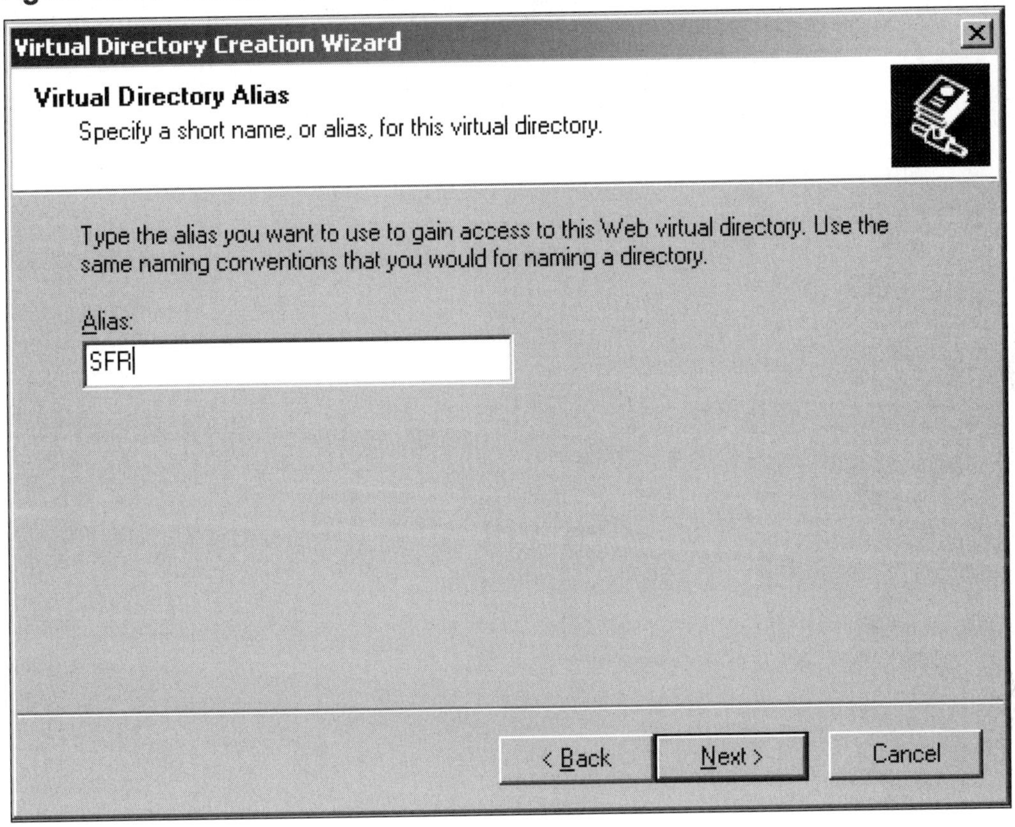

LESSON

16 Examining Software Update Services and License Management

A new feature in Windows Server 2003 is called Software Update Services (SUS). SUS can be used to download, control, and deploy updates, service packs, and patches to the operating system and its components automatically, using an internal server.

By storing the content locally, clients can download their updates locally, rather than each client retrieving the updates from the Microsoft Web site over the Internet. The administrator also has the opportunity to approve each package before it is made available to the clients. Additionally, new group policy features included with SUS allow the administrator to define the configuration of the Automatic Updates feature on client computers on as large or small a scale as necessary.

Scenario

As network administrator for Craighead College, you have decided to install the Automatic Updates Service on each client. In addition, you wish to take advantage of the server-side benefits of SUS by installing the SUS on the domain controller for Craighead College.

Lesson 16 Examining Software Update and License Management

Project	Exam 70-290 Objective
16.1 Installing and Configuring the Software Update Service on a Client	Manage software update infrastructure.
16.2 Installing, Configuring, and Managing a Software Update Service (SUS) Server	Manage software update infrastructure.
16.3 Using a Group Policy Object to Configure Updates	Manage software update infrastructure.

General Requirements

To complete the projects in this lesson, you will need administrative rights on the domain controller for Craighead College. You will either need to download the SUS software (32 MB) onto a storage device or have a live Internet connection to facilitate downloading. You will also need a Windows Server 2003 Installation CD-ROM. In addition, you also may find it helpful to refer to Lesson 16 in your Prentice Hall Certification Series textbook for further information about the topics covered by the projects in this lesson.

project 16.1

Installing and Configuring the Software Update Service on a Client

exam objective

Manage software update infrastructure.

overview

The client-side service of Software Update Services (SUS) retrieves software updates from the SUS server or the Internet and installs them. The client-side service is known as the Automatic Updates service. After installation, the service will attempt to contact either the local SUS server or the Microsoft Windows Update server on the Internet.

Since most of the computers at Craighead College are not utilized on the weekend, you have decided to have the updates downloaded automatically and scheduled to install on Saturday evening.

learning objective

After completing this project, you will know how to configure client update services.

specific requirements

Administrative rights on the domain controller for Craighead College and a connection to the Internet.

estimated completion time

10 minutes

project steps

1. Click **Start**, right-click **My Computer**, and click **Properties** to open the **System Properties** dialog box.
2. Click the **Automatic Updates** tab (**Figure 16-1**), and place a check mark in the **Keep my computer up to date** check box.
3. Click the **Automatically download the updates, and install them on the schedule that I specify** option button.
4. Select **Every Saturday** and **10:00 PM** on the respective drop-down lists. Click **Apply**.
5. To read more about Automatic Updates, click the **automatic updating** link. Close all open dialog boxes and windows.

Figure 16-1 Automatic Updates tab

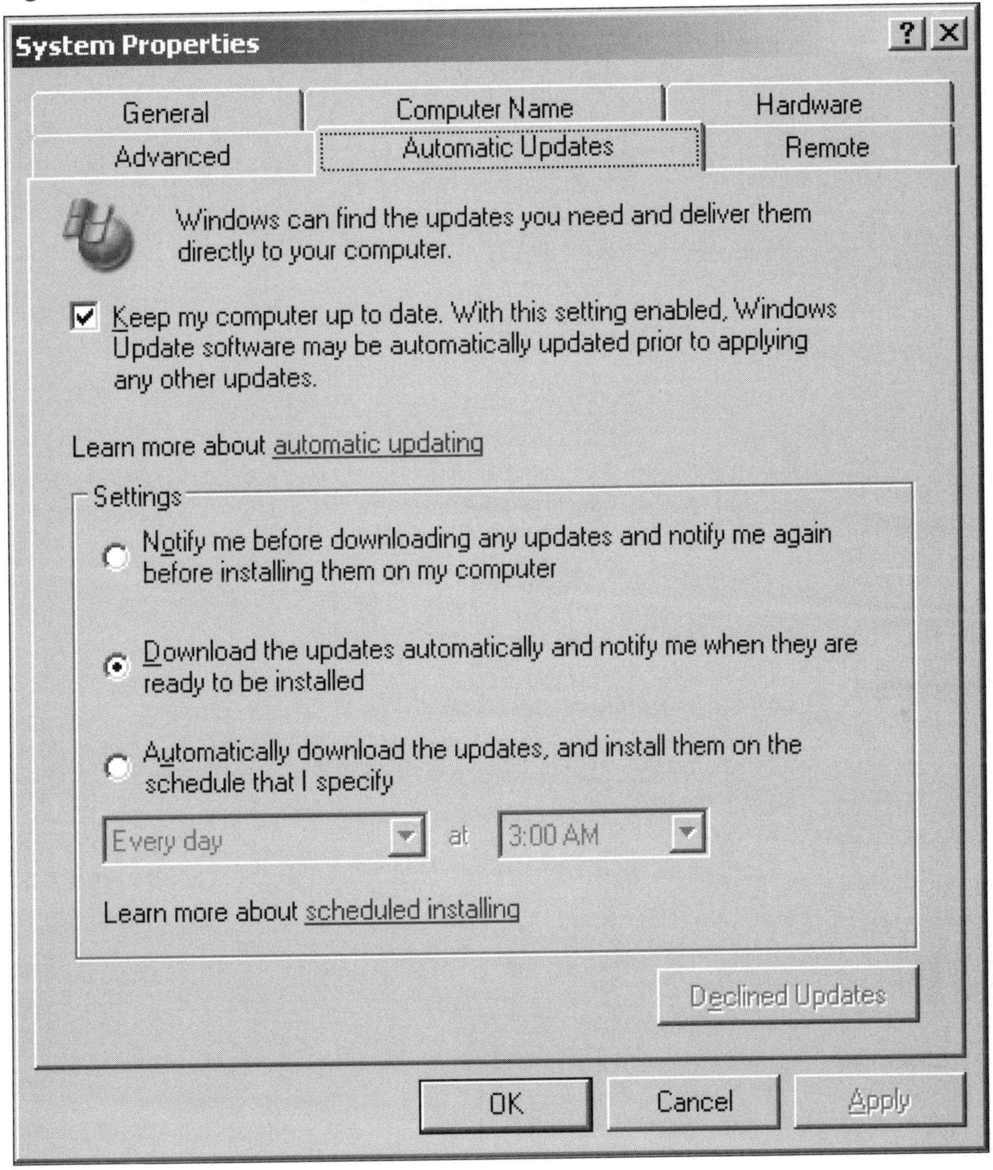

project 16.2

Installing, Configuring, and Managing a Software Update Service (SUS) Server

exam objective

Manage software update infrastructure.

overview

The server-side service of SUS is responsible for providing updates to client computers in order to reduce the bandwidth requirements for your network and increase manageability by ensuring that updates are accepted or rejected for all computers by a central authority.

The server at Craighead College will be scheduled to synchronize with the Microsoft Windows Update server on Friday evenings. The network administrator will review these updates and select the ones to approve. After the updates are approved, the clients will download and install them based upon the schedule configured in Project 16.1.

learning objective

After completing this project, you will know how to install the server-side component of Software Update Services.

specific requirements

Administrative rights on the domain controller for Craighead College, an Internet connection, and the Windows Server 2003 installation CD-ROM.

estimated completion time

15–45 minutes (depending upon Internet connection speed)

project steps

Download SUS Server.

1. Log on as an **Administrator** and open your Internet browser.
2. Type **http://www.microsoft.com/sus** in the **address** text box and click **Go**.
3. Scroll down and click the **Download SUS with Service Pack 1 (SP1)** hyperlink. Click **Download** in the upper-right side of the window.
4. The **File Download** dialog box opens. Click **Save** and select **Local Disk (C:)**. Click **Save**.
5. When the download has completed, click **OK**, and close **Internet Explorer**.

Install IIS (required for SUS Server).

6. Place the Windows Server 2003 installation CD-ROM in your CD-ROM drive. Click **Start**, point to **Control Panel**, click **Add or Remove Programs**, and then click **Add/Remove Windows Components**.
7. Click **Application Server** and click **Details**. In the **Application Server** dialog box **(Figure 16-2)**, place a check mark next to **Internet Information Services (IIS)** and click **OK**. Click **Next**. After the installation is complete, click **Finish**. Close all open dialog boxes and windows and remove the CD.

Figure 16-2 Subcomponents of Application Server

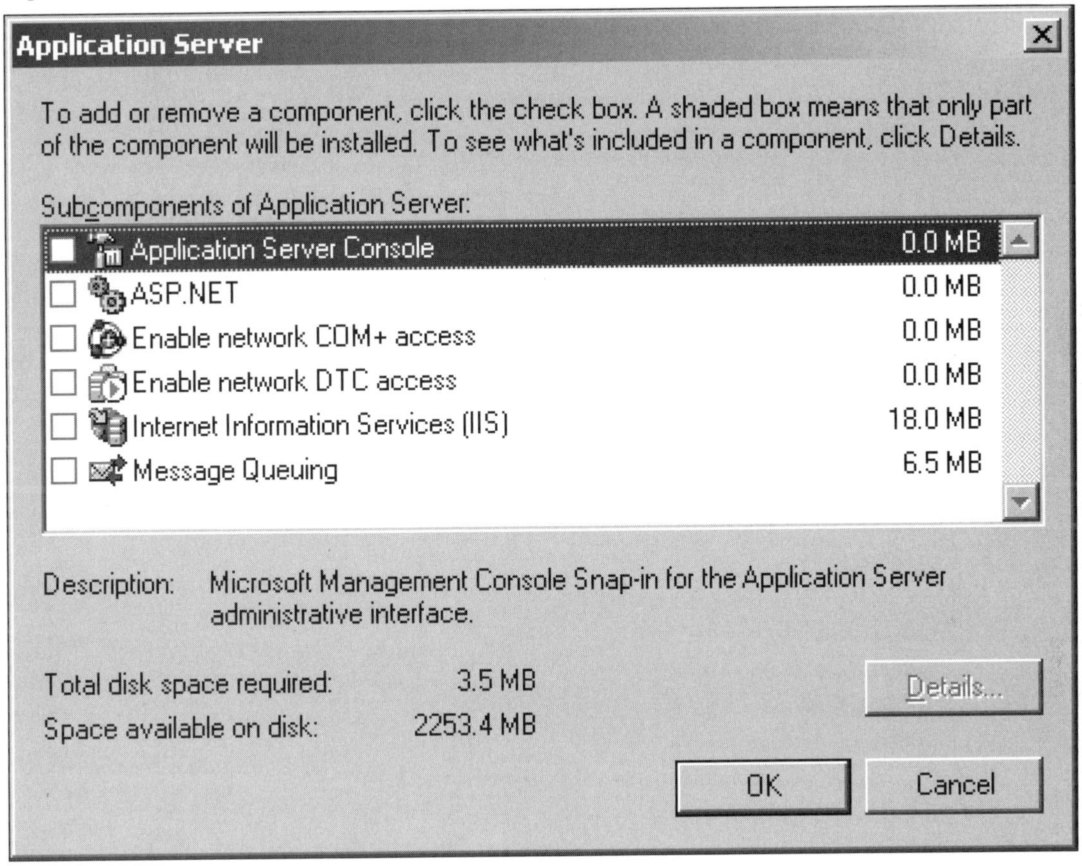

project 16.2

Installing, Configuring, and Managing a Software Update Service (SUS) Server (cont'd)

exam objective

Manage software update infrastructure.

project steps

Install SUS.

8. Click **Start**, click **Run**, and type **C:\SUS10SP1.exe** in the **Open** text box. Click **OK**. Click **Next** when the wizard starts. Read the license agreement and click **I accept the terms in the License Agreement**. Click **Next**.
9. Click the icon for a **Typical** installation. Accept the local computer as the download URL by clicking **Install**. After the installation is complete, click **Finish**.
10. When the **Software Updates Services Welcome** Web page is displayed **(Figure 16-3)**, click **Set options**.
11. Scroll down the list of options until you find **Select where you want to store updates**. Click **Clear All** and then place a check mark in the **English** check box. Click **Apply**. Click **OK** to confirm.
12. Click **Synchronize server** in the left pane, and then click **Synchronization Schedule** in the right pane. In the **Schedule Synchronization – Web Page Dialog** dialog box **(Figure 16-4)**, click the **Synchronize using this schedule** option button.
13. Select **22:00** in the **At this time** drop-down list. Click the **Weekly** option button and then click **Friday**. Click **OK**. Close all open dialog boxes and windows.

Figure 16-3 Software Update Services Web page

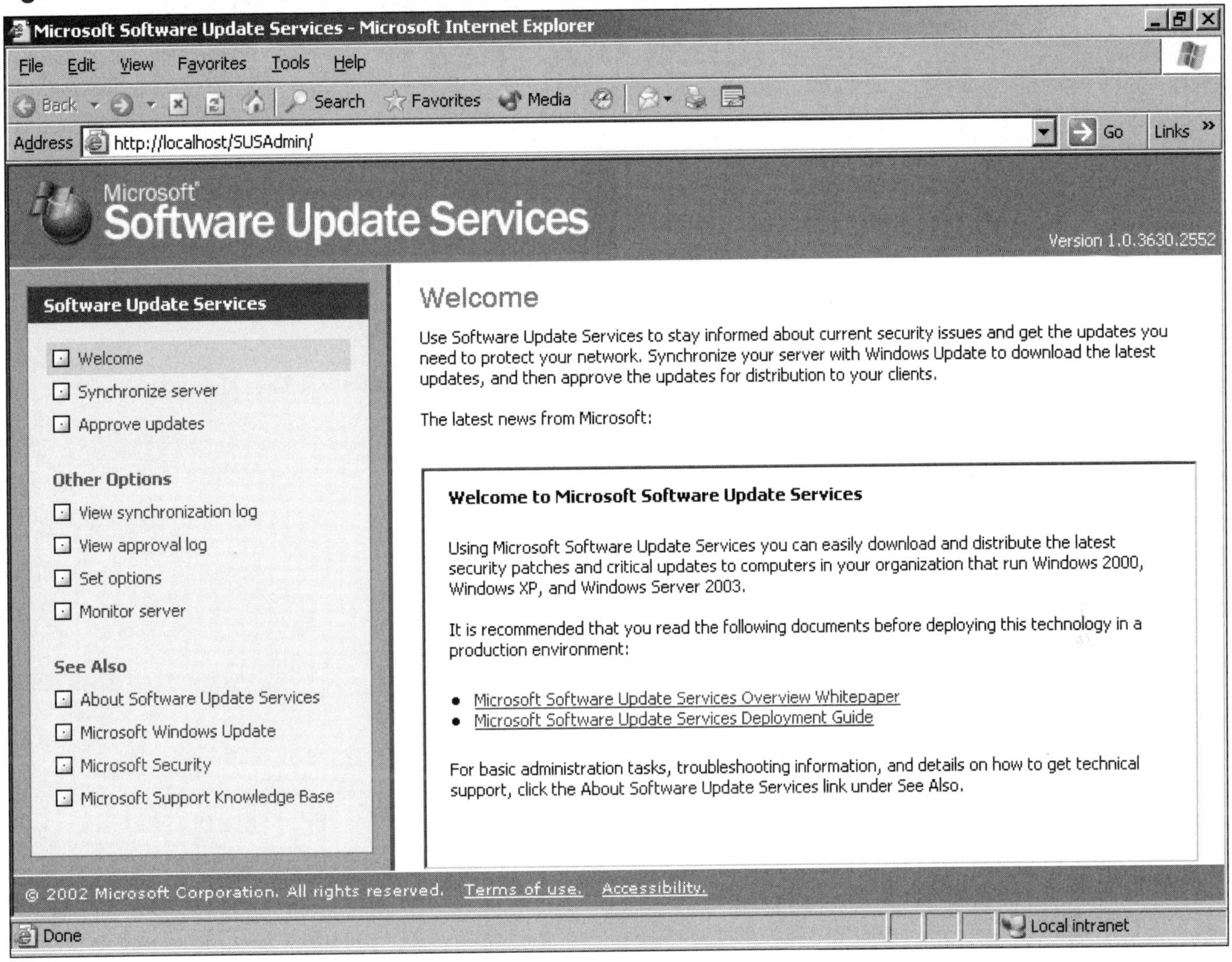

Figure 16-4 SUS Schedule Synchronization

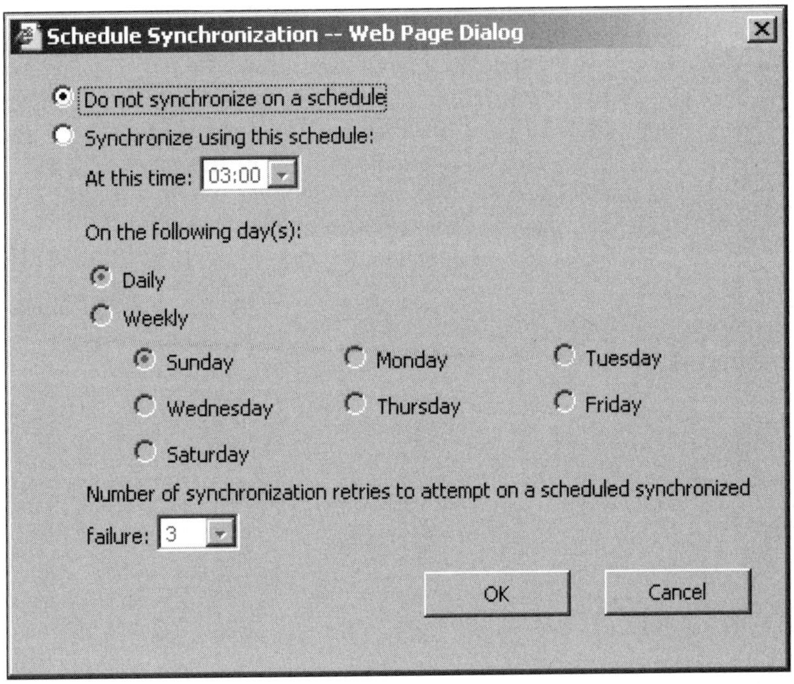

project 16.3

Using a Group Policy Object to Configure Updates

exam objective

Manage software update infrastructure.

overview

Within an Active Directory domain, clients can be configured quickly and easily using a Group Policy. After SUS is installed, a new administrative template, Wuau.adm, is installed by default. Using the setting in this template, you can modify the Automatic Update functionality for large groups of client computers more efficiently.

All of the computers within Craighead College should be configured to automatically download and install updates according to a pre-set schedule. The clients should receive the updates from the local SUS server.

learning objective

After completing this project, you will know how to configure software updates through the use of Group Policy Objects.

specific requirements

See general requirements

estimated completion time

15 minutes

project steps

1. Click **Start**, point to **Administrative Tools**, and then click **Active Directory Users and Computers**.
2. Right-click the **craighead.com** domain and click **Properties**. On the **Group Policy** tab, click **Edit** to make changes to the **Default Domain Policy**.
3. Expand the **Computer Configuration**, **Administrative Templates**, and **Windows Components** nodes, and then click **Windows Update (Figure 16-5)**.
4. Double-click **Configure Automatic Updates** to open the **Configure Automatic Updates Properties** dialog box **(Figure 16-6)**. Click the **Enabled** option button. Select **4–Auto download and schedule the install** in the **Configure automatic updating** drop-down list.
5. In the **Scheduled install day** drop-down list, select **7–Every Saturday**. In the **Scheduled install time** drop-down list, select **22:00**. Click **OK**.
6. Double-click **Specify intranet Microsoft update service location (Figure 16-7)** and click the **Enabled** option button. Type **http://*server_name***, where ***server_name*** is the name of your SUS server, in both the **Set the intranet update service for detecting updates** and **Set the intranet statistics server** text boxes. Click **OK**. Close all open dialog boxes and windows.

Figure 16-5 Group Policy Object Editor

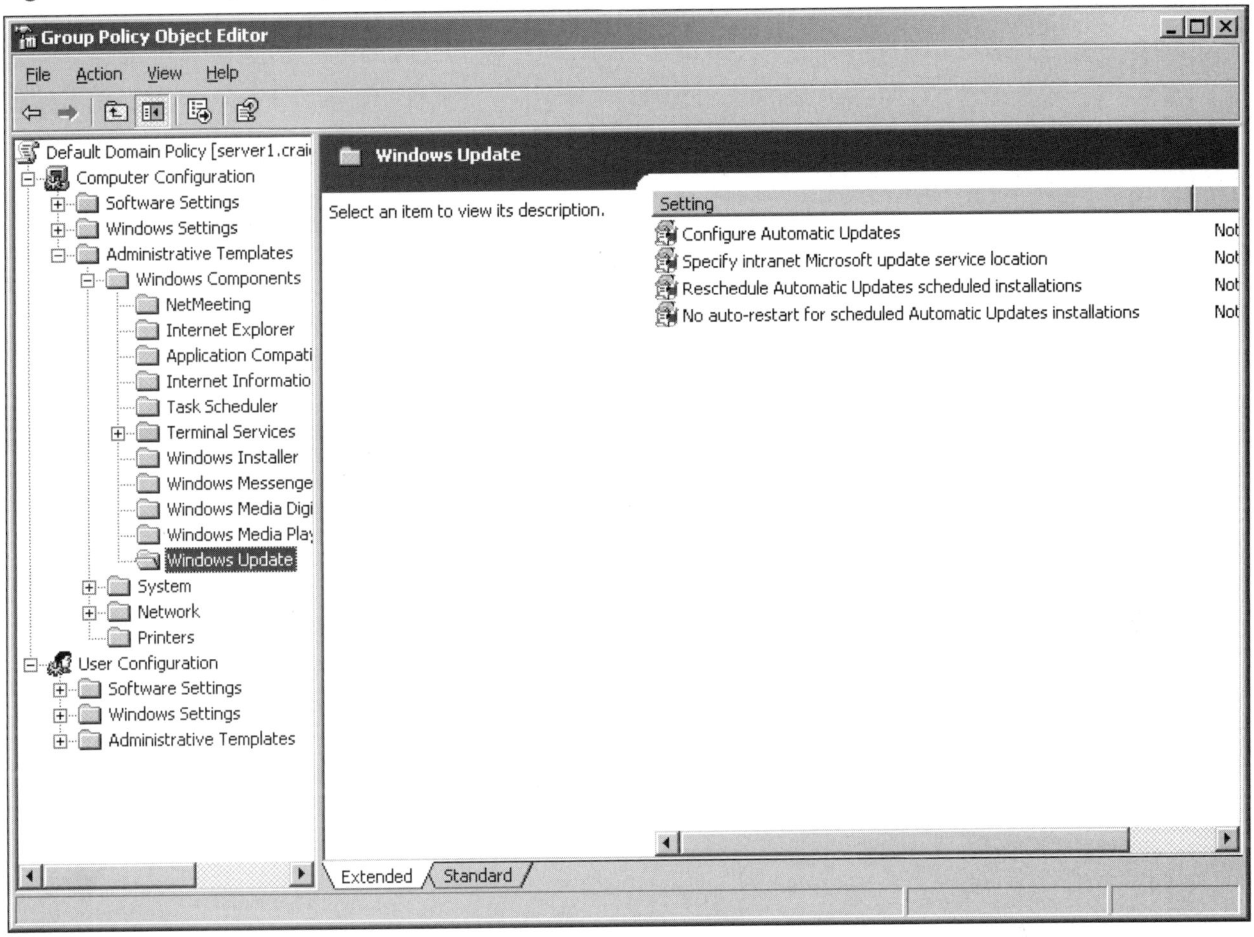

Figure 16-6 Configure Automatic Updates Properties dialog box

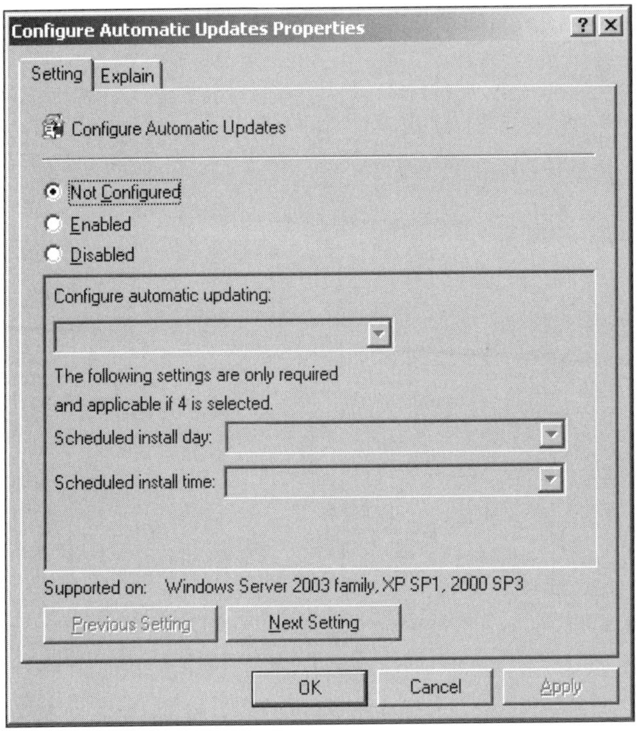

Figure 16-7 Specify intranet Microsoft update service location Properties dialog box

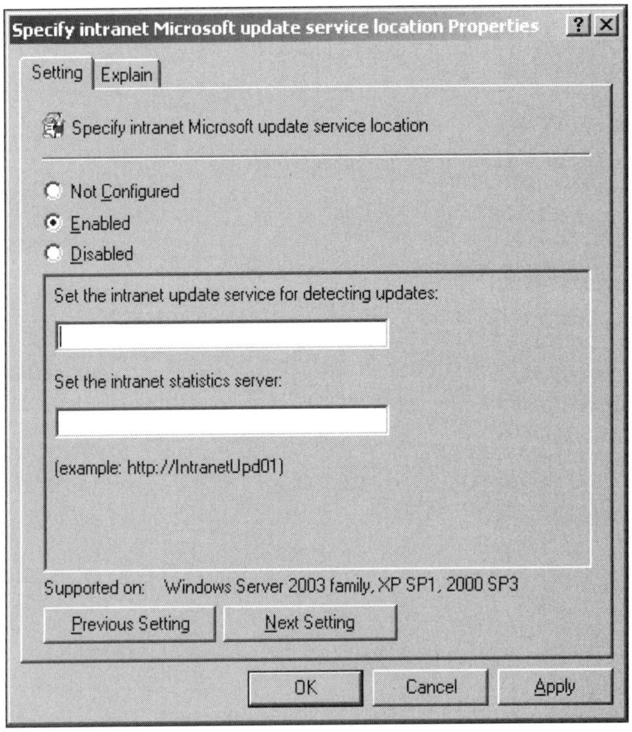